CAROL DWYER
ENOUGH

ENOUGH Copyright ©2014
by Carol Dwyer
All rights reserved, including the right to reproduce this
book or portions thereof in any form whatsoever.
First Edition
Printed in the United States of America
Book design by Austin Metze Design

ISBN 978-1-4951-2154-8

To all the people in the world I love

Acknowledgements

I'm joining the world again maybe for a little while. It's amazing how far away from words one can get when one's doing more sleeping than talking. Meanwhile it's amazing how bright a spot my mom makes when she shows up to visit me in the early morning wearing her yellow summer shirt. My brother Bobby brings by a few groceries in his crisp summer shirt. What a surprise it is to see my son Mike in his crisp suit and tie, and my daughter sharing some treat she made to cool me and my forehead down. Then there's all these incredible bright bright dots of friends who bring flowers and listen to my work and support me and encourage me every single surprising day. Last night Dana and Charlie, who I call my twins, showed up and shared a sparkly conversation about the last two summer days. They do crack me up. There's an amazing powerhouse of friends that reached in and helped make this book happen, Robert and Craig, then Charlie and Abby and Austin. That is above and beyond the eggs and milk and sugar it takes to put something together. It starts with one egg and somebody else stirs some sugar and some arm power and it happens outside of my seeing it, it happened with some big big package of love and there it was, bigger than I am.

Chocolate chips of laughter from Pyramid Lake and childhood and best friends Kathy and Danielle and Tommy and Jody and Bill, friends of such strength. God. Some friends are just there wherever you turn. And not to forget the source of writings that became this family. Girlfriends in my neighborhood and grew from support groups revolving around cancer and just supported everything everywhere.

And my brother Matt and sister Chrissie incredible with their bold presence galloping into holidays, and Connie is such a presence with her floral bouquets and floral paintings and hugs and pots of soup and Matt is sending photos of love from California and Chrissie is full of stories, almost like she is dancing wisdom and love from a distance.

My Dad left through a large portal this spring. I watched with gratitude as my loving stepmother, Mary, gracefully helped him leave.

The end is difficult to write. Please refer to Profound Sentence #442C, and see if it fits.

THE WRONG LINE

Hey! Excuse me! *Over here!!* Am I in the wrong line? Hello! HELLOOOO! Don't they hear me? *Hello?*

I think I must be in the wrong line. Someone just told me I have Stage-Four Metastatic Breast Cancer. That is not the line I meant to stand in, there must be a mistake. I was eating fruit and vegetables, going to the gym, I nursed both my children and took vitamins; if there were seven things on the LIST TO PREVENT CANCER, I was doing six, at the very least! I was only drinking a rare glass of wine, maybe that was my mistake? I'm sorry, just let me out of this line and I will drink every night, I promise. Coffee too, if that is decided to prevent cancer now, then I will drink that too, but I thought green tea was more preventative, so I was drinking that. I am so sorry if I offended the Cancer Gods. Please help me, give me my penance like five Hail Marys and two Our Fathers, but this cancer thing is a little EXTREME, no? My mother asked me if smoking pot in my youth was why I got cancer. I said, "No Mom, I don't think so. Pot was mostly home grown back then, before Reagan began spraying herbicides on fields of pot in Colombia. I smoked back in the good old days, when pot was cheap and natural."

Hi. HI. Could you help me? Yes, I seem to have misplaced my positive attitude. Do you have it? I have been pretty good, writing about the bright side of things, the "gifts" that cancer has brought me. I gave up my breasts to save my life, learned I didn't look so bad as a bald person. I had a sense of humor and made people feel comfortable around me. I worked hard not to whine or complain. I was even so grateful to find out that the tumor growing in my brain was in a fold and could "easily" be removed. Then there was the Gamma Knife radiation therapy to remove the tumor growing back…. Sorry? You don't want to hear my whole diagnosis? But this is just the tip of the iceberg. Am I in the wrong line? Is there someone here that will listen to the whole nightmare? The twist of my life from being around my children and work, to being warped around my diagnosis and treatment plan? The wrong turn I took somewhere along the line from heave-hoe-ing whatever needed to be done for my house or my Mom's, to being told, that I have more bone metastases, "Do not lift anything heavy, do not fall, you may do *light vacuuming*" Is there a class on light vacuuming? Is there a special costume, like a chiffon robe and small heeled mules? Now, I dream of walkers and canes, neuropathy and mouth sores. I have a cramp in my writing hand….Did you just tell me to *stop*? Is there another line? Is there a way *out*? I didn't mean it *that* way! What I meant is that *this* is not the line I want to be in! I want *that* line, over there that everyone else seems to be in; that line over there where people are concerned about the color of the couch and wallpaper coordinating, or making long-range plans for summer vacations in Italy. There seems to have been a fork in my road that I had my eyes closed for. Would you just let me back track for awhile so I can see where I went the wrong way? I *am* sorry. I didn't mean to be a pain in the ass, but this is so important to me. If you could just let me go back then I wouldn't have to fill out this form for Medicaid, and be a strain on the system.

WHAT I WAS DOING BEFORE I HAD TO STOP

I was working every day. Getting up reluctantly (I've never been an early morning person), but there was work to go to and Dana's lunch to be made. Dana had to leave first to catch the early bus to the high school; she occupied the bathroom applying coats of mascara to her very long dark eyelashes; they had to be perfect. I'd get the newspaper off the porch to grasp a feeling of the day outside. In the kitchen I fed the cats and made my daughter scrambled eggs with buttered toast and served them to her upstairs on the corner of the bathroom sink. I pampered her, making sure she had some sustenance for her full schedule, and because I knew she would leave my nest in a few short years and I'd be living alone. Dana left for school with her friends and I drove off to work in my quick uniform of slim jeans and a tight tee shirt; long-gone were the days of my East Village eccentricity.

I worked for the Tonner Doll Company at a job I was grateful for, a job that used the talents and skills that I had trained for, only I made clothing and costumes for dolls instead of people. I had flexibility with my time to be available for my children, time to take them for doctor appointments and be present for school functions.

My boyfriend, Robert, came up from New York City almost every weekend. He was a part-time "step-dad'" for Dana and caught her every time she ran into his arms. But Mike had gone to live with his

ENOUGH 3

father and step-mom when they moved up from New York City; he had been only thirteen and it broke my heart. Dana and Mike each became an only child in separate households. I became a Theatre Mom making costumes for the local youth theatre's musical productions that Dana was in; photographing the shows and working backstage. I joined the Marching Band parents group that held fundraisers, chaperoned field trips and statewide competitions.

My mother took care of Dana when she was sick and I had to go to work. I often left work at lunchtime to visit Mom; we'd sit outside on her deck and chat. She was always better spirited when we did this several days a week. I visited frequently and we talked things through, made lists and planned the holidays.

So Robert came up and we were a weekend couple; we had vague plans of a future together, but nothing solid. Every weeknight was for Dana and every weekend was for Dana, Mom and Robert, except when he had block parties to organize or trips to visit friends elsewhere. I could enjoy my time alone, but it wasn't usually my choice. I let the writing groups go on without me, the girlfriends gather without me; time passed. It seemed like it might be enough. Many married friends thought it was the perfect arrangement; an ex in town and a boyfriend on the weekend.

I worked with many people over that ten years, and we had evolved an exceptional team in the design room. We consulted each other on the different ways to solve the structural problems of doll clothing and we helped each other with our specialties and critiques. There were four of us in the design room and every day we talked, sharing dreams, life and angst; there were few secrets amongst us. The dolls we turned out were amazing; they still are, but I'm not working on them.

I was going to the gym twice a week and I had never been stronger or more fit than I was just before I stopped everything.

One day I showed my funky nipple to my doctor and he felt my hardened breast. He ordered the mammograms and an ultrasound. I knew it wasn't good. I saw it in the doctor's face.

Diane Epstein was the first person I called when I wasn't sure what to do next. She was on vacation, driving in a car with her husband, speaking to me about who to call for information; we made plans to meet when she got back. We'd met when our daughters were very young and became friends. I'd been seeing her for massage and acupressure. She has a calm way of communicating, she always listened and helped me not to panic, to breathe and allow the news to enter slowly.

Friday, July 24th 2009

My gynecologist was surprised by the solid lumps and the multiple cysts that showed up on the ultrasounds. "Fast growing?" he speculates because the alternative is that they have hidden from the

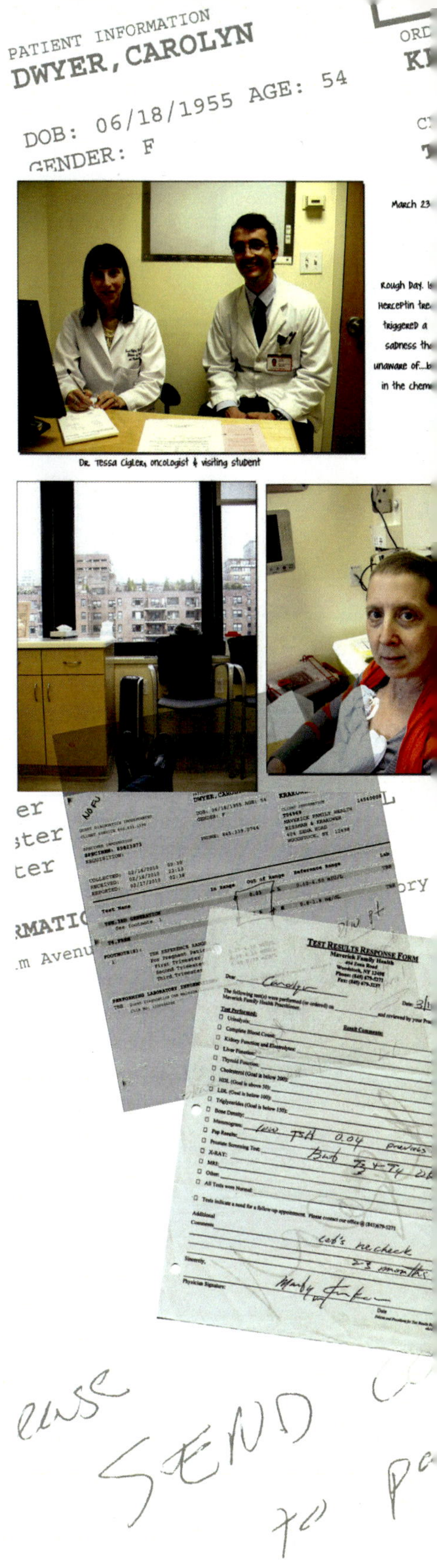

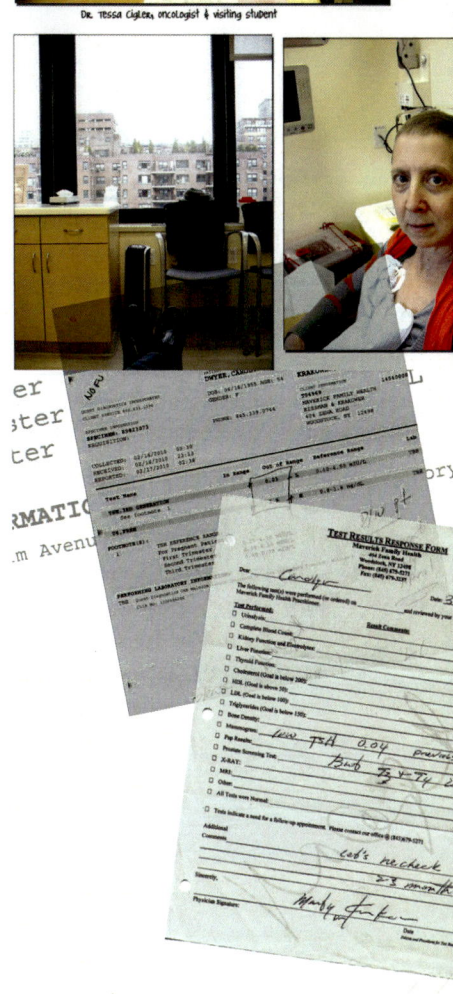

ENOUGH 5

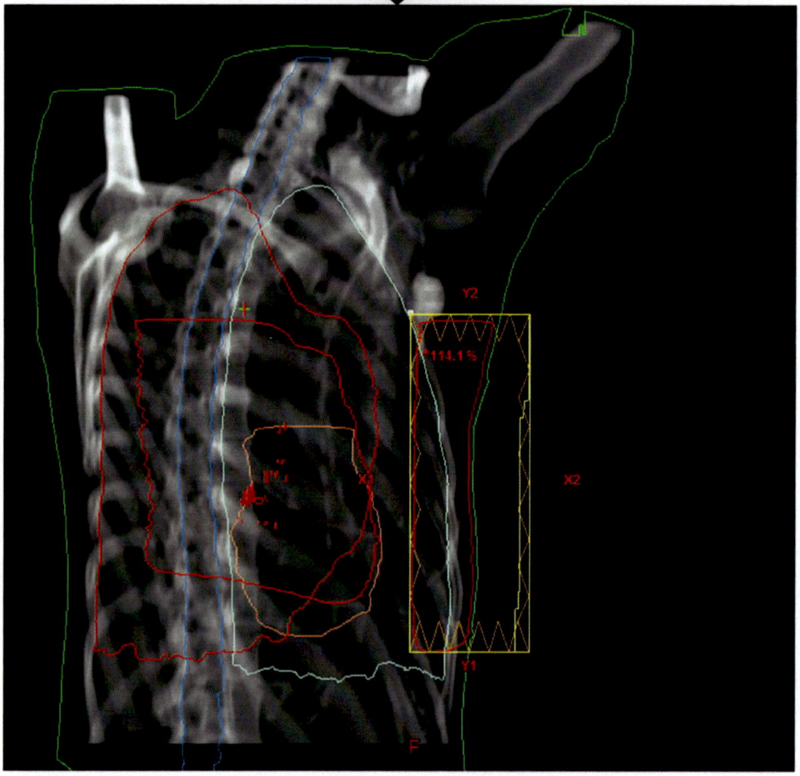

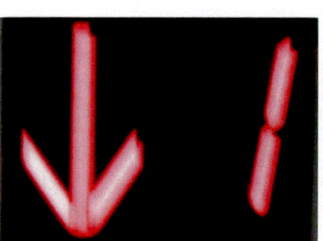

CAROL DWYER 6

mammograms I have had for the last seven years; hidden from his own investigation of my breasts. I pointed out my changing nipple years ago and we have been watching it. "It's probably just your aging body," he had told me. I have been with this doctor for fourteen years and I have just learned that I have dense breasts that can hide tumor growth from being exposed during mammograms. Why have I been having these tests? I could see the explosion in the ultrasound. I went back to work afterwards and the worry sunk in deep. I was working on a very detailed doll costume, the Queen of Hearts, and the doll's hand shredded the sleeve lining as I cried. Suzanne came over and put her hand on my shoulder to comfort me. I looked up and said, "It's so fucking symbolic. I'm coming apart on the inside too."

I have an appointment to see a breast surgeon Tuesday.

Monday, July 27th 2009

I am realizing two days later that I broke up with Robert on Mike's birthday. We sat at my son's birthday lunch Saturday afternoon and Robert seemed distracted, but he took pictures of us celebrating. That night we watched a movie called French Film which hit a little too close to home and initiated my breaking up with him, much as a romantic movie could have inspired sex. My friend is gone. I don't want to speak ill of him. He has taken his things. I have no lover, but I have a dresser drawer and space in my closet to fill. I'm home from work sick today. My back is in spasm. My whole body grieves. My tears want to flow and my belly is full of condensed breath. I am afraid to let go of this dam inside me.

Tuesday, July 28th 2009

I woke slowly. Awake before the alarm, but lying gently, listening to the sounds of morning and then "Sweet Melissa" on the radio. My body looks beautiful in the light. My breasts are still lovely, no scars; only a shy nipple, but moving forward will bring scars.

The breast surgeon was very nice and explained things well, bringing in the reasons he is concerned about my lumps being cancer. He can do a biopsy next Tuesday, but said not to change my vacation plans; it was not that kind of emergency. I sat looking at the scan on the light box. I cried to see the ill-formed masses; its explosive swirls and undefined edges. I am no expert, but they don't look good to me.

Monday, August 10th, 2009

I went to my second breast surgeon today for a consultation. She performed my biopsies in the office. She did the left breast first, "the little lump." I was not expecting the jolt. The punch of the core biopsy made me jump. I needed a little more of the local anesthesia; my tears began.

My right breast was less successful. She could not fully penetrate the firmness of the growth. She only got a few cells procured, no tissue. She felt confident that she had enough. She feels fairly sure we are looking at cancer.

MY *OLD* BIRTHDAY

"What are the chances?" she exclaimed to Dr. Doney, "The chance of having two children, five years apart, on the same day!?" "But you didn't Mary," he replied. "Carol was born on June 18th. Bobby was born on June 12th." Mom was outraged that Dr. Doney accused her of not knowing the birth dates of her own children. He had to call the courthouse to prove she was mistaken. Apparently, they celebrated my birthday on a different day one year and forgot to switch it back. Bobby's birth fixed that mistake. I grew up taunting him with, "You were born on my *old* birthday. I have a *new* one."

I woke up that morning to find a babysitter. I ran up three floors to tell my sisters. We huddled together on Chrissy's tall, double bed. Finally we heard Dad's footsteps and watched his head appear over the railing as he announced, "It's a BOY! You have a baby *BROTHER!*" We jumped up and down on the bed hugging each other. I jumped into Dad's arms as my sisters wrapped around his waist.

My mom's mother, Gramma Tugas, cared for us while Mom recovered for five days in the maternity hospital. Then Dad packed Chrissy, Connie and me into the blue and white Chevy station wagon to pick up Mom and the new baby. My excitement was thinning out as I watched Dad hold the car door open. Mom got in holding a small bundle in a yellow crocheted blanket. I sat back, pouting.

Back home Gramma turned off the bacon and

eggs to join us in the living room and hold her red-headed grandson. I watched all the excitement in a flurry above my head till Bobby was settled in a white bassinette in the middle of the room. Gramma called our family into the kitchen and everyone followed the smell of warm bacon. I stayed behind, looking over the edge of the small suspended basket that held this quiet little lump, my new brother. His fine, red hair framed a pale face covered with small red bumps. I took a deep breath as I stared at him and thought, "What is the big deal?"

August 14th, 2009

I took off for vacation at Pyramid Lake in the Adirondacks with my daughter and grand-niece. We met up with my sister Connie, her husband Richard, my niece and two nephews, for our 15th year at the same lake with the same friends. This is heaven to me. I love to swim around the island in the center of the lake, hike, eat communally and laugh. It was everything that I needed it to be this year. I withheld my diagnosis, but Connie and my friend Kelly are slow leaks, so by the time people began to "know" my news, it was slow paced enough not to blow my vacation. Instead, when we laughed and sang around the campfire, I felt the burden of fear lighten off my shoulders. This place of natural beauty and community holds my contentment.

August 24th, 2009

My very first scan was an MRI of my breasts. I opened the front of my hospital gown and the nurses helped me lay face down, placing my breasts into holes in the scanning table. They were gently centered and vitamin E capsules were taped to my nipples, exaggerating them for the imaging. Then they rolled me into the tube. The imaging sounds blasted around me and I remembered the breathing techniques that Diane taught me. I closed my eyes and imagined that I was swimming at the lake in the Adirondacks, breathing in and out, my arms patiently propelling me forward sending ripples outward. I love to have my eyes ride at water's level, watching the mirrored sky. The only sound is the tinkling of my earrings tapping together, and my breathing in and out.

August 25th, 2009

I dreamt of camp activities, nature and walks, but turned over and lost the details. Now medical stuff is creeping in. MRI was yesterday. PET scan is today.

I showered as usual, but no makeup, no food, and lots of water to drink. Again, everyone that saw me today was very sympathetic which kept me close to the emotional edge. I got my IV and sat in the "Quiet Room" for an hour (you can watch TV, but no reading). Then I was strapped in the scanning machine and photographed for 45 minutes. Again, I successfully swam in the healing water of Pyramid Lake. DONE. I waited fifteen more minutes for them to put it on a CD for the breast oncologist tomorrow. The reports will be faxed. I went home and paced, feeling too vulnerable to go to work. I cleaned my desk and shredded papers.

I went to Mom's. We walked around her garden pulling weeds and cutting flowers. It was very therapeutic for us both. I'm sorry for the worry this is causing her.

Wednesday, August 26th, 2009

I wonder what to wear for this appointment in NYC. I decided on the wrap knit dress I wore on vacation; an abstract print with blues, teals and turquoise. It looks lovely over my breasts.

IT'S OFFICIAL NOW

I sit waiting for my appointment. I am new here, in every way. I finish filling out the paperwork, and hand it to the receptionist. I sit facing a woman wearing comfortable black clothing; she looks at me with the compassion of experience. She briefly shares her successful story to put me at ease. I admire her short, stylish haircut, but have no story to share yet; it is just the beginning for me. I went on vacation knowing that I was facing cancer, but today is when I will find out the extent of it. The week I returned I had the first round of serious tests: an MRI of my breasts, a PET scan with radioactive isotope, and now I am in New York City to consult with an oncologist who specializes in breast cancer. My local surgeon, who had ordered these tests, is on vacation. This doctor will see the results first.

My sister-in-law, June, said she'll meet me here. She and my youngest brother, Matt, arranged this speedy appointment; this doctor is an associate of June's friend. June had colon cancer five years ago and will come to support me and translate the cancer lingo. When she arrives I am surprised that she has my seven-year-old nephew with her. We're called into the doctor's office, but she is not comfortable explaining the reports to me with Donovan in the room. She also needs to examine my breasts; he'll need to sit outside the door, with his Gameboy, supervised by the nurse.

Dr. Tessa Cigler shakes our hands as she introduces herself. "Well Carol, this is a bit awkward, as I am *not* the doctor that ordered the tests and I am meeting you for the first time. I'm sorry to confirm that you *do* have cancer, breast cancer, in both breasts and it has metastasized to your T1 vertebrae. You will need biopsies to confirm this, but it is stage four." We discuss what this means, as Donovan checks in on us every few minutes. It's a serious diagnosis, but I'm new here, naïve, optimistic. The doctor mentions all the new treatments being implemented to help people with Metastatic Cancer live extensively. "Even five years ago, this would have been a bleaker prognosis, Carol. You'll need to have a biopsy of your T1 vertebrae, here in this hospital. We need to determine if it's the same type of breast cancer in your breasts and spine, or if it's another type of cancer and this has to be done soon."

Outside, it is a hot day in late August. We approach the elevator and I notice a full-bodied woman waiting there, wearing a large floral print dress. She's bald under a straw hat with a large orange bow. Her arms are covered with tight flesh tone sleeves and tight, mismatched flesh tone gloves. I wonder how she could wear something so homely and uncomfortable in this weather. As I stand there, shell-shocked, nervously critiquing her costume, she smiles. She seems comfortable with herself. I realize, months later, that she had introduced me to some of the accessories of cancer.

Thursday, August 27th, 2009

My life is turning upside down, but by next summer it will be behind me. I will be recovered. I will be swimming at the lake again.

Yesterday in the doctor's office I saw so many women. I noticed many of them looked healthy, sitting calmly, reading magazines, but bald, wearing a range of wigs or hats. One woman seemed new, like me, but pacing the floor, worried sick. A frail woman passed through looking gray as death, on the arm of someone guiding her. A frail, emaciated woman sat next to me and there was the full-bodied woman with compression sleeves and gloves. Is this the spectrum of possibilities?

I am facing this cancer shit head on, not wanting it, but somewhere in here are gifts to treasure, lessons to learn. I am getting a huge one upfront – the love and light from family and friends, and care shown by doctors I have only just met. Charlie, my ex-husband, and Matt coming front-and-center like the queen's guard. My children supporting each other and loving me while continuing to live their lives. Without facing cancer would I have seen this?

VERY SPECIAL SECRETS

One day, years ago, my Mom stepped into my room and shut the door. She handed me a little booklet called "Very Special Secrets." On the cover were two young women in bras and petticoats. The younger girl looked directly at me, but nestled shyly next to her teenage sister. Maidenform Bras supplied this to help mothers, like mine, broach the subject of what to tell their daughters about their changing bodies. My Mom had noticed my swollen nipples; first one, then two weeks later the other had popped. I had been at my friend Lisa Ever's house listening to It Ain't Me Babe, when she accidentally elbowed me in the chest, trying to correct my self-conscious dancing style. I thought that's why they hurt. Mom knew better and watched for the right time to talk about it.

The pamphlet explained the simple version of menstruation and hormones, but went more fully into tips about grooming. Towards the back of the booklet were small illustrations of the various products available for their new teen audience. I picked out the *"Littlest Angel; a perfect 'first bra' with a one size magic 'Gro-Cup' of stretch nylon; it expands as your figure develops."* The elastic device had nothing to grab onto but small sore nipples and it constantly rode up my chest; straps fell off one shoulder or the other. It was not the symbol of maturity that I had dreamed of; without real breasts to put in it, it was a nuisance. I wanted to fill out a bra like my Mom and two older sisters. I appreciated

Mom's attention to this delicate matter, but unfortunately it was only my self-image that needed hoisting.

Mom's friend Mary Jane said, "Carol, I wouldn't bother wearing it if I were you." Dad embarrassed me at a family feast by saying, "You only need band aids!" The boys at school snickered too. I was tall, gangly and looked more like my father every day. Mom bought me an elasticized panty girdle too, to hold up my stockings. It was less provocative than a garter belt and held to my Mother's moral standard that *"Nothing should jiggle!"*

Friday, August 28th, 2009

I woke up thinking that someone just let go. I was dreaming of my body locked up with a key that went to the padlock on my old storefront gate. I would have to let go of my old body, the key, the padlock, to sell my business. My shoulders triangulated to create the opening of the padlock. Past employees were being replaced gently into volunteer positions for convention. Some were sad and uncomfortable letting go to new people happy to take their place, not knowing that they too would be replaced one day.

I'm focused on having the rugs cleaned in the living room and bedroom, wash windows and dust underneath furniture. Next is clearing out the garage, so I can park my car there when it snows, making it easier to shovel the driveway. I am cleaning papers at my desk. I am going into my seasonal cocoon in a more dramatic way. I'm creating my nest; nesting to cure. These images make me peaceful. It is temporary. Pulled in.

The kids came home last night after driving around in Mike's car, talking. Mike is in "charge" of Dana and she is welcome to hang out at Charlie's house anytime. He is there for her. They came back with double crème Oreos, hiding them under Mike's shirt. They teased me about needing to control myself around the cookies. I dipped a cookie into Mike's milk. I told Dana she was jealous and she teased back, "NO! Go ahead and dip in Mike's milk!" Then I took another cookie while she was distracted and dipped the cookie in her milk and stuffed it in my mouth before she saw it. Dana guessed because Mike and I were laughing and it felt sweet and reminiscent of better times. We shared a group hug, but before that I said, "It might not look pretty – ¬me on chemo. I'll have to go in deep to come out the other side." I will begin my hike up the hill. I will enjoy the view and return to base camp. My life will be changed.

I have been to the bathroom and back with my cat, Smokebomb, following me. Mila, my other cat, still sleeps on my bed. I feel at peace with visions of my convent, my retreat. I do my yoga and lay relaxing on the floor before my bridge pose. I gasp at the thought of leaving here. The loneliness of my last voyage. Light and love will help me, but I'll need to go it alone. I won't go now, but I see it will be close. How can that not change me?

Saturday, August 29th, 2009

Today is the opposite. I had big dreams, but obstinately lie still in bed and let them slip away.

I'm a slug. Catatonic. Poor me? Almost…

My great friend, Jody, reached me at a perfect moment.

She listened and then bounced comfort to me, "Carol, you'll be okay."

I talked to Dad and Mary today. Mary speculated momentarily how someone as healthy as I am could get cancer. Have I written that word much? They are very concerned and said they could help me next financially month. Relief.

Dana's going to visit her boyfriend's grandparents in NYC. Charlie is driving them down. She is stressing about which top to wear, that her boobs are lopsided. I love her. I wish telling her that her shirt doesn't matter would help. It doesn't. Her boyfriend's Gran will like her, no matter what she wears. She is incredible.

Tuesday, September 1st, 2009

"Like clockwork," the company's new health insurance plan kicks in on the day of my spinal biopsy in NYC. Bobby met me at the bus station and we walked to lunch, and then wandered around the Metropolitan Museum. I loved walking in the vaulted rooms with sunlight pouring over large Buddhas. I photographed the statues and thanked them for the distraction and peace I found amongst them.

We arrived at the Weill Cornell Hospital and were led from the office to the basement radiology department. The doctor performing the spinal biopsy was amazing. He talked to me the whole way through, describing every incremental needle insertion. "Now we're going to run you through the scan. Now I'm going to push it in a little more." This man and his team do many of these procedures every day, but he was as patient as if I was the only one. He seemed to enjoy the challenge of his work and I felt confident. There was a team of people in the other room looking under microscopes, testing my cells, to see if a big enough specimen was procured. The doctor was hoping to get the results needed without penetrating my bone and was successful. Everyone seemed pleased, especially me. They were able to confirm that the cancer in my breasts was the same in my spine. I presume that treating one cancer is easier than treating two. It was nice to have another test behind me.

CIGARETTES

Cigarettes intrigued me in the sixth grade. I caught my teenage sisters smoking and my Dad, too. After school my friends and I always went to Central Market to buy candy, displayed right next to the cigarette rack. While a few girls paid for the Necco Wafers and Junior Mints, someone else took a turn pocketing the Winstons. We were good "Catholic girls" though, and always left fifty cents at the end of the counter, near the stack of brown bags.

We walked over to Linda and Leslie Ruff's house. They discovered a wooded area behind their garage, perfect for our investigation. The holder of the pack doled out cigarettes and passed matches. We each lit up and inhaled, coughed, choked and felt lightheaded. We practiced for days in a row discovering "dirty pictures" and empty beer cans from other explorers. The code phrase for the activity was, "Do you want to go to the *LIBRARY* today?" With that we could ask friends to come smoke with us in front of their parents.

We practiced inhaling until we stopped choking. Next was learning to exhale through our noses, like they did in the movies; it looked so glamorous. My personal goal was to exhale as a performance for my sisters. I wanted them to know how mature I was.

Mom wasn't home one afternoon, and I found Connie and Chrissy smoking cigarettes in the kitchen. I surprised them by taking one, too. I casually exhaled through my nose, glancing to see if they noticed. I imagined that, for a moment, they had seen me as

their equal. It was an unfair race being the little sister; always behind them, always running to catch up. I was satisfied by my exhale though, and never smoked another disgusting cigarette again.

September 7th, 2009

TEAM HELP has formed and they met at my house tonight: Jody Sterling, Diane and Kate Scott-Childress (SC). They talked about what I'll need. I have no idea what I'll need, but they've been researching and began discussions about fundraising, food during chemo, help cleaning my house, rides for Dana…I am overwhelmed as these friends lift this weight off my shoulders. We talked about my breasts. I showed them my skewed nipple in the kitchen. They all looked and someone says, "You're not as big as I thought you were!" and we all laughed like we're still girls. I took the first photo of our group to document *us* in *this* time.

Diane went with me to the doctor's office to listen and be an extra set of ears. I have trouble remembering all that is said or suggested. The doctor talked about surgery for my "port" to make chemotherapy easier. Diane asked questions about the port and was enthusiastic about it being an *Infusa-Port*. Diane got the doctor's permission to be in my operating room to do her specialty: Transformational Healing.

September 8th, 2009

September 9th, 2009

I had surgery for my Infusa-Port. They weren't going to let Diane into surgery, even though the surgeon had no objections. Another great friend, my hospital "Guardian Angel," pulled strings and made it happen. I am so grateful. Diane was holding my energy and helping my body to welcome the port for the ease of my chemo infusions. It all went well. I can't help but feel so lucky.

I need some time to heal before they can use it. The port is in my upper chest attached to my carotid artery.

September 11th, 2009

I dreamt of chemotherapy on a roof top. I was trying to figure it out with no instructions. Which direction do I lay? For how long? A few people lay on other roof tops – over and over – this way and that way. I lay sprawled on the roof with my arms, legs and fingers spread.

Then I'm in a neighborhood – no sidewalks, rural, a small town with blocks of houses and lots of elderly people. When I walked around the block I saw an elderly woman sitting in a rocker on a porch, then a home for older men in the firehouse. I looked through the window at the guys reading and trading books; they're bearded but not that old. There also was a very old man in a suit that walked around and around and around the block in his suit with a cane. I am in a car with Mom driving us around the block, but she cuts through the middle on a grassy road.

Slept poorly last night. I woke forty-five minutes after going to sleep, one hour after that, 2:15, 4:20, who knows. I'm conscious of getting used to my port; the stretched skin, the bump and the residue of ache.

I had a nice ride with Charlie to New York to see Dr. Cigler again. Long car rides were always comfortable with Charlie. Now we discuss our children, all the old friends we have in common, old stories we share about our lives together with his family or mine. We avoid hot topics that we know push each other's buttons; we don't need to touch underlying differences. Charlie took notes and recorded our appointment, which was handy later, on the way home, to replay and clear up a difference about what we heard. So, I'll go every two weeks for chemo, three to four hours per, and then get a follow up shot the next day to boost the white blood cell production. Dr. Cigler said she will call my Kingston oncologist, Dr. Andrade, and discuss my "unique" stage-four breast cancer. She plans to treat for CURE.

Matt followed up on the phone with a lecture about using the "best," being willing to come into the city for it, Fighting with the Best, Going in the Ring, SCIENCE, NOT OPTIMISM. I am optimistic with Science. I know I will get through this. I feel ready for the gauntlet. I am not afraid or hesitant. Everyone can worry, lecture or cry, but they do not know my path as I do. They can hand me cups of water, but it is my race. I know this will not kill me now. I will be more finished when I leave this life. This path is closer to clarity, but not death.

UNCONDITIONAL HEALING

"The conventional view of illness is that it possesses no intrinsic value or worth, and should be resisted and discarded at the earliest opportunity. Consequently, if an illness or disability is chronic or life-threatening, we often feel a loss of self esteem and self-worth, and a sense of isolation or alienation.

The more expansive view of illness is that it is a profound opportunity to confront questions of mortality and fundamental well being, and offers us the means to experience our genuine nature. This is the view of illness that we explore and practice together."

Jeff Rubin

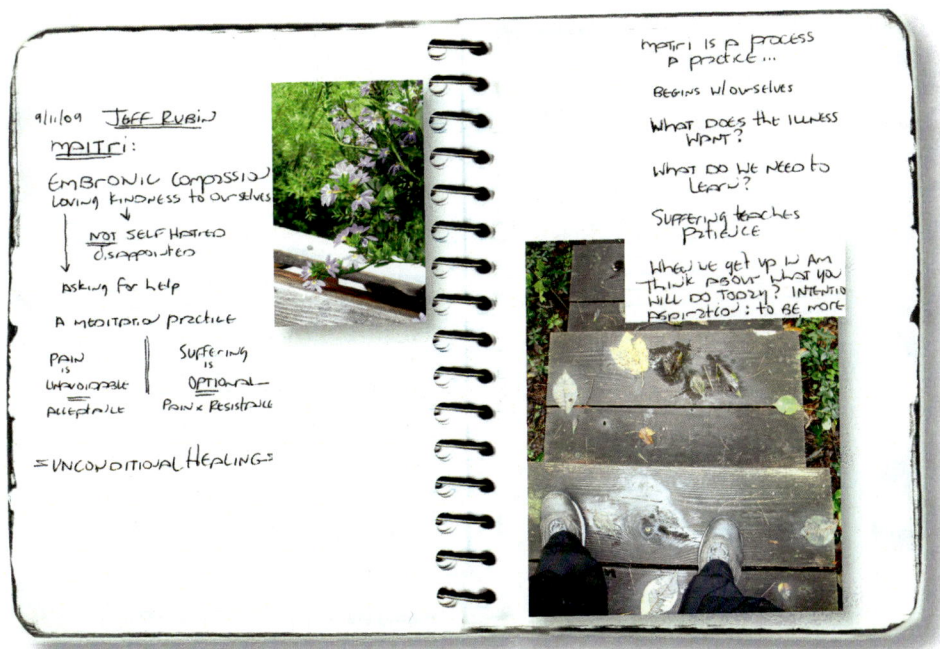

September 12th, 2009

I dreamt that my NYC friends, Tommy and Danielle, were driving me to an appointment in my room that had pinwheels taped to the walls to catch the wind. I showed Danielle my new corset I made for convention, black satin with light teal piping and wedges of color peeking through looking stretched. She was silent and I reassured her I would wear it again. I would stuff the cup after my mastectomy and use it as a foundation garment under evening wear to look normal.

It's 8:45 am in real time. I just had an anxiety dream of missing my appointment with the local oncologist. I am good this morning. I slept on my right side and had a deeper sleep after I turned over. I need to RSVP my friend, Jennifer, that I can't go to her wedding: hair loss 10 – 14 days after first chemo. Prepare for it.

Kate SC took me to my appointment with Dr. Andrade today. He had discussed my case at the "tumor board' that morning, where radiologists, oncologists and surgeons confer on procedures. They are all in alignment with Dr. Cigler's recommendation. Great. Monday: I get an echocardiogram. Wednesday: 1st chemo

By next weekend: 1st short preparatory hair cut.

Tonight I went to hear Jeff Rubin's workshop on Unconditional Healing at Sky Lake Lodge in Rosendale. He spoke of maître – self caring. I have a lot to learn.

September 13th, 2009

I had a powerful dream of walking down a hallway and suddenly, to my right, there's a large opening in the wall. I look through it to the outside; a view of an ascending yard, like a child's drawing. A tree grows midway up the slope. It gives the impression of a graveyard though no gravestones indicate that. I am looking through glass at the scene of my death. I reach, expecting to find the knob to open a door, but there isn't one. My eyes follow the wooden frame and I realize it is a window, not a door. I don't have to enter. I woke and told my daughter that I'm going to be okay. I'm not going to die now. My cancer is a window to mortality, not the doorway to my death. Now I feel less afraid and can afford to take a good look before continuing on my journey. I'll be grateful for this glimpse, when later in life I'll stand here again with an invitation to abandon this body that will have served me well. I have much love to share first, more experience for my spiritual resume.

I woke up in pain this morning. I was laying on my right side, my usual favorite way, and I woke with pain on my left breast, bottom center. I realized it wasn't a dream, but real pain, and rolled over.

I spoke to Robert today and told him of my progress. The next time I see him I'll be bald. He told me he has felt my beautiful round head and I will be fine. I told him that my port feels like a cocoon under my skin. It's part of my transformation.

Work with Diane: *This is the gold mesh that I lay on to separate the dark cancer from the light of my body. My light filters through, but the cancer gets caught and removed. I travel through my filter several times every day.*

There are going to be thousands of little goldfish — so tiny in my chemo solution. They'll blow colorful bubbles in the bag and anxiously wait to swim in my body and ingest the cancer. They each ingest a dozen cancer cells and replace them with healthy cells as they paint the area with their bodies. The fish carry the cancer cells out of my body and transform it to positive energy, replacing the darkness with light. They will come in my body on Wednesday for the first of sixteen journeys.

The cancer is my raw, rough, unformed self. It is unfinished, heavy and lumpy. I have polished much of myself, but this lumpy clay is what I have not dealt with and is part of the disease in my body. The process of chemo and surgery will breakdown the un-needed and un-useful clay mess in my core. Diane's healing work and my friend, Therese's acupuncture will help me through the process. I am being refined, filtered and loved. My ego is softened and gaining a broader view; my understanding of life is growing.

My images are expressed with Diane's guidance, but they are my healing images, unique to my journey.

September 14th, 2009

I went back to work today. Joe, our design-director spared me the meeting that everyone else had to attend. I finished a doll project, a Bette Davis hat, and began another. It is a working meditation, keeping my mind on the project, always coming back to the project. I left at 1:00 pm for my echocardiogram. I found it fascinating to watch. I saw my aorta. Then I stopped by my surgeon's office and she had a look at my "Infusa-Port." She said to be careful, but go ahead and do my yoga. I won't do a bridge pose or shoulder stand because of the tumor in my T-1 vertebrae.

Then I stopped by Mom's for my surprise gift. I opened it with Mom taking pictures and Connie had sent me a prayer shawl and she made it! Mom said she'd been knitting furiously "behind my back" at the lake. It is beautiful shade soft blue, calm and peaceful and the healing colors I visualized for my port.

Tons of emails! I'm trying to respond to friends, just a note. I love and appreciate the unbelievable response. Dana and her boyfriend cooked last night. They were so sweet to be with. They made cookies too.

It was a wonderful day. It is complete with Mila lying by my side. Her colors look so gorgeous on the flannel duvet. Goodnight.

Tuesday September 15th, 2009

I actually touched my body…loved my body and enjoyed it. I have been asexual without Robert. It's good to know I am still a sexual being.

My dream had Janet Leacock in it, but Dana's alarm snapped it shut. My chemo is tomorrow. Last night I emailed more friends with my Health Updates 1,2 & 3 so they aren't left out of the loop. I'll let them hear it from me.

I ran to New Paltz after work today for pre-chemo acupuncture session with Therese. It was very powerful. She worked points near the bone on my lower leg that gave a feeling of movement downward. She said to remember it tomorrow, to keep everything flowing downward –

that's the right direction. She placed a needle in my mid-section that gave a powerful sensation. Therese told me it was a point of Unification and gifted me a beautiful Celtic amulet to wear for healing.

Therese walked me outside and showed me the plant Artemisia growing wild along the side of the road. She suggested taking a sprig of it to place under my pillow to enhance my dreams. I carried it gently home.

I stopped by and visited my old friend, Sally, to share my news in person. I told her that I wanted her to see me well and picture me well, so she wouldn't worry.

I got home to a phone call of good wishes from Kate SC. She began a Facebook page called "Friends & Family of Carol Dwyer." I checked it out and wrote a note on the page. I posted that I go for my first chemo tomorrow and for a short haircut on Thursday (in prep for chemo hair loss). I feel expansive tonight, positive, picturing chemo and glad to have my big sister Connie coming with me. So much love. I am grateful.

Wednesday September 16th, 2009

I dreamt it was my birthday. I was wearing my reading glasses decorated with rhinestones glued on to 1950's cat frames. I was preparing for fun! It was a surprise birthday party at my chemo session! The place was packed and everyone was singing to me. A little boy enthusiastically banged on the table and my late friend, Mark Truman, began clapping his hands to his thighs for the little boy to follow and they marched through the festivities. Mark winked at me as he gently fixed the problem, while being sensitive to the little boy's feelings. What an interesting way to celebrate my birthday!

Purification begins today – my birthday, in a way – the new me. Dana kissed me and is off to school. I sit in bed writing.

✯✯✯✯✯✯✯✯

I went to work at 9:00 am and lasted until 11:30 when I left to go home. I ate my light lunch and vacuumed until Connie came to pick me up. We got to Dr. Andrade's office by 1:00 pm and began to laugh right away and have fun. She had worn the "perfect outfit" for chemo, a crisp white shirt and black pants like the angel that she was for me today. I also teased her sitting there knitting while I had my first chemotherapy infusion. I called her "Madame Lafarge" who watched the guillotine decapitations while knitting during the French Revolution. I'm feeling a little "wooshie," not high, but not *not* high; not nauseous, but not *not* nauseous.

Thursday, September 17th, 2009

Nauseous, lightly, enough to be nervous or are my nerves making me nauseous? *Blue,* it is a gray day outside. It is my first post-chemo day, adjusting, trying to find comfort in the beginning of a changing normal.

I got up for breakfast and anti-nausea meds. I hate to think what this would be like without them. I feel random aches and pains in my bones from the second drug that my nurse, Jody, gave me yesterday. It is pumped in more quickly. I want to lie down, but I'm afraid to give up. Maybe I'll shower. I made some ginger tea.

Friday, September 18th, 2009
Reality Check Day.

I made it to work for two and a half hours sporting my new hair cut, but nausea won and anxiety over nausea, and sadness over not being able to keep up the pace. Falling, or failing? I left and went to Mom's house. She was showering, so I made myself comfortable on the back deck's lounge. I relaxed with the soughing of the trees and the distant Thruway traffic hum. The squirrels scampered in the trees overhead, dropping nuts. My body was half in the sun. Mom came out with a blanket, pillow and a chicken sandwich. Noon. 1:15 pm. Mike and Charlie stopped by to check on me. 2:00 to 3:00 I slept. 4:30 I got up. I came home and Kate SC called. She was okay with my grief. I appreciated her tone, her acceptance.

"Mom-Mom," Charlie's mom, called me back. I was relieved that she was okay after her fall yesterday. She told me to be strong. Mike brought Dana home from shopping. My neighbor brought me a bouquet of roses. Dana fixed me soup and toast. We watched most of Breakfast at Tiffany's before she joined friends at the diner, so I watched Mozart and The Whale that Connie had left for me.

Dana came back with a stomach-ache and we watched the rest of Tiffany's. I am crying tonight, crying that I really have to go through all this, crying that Dana has to watch me go through this; there is no Fast Forward. Dana saw me cry. We cried. Mom saw me cry too. A big, blue day.

Saturday, September 19th, 2009

I am better than yesterday.
I decided to be.

Sunday, September 20th, 2009

It was a good day, almost normal and very social. I sat on the porch and got visits from Patti then Sally, and later with Jody and Bill Sterling. I am overwhelmed with love and kindness. My brother, Bobby, helped me disassemble the dining room table and set up my studio so I can sew in the comfort of my own house instead of the cold studio over the garage. Charlotte brought soup which tasted so good. I'm constipated and trying an over the counter remedy suggested by one of my friends. Reading: In The Time of The Butterflies by Julia Alvarez for book club.

Monday, September 21st, 2009

I was in a 1950's boat, like a big old car, moving slowly around other boats and people selling boats. Then I'm in a traffic jam of boats full of older women from the 1920's and 30's wearing fur coats and old fashions, trying to leave a party backwards and finally all jammed into a canal parking lot. I left with an Asian woman who wraps a sarong around me to slow me down. We get quite a laugh out of this. I'm walking with the gait of a Geisha, with my body wrapped in a large cloth. We are walking down the city street, then in a museum with beautiful walls. We are walking through Parsons and see my old teachers. We are walking gingerly on a black fire escape outside of a large building, but it feels to be getting frailer and frailer, rusty, diminishing…I am leading as the stronger and more confident of us, but restricted by my sarong. I can no longer see the escape in front of me. I am groping in the dusk. I am groping the disintegrating ladder and say we need to turn back gently, quickly, quietly, before the whole thing becomes dust in our hands. I woke up as we were gingerly beginning to back up the frail fire escape.

My neighbors Anne and Ray stopped over to talk. Ray said not to worry about snow shoveling this year. Anne is organizing a Bike-A-Thon fundraiser to benefit me, at the gym where she works and I'm a member. I am in a space unknown to me.

Tuesday, September 22nd, 2009

I dreamt that I took a big poop. I dreamt I was turned on sexually. I dreamt that I had to get dressed to lead an army. I am standing in a country driveway, near mailboxes, looking for my underwear and my mechanic is driving a wagon up to the property. I am yelling for Dana to help me find my underpants! Then I have to feed the rabbits. Usually, I travel all this distance and there is old food to take away and new to put out, but this time it is all empty. No old, no new and I'm so far from home; where will I get the food to feed the bunnies? Why wasn't I warned that there was no food?

Oh my God; I have never been so depressed before. It's worse than flat. No way out, but through. I want to lie down to sleep and wake up and be done. I am still working at my job and already in overdraft in my checkbook. I feel angry and disappointed by my life. I wash my hair and wonder if today is the day my hair will begin to fall out. I am pissed off, sad, lonely. Dana is amazing, but this is too much.

NIGHT: I worked through an array of thoughts and emotions today. Right now I feel good. I have gone to the bathroom. I've bought and eaten prunes, answered emails, and took a walk. It feels so good for me!

Katie SC and Jody both checked in on me. Dana had fun eating Chinese food with her friend, Faith, while watching video awards on TV. Bobby called to remind me, "You are not your thoughts." I forgot to transfer money to my checking account.

Wednesday, September 23rd, 2009

I dreamt I was watching Hugh Jackman and Anne Hathaway's big Academy Awards dance routine only Anne wasn't there, just Hugh. The queen was coming for tea and I was imagining a huge spectacular banquet and performance in this bank plaza with a simple fare of yogurt, granola, raspberries and tea, along with their show. How would I get in touch with Anne? Does she still have that blue dress? Would she do this on the fly? The space, the dishes, the help??? It is 11:35 am and the Queen will be here at 2:00 pm! How could that be enough time?? Impossible! Hugh Jackman was kind throughout my decision process.

Robert called up and left a message that he'd be able to come up this weekend and help clean out the garage so I can park in there this winter.

Thursday September 24th, 2009 @ 4am

I dreamt I was in NYC and Donovan had a jam session on a rooftop. I walked downstairs and talked to two women cooking food at a counter. We all had the same haircut. They said I'd be good at sales for them. As we talked, different siblings and nephews passed through and I introduced them, Bobby, then Everett being all sweaty and charming, Donovan with a soda and not saying much, then Connie and finally Matt, like he was the star.

It's so muggy and hot. I hear Dana tossing and turning. I am a mess. People are pouring out concern. I have stage-four breast cancer, but feel like a fraud. What the fuck is wrong with this? I am so stressed today, letting other people help me. Why am I so resistant?

I'm struggling to be normal. What the fuck do I want to do? I have to face my fears. I have to acknowledge my anger, express it, and through my cancer, take charge and shape the next section of my life. I want to be of value; creative, loved and loving.

My lower back is killing me today, like I need to shit a constipated brick that is lodged in my back. Co-worker Suzanne handed me an envelope with a check in it from her and husband, Jim. She said it can be a loan, but not due until the year 4034. I am fucking floored. Mortgage for two months plus just like that. "The circle," she said. "We're paying back to the circle…"

Friday September 25th, 2009

I dreamt of facing my illness, going to the doctors, going from room to room, preparing and finally into a hospital gown. There were three doctors: one strong, two that were weaker and nervous, walking ahead of me. I am alone in a closet dressing room in my hospital gown, going to confront my illness.

Then I'm at work working on a hat. After every step of working on a game at convention, I stroke the hat with a damp sponge. Oops. It shrinks and pulls away from the frame, oh well, try, try, and try again. At the end of convention we pack up like it's an empty circus tent. I ask Joe for time to pack. I am in a garage. The cement floor has a worn brick color paint. This will be my space for this time. I look around and need help to prepare. I would like to clean and repaint the floor for starters. Does it have walls? One direction yes, but the other side has cyclone fence. There is a dip in the floor for drainage. I can at least wash it and it will dry, but I must do it before the cold sets in. I dip my foot to the drain and feel a chill from deep below. I will need to cover it for warmth. There is another flaw in the floor that I see as I round the first drain, Oh my God! It is a natural formation of crystals! Primeval, rough and course, sharp and splendid; a valuable find to keep or sell. I have reviewed my healing space.

I fell back asleep and dreamt that Robert slipped up behind me to snuggle. I tried to resist, but I enjoyed the comfort, but I did separate to communicate my feelings, I had to, and it was good.

Dana had a nightmare and came into my bed to snuggle for the first time in at least a year. We ended up talking from 3:00-4:30 am, both of us exhausted, but happy to share this open and honest time. She shared early childhood memories, talked about enjoying school and getting more involved in it. She's not doing the youth theatre this season. She talked about classes and plans for next year. She also spoke about how overwhelming it is when confronted by people who heard of my cancer, asking her sorrowfully in the hallways of school, "I'm so *sorry* to hear about your Mother!" or "Please let me know if I can help in *anyway*…." She's finding it hard to not cry, but she was grateful for our mutual friend, Carole, who seemed to be able to ask Dana the right questions, "Dana, how are you feeling these days? Is there anything that I can help you with?" She allowed Dana to open up about her feelings, be heard and consoled.

Saturday, September 26th, 2009

Robert and I attacked the garage and we accomplished it! It is now raining and the car is dry in the garage! Steve and Sandy were walking by and stopped to chat, then Lisa drove up and stopped, then Katie. It was a driveway party, a fun respite from our task.

September 28th, 2009

My blood count was great! I'm preparing to go for round #2 on Wednesday. Nice talks with friend, Joanna, tonight and then Danielle. I feel open to all the people I have ever known and loved. Anne finished the poster for the Bike-A-Thon Event at the gym coming up in October.

October 4th, 2009

Mike and his friend came over today. He brought me beautiful and thoughtful gifts including healing stones that he selected specifically for their traits. We sat out in the back yard and I told him my hair was falling out. I have been shaving his hair for years, half way up his head, leaving the rest long. In fact, having the shaver in my possession was a tactic to have him come over to visit me.

"I think it's your turn now Mike. Would you shave my head?" We set up on the back lawn and his friend took pictures. "Mom, this shaver is too dull! It will hurt you, but I'll just cut it off." Half-way through he asked if I still wanted bangs, but I assured him that it all needed to go. When it was all done he kissed my head and got a loose hair stuck to his lips. We laughed out loud and it was the best experience that could be. Who'd have thought that this long-haired woman would ever let it go? I never would have been brave enough. Now I actually find it fascinating to have no hair; I dare to say it feels empowering. I am free. Chilly, but free! Going without hair reminds me of the power I felt going braless as young teen.

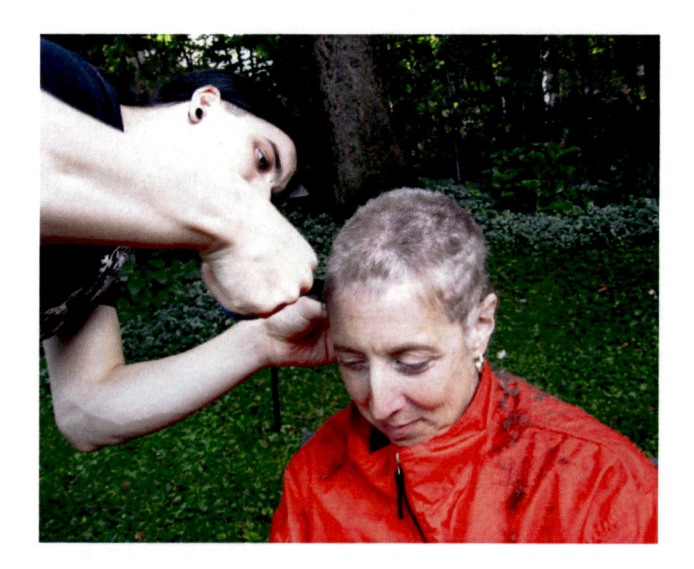

1970 - SECRETS EXPOSED

Mom decided after my first "Training Bra" introduction, that a padded bra would be better suited for her flat-chested daughter. "A little padding will improve your self- image," she said. That was sort of okay, except when the girls at school gossiped about our friend saying, "Her bra must be stuffed because her boobs are too high." I began to feel concerned that my underutilized undergarments were discussed publically too. They might say mine were stuffed because they were too low, but that's where my bumps were on my long torso. Insecurity hunched my shoulders forward.

While camping with my friend Kathy and her family in Lake George, I met a boy named Rick. "Love the One You're With" came on the radio in the Teen Center and inspired us to go make out in the park. I desired the practice of passion. We lay down kissing and then he slid his hand up to feel my fifteen year old breast. I pushed his hand away. I felt very passionate at the moment, but if he felt for my breast he'd only be feeling the padding of my bra. He would discover my dishonesty; I felt embarrassed and we stopped there. It was the arousal of my passion, combined with the imminent danger of humiliation that helped me take the next step into teenage rebellion.

It was a few days later when I made the leap and came out of the house, braless. I was wearing a soft yellow Henley tee shirt standing on the front porch when my Mom saw me. "Carol! You can see right through your shirt! I can see *everything*" she said in a low voice as she looked quickly, side-to-side at the neighbors' houses. Standing on the top step of the porch, I pulled my shirt taught against my chest, making everything more distinct. "*You can?*" I asked. My poor mother did not know what to do with me, but I felt more comfortable with this forthright stance; I felt empowered. What you see is what you get. I accepted that I was small-breasted and stopped faking it. I grew my hair long and wore my bell bottoms low. Self-confidence is more important than breast size, I discovered. I was growing with the times.

It was the changing of the fashion guard; from the dichotomy of my big sisters' Doris Day and Marilyn Monroe ideals to my Twiggy. Fashion shifted from the forced cleavage of bras and corsets to the braless, natural shape of the loose breast and nipple. Small breasts were more fashionable while large breasts never lost their sexual allure. I was content to own mine.

****

I ran to Dietz Stadium to see the Kingston High School marching band Field Show with Kate, Rennie and Elias. It was exciting and fun to see the band perform their well rehearsed show. Back home I cooked rainbow Swiss chard with garlic, yellow tomatoes and coriander over rice. I watched She's Just Not That into You and when Dana came home she insisted that I would love Stepbrothers. We laughed out loud!

Monday, October 6th, 2009

I dreamt of living in the East Village and my boyfriend kept talking of repairing the roof…blah, blah, blah…railroad apartment that's so small and funky, but why do we have to store Mike Tyson's art collection in our apartment?

Bleeding cold sore on my lip. I came home after work and was glad that Dana was at her friend's house because I needed to cry, wail and sob. I had been close to it all day. Poor fucking me. Sally left a bag of groceries on the porch and Danielle sent a tee shirt from a breast cancer run. It's a beautiful color with beautiful thoughts coming my way. But is my throat funny? Glands? The doctor will prescribe antibiotics automatically. I'm tired, and went to bed early last night, 9:30 or 10 o'clock, but I woke at 3:30 in the morning after *dreaming of being on a cliff in New York State during ancient Indian Tribal times. Dana, another friend, and I, had to jump to safer ground. Our friend was not in shape for this survival mode situation. I suggested jumping to a tree and climbing down. I jumped. Then we're on a train going over a bridge through a tunnel. One side of the train was glass and we could see the wall of the tunnel that looked like an archeological find of an ancient American Indian mural, but the train was going too fast to see it well.*

The hot flashes of menopause have returned, anytime, day or night, I get a full flush. The left hand pinky and next finger occasionally have numbness from the chemo.

A friend at work buzzed my head clean today. The hair stubble is gone. I got tired of people asking if I was going to buy a wig or not, so I went to Colombia Beauty Supplies and bought one; dark red. I got angry today thinking about everything that I did right, but still got cancer.

Easy left-overs for dinner tonight with Dana. We watched more of Seinfeld. I was sad, and tired; Dana soothed me with sweetness and a head massage. She fixed our dinner and cleaned up while I snoozed. My brow is furrowed. Bill is taking me to the bank tomorrow to set up an account for my friend's fundraiser to help pay my upcoming expenses.

I was disappointed that today was not a super UP day. It's bad to have expectations and then I felt worried about carrying on.

Thursday, October 8th, 2009

It's a better day already.

I dreamt I was watching an old couple help each other on the side of the road, in the middle of nowhere. We got off the bus. I was talking to a man with black hair, a stranger. He told me to get it off my chest, to tell him what was bothering me and I did. I let him have it. I blasted him! I ranted and raved! I let it all out. He told me I had to tell Robert. I had to tell him of my disappointments. I was with Robert in Hudson Falls, on a street a block away from Gramma Tugas' house, sitting on the curb. The Disney Parade was going to pass, like in my childhood days. I told him calmly of my decision, reasons, and disappointments. He tried to counter, to respond, to defend, but it was not time for him to talk. It was for me. Then we were in the parade with Disney characters. I ended up holding Cinderella's blue ball gown and I stood on Gramma's corner holding it out to the actor as she passed by on the returning trip. She was relieved that I didn't try to keep it. She would have been financially responsible.

Another low day, but I went to see Dr. Andrade and got checked out. I felt better knowing that everything looked okay. I saw Anne, Ray, Kathy and Jody across the street at "Thirsty Thursday." I bumped in to Carole briefly and spoke on the phone to my oldest sister, Chrissy, and her husband, Kurt.

I am working on being here now.

Now is a good place to be.

Uncertainty is certain.

October 9th, 2009

An incredible day, another incredible day. Yesterday while I was at the doctor's, Jack Kralik, our VP, announced that anyone who wanted to donate sick days to me could do it by filling out a form. Within a short time they compiled over four hundred hours. "Enough," Jack said, "to carry me through treatments without having to go on disability." Breathtaking. The goal of returning to work was placed squarely in front of me. "Thank Julie," he added. "It was her suggestion and Robert Tonner approved it, of course."

Saturday, October 10, 2009

Epic dream involving staying overnight at a crash pad of some kind with people I didn't know well. We all slept in a row on the floor and people left one by one. I finally got to pee but wasn't paying attention and it was hitting the seat and spraying onto a box of someone's stuff that was too close to the toilet. I went to wipe up and realized that another guy had shit on a towel and left it! And on the other side of the room was a dead body which I placed behind the chimney as new people began to filter through. Later I looked and the body was in a different position, feet up the wall and head, with a hat on, partially sticking out.

I smoked pot last night, two tokes again. I enjoyed making myself dinner and watched <u>Happy Feet</u> *while I ate two plates of rice noodles, kale, broccoli with peanut sauce and salad (munchies). My doctor assessed that my lower energy was due to weight loss – munchies helped.*

Sunday, October 11th, 2009

A day of wonderful health and energy! I got Dana to band before 8 am. Mike Schneller came over at 10:00 am and cut my shrubs. Bobby and Chloe came by and cleaned up the yard. Chloe looked like she was working hard out there until I looked closer and realized she was raking with one hand and texting with the other! Cousin Jess picked up Mom to repot my plants. Then she cleaned the bathrooms, vacuumed and helped with windows. Mom was pushed outside her current envelope, though she looked nice and got a lot done. I put clean sheets on my bed and the flannel duvet on the comforter for the colder months ahead. I took pictures of the day and loved having a clean house.

Dana came home from the band competition, they placed 2nd in their division, and then she worked organizing her room.

Work with Diane *for a Pre-Chemo Transformational Healing session: I visualized my cancer – black lumps – dead – not living. Quickly reproducing cells of science? No, mine are dead, no longer growing, no longer needed. They woke me up to a fork in the road that I needed to take. They woke me up to the self care that I needed to learn. "NUMB-LUMPS," lumps of numbness, lumps where I put my* *swallowed emotions and feelings; lumps that grew from my "Danish Reserve." As a young girl, I learned not to trust what I felt. I felt something was wrong in our family, but was told, "Nothing's wrong." Diane was grateful that I now had a place to put feelings to help me survive and now I can learn to express those feelings and no longer need to store them in my breast pockets.*

She also had me visualize a year from now and I was dancing at a party, swinging my hips to Latin Jazz with a partner, laughing, stylishly dressed; I was happy, connected by my cord to NOW, present.

NOTHING IS WRONG

Mom told us everything was okay. She was mixing powdered milk into the milk bottle when I wasn't looking; she knew I would taste the difference if I saw it happen. Nothing is wrong; everything is fine, but the tension in the house couldn't lie. My teenage sisters were in high school, it was the late sixties. My family was part of our fractured culture; the disappointed trying to live the American Dream.

My father was working a lot and my forty-year-old mother was furious to find out she was pregnant with her fifth child, after a seven-year hiatus. I was not eager to help Mom make her and Dad's bed that morning. She screamed at me across the sheets, "You have to help me! I'm exhausted and pregnant!" I was eleven-years old, and stunned by her anger. I grabbed the sheets and pulled them up on Dad's side to help make the bed.

Dad came home and showed my younger brother and me his big check. "Look at this kids: $10,000!" he exclaimed. We did not know about business, overhead, or cost of living, but were impressed by Dad's big check, maybe this was the "ship coming in" that he always spoke of. He taught me how to play cards, gin specifically. I was so happy to spend time with him again and learn how to shuffle cards. He praised my skill, sometimes I even won the game. Mom grumbled through the living room. I wondered what her problem was, Dad was spending time with me, his "favorite"; we played cards until dinner time. The tension between my parents made the ground tremble under our feet.

I woke very late one night. Crash! Crash! Crash! Mom was screaming. My sisters on the third floor didn't hear it, but my room was on the second floor. I crept down stairs, tip-toeing towards the kitchen and saw Mom by the sink, furiously throwing dishes at my father who stood near the doorway, ducking. "Mom! Dad!" I yelled. "What are you doing?!" They turned to look at me surprised, caught in the act and shooed me back off to bed; defused for the moment. Everything was fine.

It was Easter dinner at Gramma Tugas's house. The sun pouring in four windows, past the African violets, the set table sparkling with simplicity. "Carol, straighten your shoulders and pull your hair out of your face," Mom orders. Uncle Al, her large quiet brother, his intelligent wife, Aunt Betty, and their son, Lee, are finding their seats around the table. Mom helps Gram put the main course and side dishes in the center of the table. She's added a hair piece to the top of her head for a pouffier bouffant hair style. My mother is uncomfortable with silence; she fills the room with chatter about the dinner, Gramma's new dress and the weather. Aunt Betty mentions a book and my cousin Lee makes a comment; they banter back and forth with their opinions about English literature. I want to be like them. I wonder how old I will be when I'll be able to discuss books or have opinions about politics. Mom is insecure in this department; it makes her nervous to be unable to form an opinion.

She throws out a comment about the dishes. "*MY* dishes," she wonders out loud, "I can't imagine where they've all gone!" I know the answer to that one. "You threw them at Dad, remember?" Mom gave me the *look* while everyone else was chuckling. Deep down I knew everything wasn't okay, but parents don't lie.

Friday, October 16th, 2009

Hot flashes like a furnace out of control. I lost my hat and hankie while tossing in bed. I watched all eight episodes of <u>Weeds</u>' first season on Netflix. One of the lead characters discovers that she has breast cancer and her whole process runs only two episodes, from discovery, chemo, baldness, to surgery and reconstruction. WOW! I was lying on the couch, absolutely feeling the minutiae of discomfort from chemo and I thought, "I want her cancer: the kind that can be fixed in two episodes."

Therese came for an acupuncture house call yesterday. As always, we had a wonderful visit. She reminds me to bring the flow of energy down through my body. Mom came and took me for my Neulasta shot (post-chemo, white-blood cell booster) in the afternoon. She talks about taking me to chemo, but that's a long visit. I think taking me for a shot is enough.

I reclined all day. Slow. Low. Skipped anti-nausea medication last night and tonight, too. How will I do? I smoked two puffs of weed this morning, ate breakfast and watched a stupid movie on a DVD in the TV room. Then I went back to the living room couch for Cool Hand Luke on my laptop. Tonight I watched two documentaries: New York Dolls and Valentino. Then I watched The Last Emperor. I enjoyed both pieces of history.

Kate SC brought me chicken pot pie for dinner tonight with salad. After that, Dana ran off to the movies with a large group of friends. Her PSAT's are in the morning and I might have to drive her!

Sunday, October 18th, 2009

First dream memory post Chemo #3: I am walking down a busy avenue looking for someone to weave fabric for a new coat. Vendors speckle the street; there are painters and miscellaneous sellers of wares. There is a narrow loom and someone tells me it is $90 a yard for fabric. I see a woman in a wheelchair painting canvas. It's thickly painted. I think it would make a warm coat. I notice her style is different from before and she explains it's the influence of her old lover. I enter a building and when I come back out I am in pure fog and blustering rain. I can barely make out the direction to go and tell Dana that I'm not there. I have gone to shower.

I woke up like a normal human today, but lethargic? Heartburn?

Connie and Richard called from an artist's tour and she pep-talked me about feeling down. But down is not falling into negative. Dana went off with friends. Should I walk? I'm restless, but not full of energy, or not full of energy because I'm not using it?

Monday, October 19th, 2009

Dreamt of perfection over and over.... I was expected to get it right, keep going, get it right. I HAD to get it right, putting little tabs on wigs....

Tuesday, October 20th, 2009

I dreamt it was time to let my storefront and apartment go. It has been years since I was there. I wanted my machines and to make stuff. I walked through the store and out the back door and up a flight of stairs. Wow! Am I out of shape? Wait. I walked through the vestibule using the key to enter the apartment building. I had keys to find my apartment up the flight of stairs, but there was a family in the apartment that I thought was mine. She invites me in to sit down and talk. She's been there since 2006 with her three kids. Maybe my apartment was downstairs in the back? I should go look. I hope he has not dumped my stuff. I hope it is still there to find, to own.

312 EAST NINTH STREET

It was turquoise when I first moved there, with orange trim and cracked glass in the front door window. The street had quite a few empty storefronts and the landlords allowed people to live in them just to have them occupied. I met the agent renting out the 312 East Ninth Street shop, and I was her best bet. It was October 1975, I was just twenty. She said I could have it for $150 a month with three months to give her a deposit for the same amount. The contact paper stuck to the display window and volcanoes of wax on the floor didn't dissuade my vision for the space; I saw its potential and mine. This was what I wanted.

I cleaned it because I wanted to clean it. I set up my plywood cutting table on saw horses and I wheeled a large canvas mail cart underneath to hold fabrics. I slept on the floor until I cleaned the back room and then I slept on the floor back there. I had my drawing table and a large stump that I used as a stool, a big comfy chair, a vintage ironing board, an industrial sewing machine, and not much else. I raised my self up by my proverbial bootstraps. I kept yogurt, black raisin bread, peanut butter and jelly on the window ledge outside in the winter months until I found a small fridge that I put in the same closet with the pull chain toilet. My clothes hung over the fridge. I had a low, flat sink in the back room, but I went to my friend Sandy's apartment down the block when I needed a bath in her kitchen. She gave me a copy of Diet For A Small Planet as my first cookbook. Mom gave me the family's old electric frying pan. I lived sparsely and efficiently, the captain of my ship.

I was in my fifth semester studying fashion at Parsons School of Design, and, finally, I was living alone. Last spring, while still living on Carmine Street with my old boyfriend, I'd begun a business making wrap vests out of recycled denim. I sold them to friends at school and a couple of stores uptown. I was testing the "No Denim" rule at Parsons when I made myself a sleeveless jumpsuit from old jeans. The center front neckline was open from the high mandarin collar to below my breasts where it began wrapping securely with long thing straps tied at the waist. The torso fit close, releasing into stovepipe pant legs with a recycled jean pocket on the side. I wore it daily with a t-shirt underneath for school and, more than once, I dressed it up by removing my shirt to expose a deep and secure décolletage. It had a very strong tease factor, but no breast exposure or garment failures ever occurred. I bought a pair of clogs and when I walked confidently down the dark streets at night, I could make grown men look over their shoulders with trepidation. Survival in 70s NYC was not for the meek.

I shared my new workspace space with friends from school to do projects late into the night; the wild East Village was right outside my storefront window. Junkies nodded on stoops across the street, reasonable men I knew in the daytime were aggressive alcoholics at night, and creeps hid behind signs in my window. I kept the rusty gates locked even when inside.

I swept the front stoop of the shop and moved the garbage cans away from my window. I rallied our building's tenants to organize for heat in that first winter and to keep our block clean when the spring came. I cleaned and cleaned until it began to look like something. I grew plants and sewed my vests and school projects. I left school in January and began to sew for other young designers and make their patterns. I rented the other store in the building and hired employees. I worked to build up the space for four years until I began my own line exclusively. I gave my friend's son the summer job to paint the front of my shops bright red enamel with painted silver gates. I bought woven black labels with white letters that spelled Carioca to sew inside my clothing designs. I introduced myself, my label and my shop as Carioca. Thanks to the fabric store owner on the corner of First Avenue and St. Marks Place, I began to buy fabric on credit and I spent the next six years making retail clothing for women like me, who wanted everything with deep pockets in comfortable fabrics, and versatile components. I opened each season with a fashion show where friends and clients modeled my clothing at local restaurants.

I was an entrepreneur staying up late into night enjoying the quiet focus of my work cutting the paper patterns and the beautiful fabrics to prepare for the next day's work. Janet and Michele opened the shop in the morning while I went to Veselka for breakfast. Max often saw me coming and prepared me a surprise omelet to place on the counter when I sat down.

During the day it was hectic keeping the work flowing while I helped my customers choose their clothing. My friend Shaindl often helped me with inspired window displays, repainting my second hand mannequins, and helping me to accessorize my collections.

I got an apartment upstairs and renovated all three spaces with the help of a friend who was in construction. I had a new red and black sign painted for the shop and a business card to match. I only wore my own designs and stuck to my signature colors of red and black. My hair was long again and I bought shoes and lace-up boots to match my outfits. I was always dressed well.

I was a local character in the village play, one of many who owned small businesses in the area or lived in the apartments above. There was that tall haircutting actor in the middle of the block who loved to announce boldly that he was a *THESPIAN!* The two old brothers who owned the Ninth Street Bakery, sweet and eccentric Willy Rizzo owned an eclectic shop packed with vintage clothing and for awhile the Bread and Puppet

Theatre had a New York residence across the street from my shop. Benny was a very short old man, who sat outside the building next door on a stool in his three piece suit, hat and cane, smoking his cigar for hours on end in the afternoon. A few older women from the Ukraine, came in and out of buildings where they cleaned the hallways and stoops of tenements. Mary was my favorite, in her babushka and old, tight sweater over an old dress with thick stockings. She'd wave her arthritic hand to me and nod as I swept my own stoop, always asking when I'd marry and have babies. Her face was rich with stories. Being in a storefront meant meeting just about all of the neighbors passing by.

Sweep by sweep, cut by cut, I made the store and the things to sell in it. This was my dream, not the dream of marriage like my mother's or the Parsons' track to Seventh Avenue, but my own track from the rough and tumble sleeping on the floor days to getting written up in the local papers as a young designer to be on the lookout for.

In 1982 I met Charlie and fell in love. The new landlord tripled my rent with no lease. It was happening all over the city. Small shops that held neighborhoods together, providing local color were being forced out and replaced by larger chain stores. Charlie and I got married in '84. I cut my hair and broke my habitual dressing in red and black, wearing blue lace for our wedding. I researched the possibilities of moving my shop further east or going wholesale in a loft uptown, but I closed my gates in January 1985. I pictured children in our future. I was turning thirty and broadened my work experience with a job at a children's wear company. I studied millinery and traveled with Charlie, who played Javert in the First National Tour of <u>Les Miserables</u>. I delivered our son, Michael, in Chicago. Back in New York, when he was six-months old, I took a teaching job

CAROL DWYER **48**

in the fashion design department at Parsons. When Mike was 18-months old we moved upstate to a small house in St. Remy, New York. Dana was born there, at home, with a midwife and I commuted a few days a week to teach. Charlie and I divorced in 1996.

I still go back to Carioca in my dreams. I still have the key to get in, just like my childhood home at 15 North Main, or my Grandmother's house at 18 Walnut Street. When I look through the decades of journals I've written, these are the places that I haunt, but a dream of 312 East Ninth Street is always a powerful dream of knowing who I am or looking for what I left behind. It's a place full of memories and stories and I remember it like being a cowgirl living in the "Wild East," with people living on the edge. But it was a small town too, a village with safety in knowing who your neighbors were and many of us helped each other. My East Village experience fed my childhood roots to grow into the woman I've become.

Wednesday, October 21st, 2009

I dreamt I was preparing for vacation. It was a massive endeavor packing everything up. Many other people arrived, and were they going away too? Or helping, but not very well? My house was all packed for vacation and it was made of glass, like a greenhouse. Everyone looking in could see I was all packed up in suitcases and boxes.

Dana crawled into bed early before her alarm went off, with a stomach ache. She was awake, but should she get up? I got her to go back to bed after a snuggle and shared head rubs. Now I've slept in too. I feel normal today! I hope she does too and I could drive her to school.

Yesterday Mom took me to buy my second wig, her treat. I'm a blonde this time. The first thing out of my Mother's mouth to the saleswoman was, "My daughter needs a wig. She has breast cancer." Mom was very happy with the light blonde wig we chose.

My neighbor, Ann Warman, left the funniest message on my phone today…. I cracked up and left it on to listen to again! "Carol! Please throw out the soup that I made for you. I just tasted it and it tastes like wallpaper paste! Throw it out and don't tell anyone that I made it!!"

I took Dana shopping today. It was fun helping her: I hung up the clothes as she plowed into the next garment. I love her model walk and her pouty look in the mirror. I was energized speed walking through the mall, but my body felt how long it's been since I've done this level of activity. I heard people cough and sneeze and felt vulnerable being exposed to the public with my lowered immune system. I was conscious that it might be awhile before we do this again. I wore my new blonde wig all day and got lots of compliments. It was fun being a blonde. My head-hair stubble is noticeably falling out. My facial rosacea is noticeably clearer, a good side effect of chemo? I am rich with hot flashes, power surges.

I had a nice talk with Jack today about our families. I made him a night cap like I've been wearing around to keep my bald head warm. He said he admires my ability to live with cancer. I am grateful for feeling well, except for the discomfort of the cure.

I'm feeling anxiety for the upcoming fundraiser on Sunday that Anne is organizing. She's done an amazing job. I want it to be successful and fun for her because she's put so much into it! They have raffle prizes of a helicopter ride, a fat-wheeled pink bike, Tonner Dolls, manicures, and a Herzog hardware gift certificate. Someone at the gym made 100 pink ribbon cookies with an inspirational word attached; lovely. How do I look or stand or be at a fundraiser for me? Anne replied, "Anywhere you want!" I need to be here now and appreciate all that everyone is doing for me; the gift, the lift, they feel good helping me and they want me to feel better. I begin to lean forward into the unknown of tomorrow or Wednesday and I feel anxiety over the chemo feeling. That doesn't help me.

Dana and I made big salads with roasted chicken, apples, pecans, feta and raspberries and ate them watching three episodes of <u>Seinfeld</u>. It felt so good to laugh!

October 23rd, 2009

BIKE-A-THON

Sunday, October 25th, 2009

    I big, blue-sky, spectacular day! Dana, Danielle and I arrived at 10:45 am to see a full spin class in action. Anne greeted me in a pink wig and I was wearing one too. The energy was amazing…. Raffles, and old friends, so many of them riding in the spin class and others milling about, talking to each other. My neighbor, Billy, came with his bagpipe crew and performed. I counted at least fifty people that I knew including women from my dentist's office, friends from book club and work, old and new neighbors, plus my family. Other people were there too from Anne's early morning spin class and they came up to wish me well!!! The day was a financial success, but more importantly, it was a spiritual lift to see the collection of people that care for and support me. My nephew Mike took some wonderful pictures of this once-in-a-lifetime celebration.

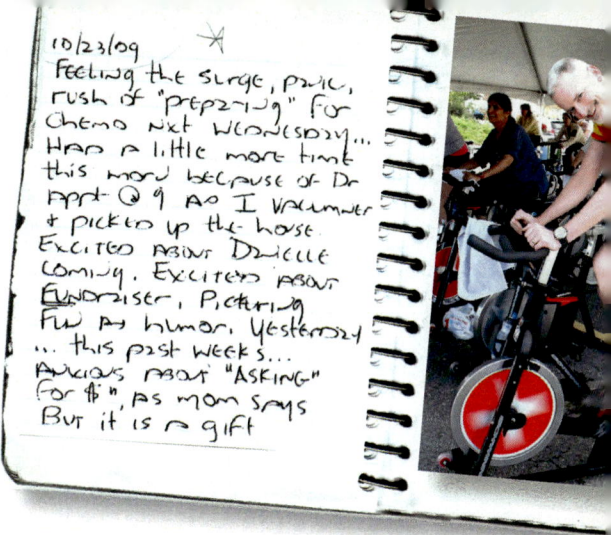

    I was very OUT today and now I need to pull back and focus inside. Breathe. But what a wonderful party. Anne was jumping up and down she was so happy with its success!!!

October 27th, 2009

October 28th, 2009

    I dreamt of chemo preparations…a line of people shopping for clothes…confusion as to whether that person claimed that dress or not… circular, not linear preparations…are they helping me or someone else? A plant not doing well…chemo's fault? No, it just needs a little water. The cactus needs water. Help gets a little more specific. Someone suggests an outfit I should try on to wear for chemo.

Work with Diane: I told her I felt "wonderful and buoyant from the support at the fundraiser on Sunday, but now I need to get grounded to focus my energy inwardly for healing." Diane asked me to clarify about this "needing to get grounded?" It began to sound like my "Coulda', shoulda' woulda'" voice, the voice of Sister Josepha in the third grade, "It's not time to be happy! Go stand in the corner and think about that!" I had a flash of Gulliver's Travels and the Lilliputians… I'm a large helium balloon in the Macy's Day parade and the people supporting me, loving me, helping me, are on the ground holding the strings to keep me grounded. Maybe I can stay full and buoyant and happy? Maybe I don't need to deflate and look inward or change from this state of love in order to heal; I have a grounded connection to people who love me.

I stayed up late writing some more thank you notes and have many more to thank. I have so much to be thankful for.

11pm
SELF Portrait
10/28/09
4TH CHEMO

* Forgot Emedos before treatment. Took the other one, but feeling ok….

* After 10pm I smoked in my new bowl. Much lighter in the lungs. Relaxed.

Sunday, November 1st, 2009

I dreamt of playing with a yarn doll on a tall bed with a muddy stream flowing next to it. I dropped my doll accidentally into the muddy water and I let it drip dry on the side. I am on my tall bed putting her yarn doll fathers away into a multi-sectional box, but the last one has no shoes. I pack a piece of silver and a piece of quartz that might meld into a pair of magic shoes. There is time that goes by. I am on an escalator in a department store with disappointment layered on each floor, until I finally rebel and open the box to show my doll her father's shoes: my boyfriend, your step-father, your father (each has an extra layer of blanket between them); I am peeling back the blankets and am going to reveal the melded silver and quartz shoes, but I am distracted by the audience gathering around my tall bed and the layers of blankets are thicker and thicker on each doll that I expose to the yarn doll muddied in the stream…

UNCONDITIONAL HEALING SUPPORT GROUP

Darcy drove me to it at Sky Lake Lodge. So special; so many kinds of suffering that cancer can seem light weight sometimes. They plan to meet again in December and I hope that I can make it.

Monday, November 2nd, 2009

Back to work. Blonde wig and makeup. Starving after breakfast. Tired by lunchtime. I took a nap at Mom's before I ate.

I have a nice little crop of projects going at work: Anne Hathaway's school uniform in Princess Diaries, a guy from Twilight, and fixing a production sample from Prince of Persia. I always like to have a few projects to bounce around with. I am debating about attending the Tonner Luncheon Event. Doll collectors come to be entertained and play and enjoy the company of fellow enthusiasts, not to be reminded of "Carol has cancer." I'm not ready to answer lots of questions either, but feel to recede gently and let Robert Tonner's fans have fun!

Dana and I ordered Chinese take-out and watched a movie tonight. She put her head on my lap and I stroked her hair and both of us fell asleep.

Tuesday, November 3rd, 2009

I slept through until 5:00 am dreaming that I was working the entire inaugural ball for Michele Obama – very Balenciaga (duchess satins, high necks). It is just before the final fitting and every piece needs changes. I'm trying to maintain order and rally my help. Anne was part of the event and I made her an ensemble that was very costume – too costume for her, including the large hair-do wig, poufs at the hips and train in the back. "Try it without the wig!" I suggested. "Make it yours!" Meanwhile I have to finish Michele's gown and she is stepping out of her slips and shoes…is she deciding to wear something else? Chaos is near. Alterations. Difficult fabrics and all at the last minute!

Wednesday, November 4th, 2009

I dreamt of going home one evening to my apartment in the East Village, mid-block on East Ninth Street. I stopped in the shop downstairs and the guys were selling me a large ceramic vase with a lid and, of course, I would have to take the table too. It created a "we'll take this and you take that" situation in order to accommodate the vase. Suddenly I have their dog! My daughter, roommate and I are rearranging the apartment to accommodate the dog. Will it bark all day in our apartment and get us in trouble with the landlord? Then we are helping the guys rearrange their apartment, too. Like we will all live together in the apartment along with one of their parents. Moving tables, I gather a dirty tablecloth and curtains to wash in my apartment. We are making sense of shared space and eliminating pieces that don't make sense anymore; like a table we try to use for dinner, but it's too low for his parents and we use the other one instead. I end up in a crib under the stairs and we have to rip a side off to get me out. What about the big dog in our apartment?

I spoke to my oldest girlfriend, Kathy, last night. We lamented that this is what it took to get the girlfriends, her, Linda and Leslie, here for the first time. I planned to make a pot of chili for their visit. I spoke of my schedule being freed up since I broke up with Robert, how it was difficult when he and I only had weekends to spend together. I've been seeing lots more of my friends since we broke up – or is it since I've had cancer? Both.

KATHY WELLS

I was thinking about it being no coincidence that I would attract a friend of my very own when I was five years old, the same summer that my brother Bobby was born. Dad had carried me as a child to the point that Aunt Margaret said I'd never learn to walk. Mom told me how she used to put my four and five year old sisters out in the backyard to play, so she could give me her full attention while bathing me in the sink. Then, at five, the party was over. Mom was inside caring for the new baby and I was put outside to play in the sunny backyard, alone, looking for something to do.

I sat in the fenced-in yard, in the shade of our lovely little lilac tree, diddling with twigs and stones in its roots. My ears perked up when I heard voices of children playing in a yard nearby. I scrambled to peer through the chain linked fence, over the short shrubs. The trio saw me and wandered over to my back gate. We were shy, but curious and I lifted the u-shaped gate latch, inviting them in to play. Kathy was the oldest, two months older than me, and she became my very own best friend. She wasn't a younger sister of my sister's friends or a child of my Mother's friend. Kathy Wells was *my* friend, from that memorable summer day that we first met.

It was the summer before we began kindergarten that her family moved into one of the four apartments in a big house on Albany's Western Avenue. The house ran perpendicular to the back yards of the row houses on North Main Avenue, where I lived. It was very exciting to realize that we could wave to each other from her second floor dining room to my bedroom window and call to each other without using a phone. I was worried though that when Mom spanked me over her knee, with my pants down, that her family would see me. I looked over my shoulder to see if they were looking.

I had never eaten at anyone's house without my Mother before, until going to Kathy's. I had already met her younger siblings, Nita and Donnie. I joined their family at the long, well-used dining room table. Her parents, Roger and Monica, and Nana, sat at the ends, while I sat on one side with the youngest children, facing the three older siblings; I could see my house behind them. I felt all eyes watching me as I was asked which TV dinner I wanted, but each dinner had something that I wouldn't eat. Monica lost patience when I admitted that I didn't even like cucumbers. I shrank in my seat as my finicky eating was exposed. Kathy sat next to me, but I had to answer for myself if I wanted to stay. I made a random selection and did the best I could.

My first sleepover was at Kathy's, too, and we went to bed giggling and wrestling naked under the covers. Monica came upstairs to kiss us goodnight and we knew instinctively to pull the sheet up to our necks so she didn't know we had removed our pajamas. We touched each other's bodies and I remember being surprised by how good it felt; I had known nothing about this before. For days we continued being amazed with the sensations of our bodies until Kathy's eldest sister, Eileen, looked down from the second floor porch, on us in the back yard with our pants down. She screamed at us that we were bad and disgusting and she was telling our parents. I was sent home, mortified.

I was uncomfortable "down there" and told my Mom. She escorted me to the bathroom. "This is the only place you *ever* pull your pants down!" she declared. We looked in my underwear and found a small feather. I looked up at her surprised and that was the end of that.

November 5th, 2009

I picked up the names of people that sent checks to the bank account that Bill established for my medical expenses so I can send thank-you notes. The checks came from all over! I am in awe of the energy flowing my way. To *not* worry. The flow carries me on a cloud or a raft slowly down a stream…no danger…calm…protected by the love of these friends.

Friday, November 6th, 2009

The Tonner Doll being auctioned off for my benefit was a big success today. They told me about it at the company dessert gathering tonight. I enjoyed seeing everyone from the company and guests that are in for the big event tomorrow, but told Robert that I wouldn't be attending the big event tomorrow. I don't want to steal any focus off our collectors enjoying themselves.

Saturday, November 7th, 2009

Suzanne called to tell me that Paula, a friend and Tonner doll collector, bought the second doll that the company raffled off for me. "She must love you a lot," Suzanne said.

Sunday, November 8th, 2009

I dreamt Joe was leaving for the day and I didn't have much work to do. I was waiting for supplies to finish my projects. He said he had planned to wait until I was back from my time away, but gave me a green car key to a company car. I went to see it and it was so low to the ground that the roof was clear. It was so low that when I reclined my arms couldn't reach the steering wheel. I hyper-extended my arms and took it for a ride, but it was scarily out of control and I drove a block and came back. I am not familiar or comfortable driving lying down and I was driving in Brooklyn with big wide boulevards and I could have easily gotten lost. Then Joe was asking directions in Brooklyn and I had no answers for that.

Then I'm on a golf course with a small car. I am told to mow a section of the course. I go to the dressing room closet to get the key and instructions for the mower. The owner comes in and is dubious about my capabilities. There are women changing in the dressing room and it is sleazy of the owner to be stalling there. I go to bring things back to my little car for storage and I notice that a lot of the terrain is rich with plants instead of manicured turf. I walk too close to the swamp and my foot slips into the sucking mud and it is difficult to pull my foot out and I re-slip in again…I don't remember mowing or seeing a mower, but I drop stuff off at my car.

I watched a YouTube video of a five-year-old golf prodigy that had eye cancer at three years old, but has had a perfect golf swing since two. There was another video of a TED lecture where a doctor who studies brain function described her personal experience having a stroke and how it affected her brain. She saw it as an incredible opportunity to study the brain. I saw these videos as links to the Unconditional Healing Retreat philosophy; the exploration of our illness and its meaning and purpose in our lives, the gift of it, a re-focus of priorities.

I had a wonderful visit with Linda, Kathy and Tom, Leslie and Jim, talking, eating and doing yard work. They put away all my lawn furniture and my garden to bed for the winter. I joked, "How many friends from Albany does it take to get Dana to rake leaves?" But I was teasing – she's an ace and worked hard and talked to everyone. Jim hung her mirror over her vanity, too, to help pull her room together with the final details.

My mouth is very uncomfortable. The left inside cheek has a long sore. "Magic-Mouthwash" holds it for a brief time. New normal. For now. This too will pass.

Monday, November 9th, 2009

I slept poorly with the monster in my mouth. It seems to magnify in my sleep – throbbing and swelling, being bitten or exacerbated by clenching my teeth. I lay in bed for hours before Dana's alarm. I dozed again while she showered and dreamt of looking for a place to go to the bathroom.

Wednesday, November 11th, 2009

I woke to take my anti-nausea medicine at 5:00 am (with a banana), but many times before that, too. I was relieved that it didn't make me nauseous. I feel fine.

I dreamt of East Ninth Street and my shop. The check-out counter was closer to the front door. People lined up along the east wall; some for the register, some for the bathroom. It's so busy; I wonder how I will keep up with making the clothing and pay attention to everyone. I'm not worried, but curious. Some people seem to be waiting for us to eat. They form rows and chant with maracas, and when they stop, they hoped they hadn't freaked out my customers, I said I liked it. I think its healing energy. Then I walked out of the store. I don't remember someone taking over. I don't remember locking the front door, just breezing out… going to eat.

I dreamt of being in an apartment with lots of elderly women. It begins to rain a windy spray in the windows and we rush to close them before everything gets damp. The window to the left shuts easily. The window straight ahead seems to have not been shut in years. There is a vine with thick stalks weaving through the window ledge, preventing the window from closing. It takes great strength to saw through the vine and pull it away.

Then I'm alone in a room. A flash of lightning stops me in my tracks. I duck behind a table because I expect the thunder to be as powerful as the lightening. The most powerful silence follows, instead. No thunder, no release, no balance, is the storm far away? Or is it some kind of powerful new storm that you can't know what will happen because there is no old "normal" to go by?

Work with Diane: last night on TAXOL, my new treatment…TAXI YELLOW… a vehicle to transport me through this portion of my chemotherapy. It will sweep through and gather dead cancer cells to carry to the drains to excrete out of my body. It's a bright yellow taxi to transport me to the other side of chemo. My first trip starts today.

Anne Warman drove me to chemo today and kept me company for two hours. Then I had a good deep rest. My son, Mike, picked me up from chemo and brought me home. It was five hours total. The kids ran and got us sandwiches down the block. I watched an old Sherlock Holmes flick, Terror By Night, followed by a French film called Two Days in Paris. Dana joined me for two episodes of Ugly Betty.

November 17th, 2009

Bad Day; I made it until lunch at work, distracted by wanting to leave. I didn't want to get out of bed. I'm disappointed to feel bad, judgmental, trying to measure up to the productivity around me. I ate lunch with Mom and came home to nap. Dana and I ate dinner watching Being

<u>There</u> starring Peter Sellers from 1979.

I worked some photo album pages tonight; all those smiling chemo pictures make me look like I'm holding up well and making the best of it. Right now I'm thinking of mastectomies and recovery with Smokebomb purring by my side.

November 18th, 2009

I dreamt that I went into the garage and a whole wall is glass shelves, full of glasses and glass bowls and it's all wet, dripping wet from the rain, rain pouring from the top glasses to the lower ones, like a waterfall. I pull a glass carefully from the wall. I am thirsty.

The holidays approaching has brought forth feelings of sadness and loss. No creamed onions at Thanksgiving; I couldn't make them without Robert. I sit on the edge of my bed, bald, facing the holidays and mastectomies, and wonder at our eleven-years together and how I released it like a kite.

Thursday, November 19th, 2009

I dreamt of being at a Tonner Doll convention. It was the end of the event and people were coming up to me and sharing hugs. Very sweet. There was much concern for my health. The next event was a fashion show and somehow I was going to make a red charmeuse evening dress before the show. I was in a room organizing pieces. There really wasn't enough time to make the dress. Then I'm walking through a room helping students hang their rough projects for a menswear assignment. We will be perfecting the pattern and producing the samples. I remember I need to tell Tonner that I didn't make the red dress.

Friday, November 20, 2009

DANA WENT TO SCHOOL WITH NO MAKE-UP!

Work with Diane at 4:00 pm: *Ended the session with a vision of a hike a year from now, with Dana…walking uphill full of my energy on a sunny day* *with melting icicles, trees, a view of the river with both Dana and I taking pictures of it, smiling. We're on the other side of all this, enjoying each other's company and my unmeasured energy.*

I welcome my next treatment of Taxol...taxi – Bright Yellow – driving inside me and sweeping cancer to my natural elimination processes. I filter through my golden orange cloth and there is less and less cancer for the cloth to disintegrate. The Taxol, the cloth, are all doing a great job of filtering the cancer out of my body.

We took some time for me to acknowledge my breasts, to be grateful for them, to begin to detach from them. I am in my winter cocoon and the spring will bring a new style of being and dressing.

Where I want to SQUIRM is called my "working edge." It is the place where work happens. Grief and my whiney voice make me squirm.

Saturday, November 21st, 2009

I had a Beautiful day with Dana shopping at the Farmer's Market. We ate brunch with Rennie and bumped into Jody and Bill. They were checking out the Church on Albany Avenue for the January 10th, 2010 party/fundraiser/concert.

I have been "Photoshopping" my chemo pages for my album. It puts things in perspective – I used to have hair – but they say I still have the same smile.

Sunday, November 22, 2009

I dreamt I was in the hospital with Mom. Our beds were side by side. There is something wrong with my arm. The staff brings Mom food, but not me. My status, I find out after many meals have passed, is "non-food" status. Something to do with health insurance, I suppose. I call Bobby to come back, but he disappears before he helps me. I go out with Connie in Hudson Falls to forage for food. We find a place almost ready to close. They bring Connie a big salad, but don't tell me that they have no sandwiches; they just don't bring me food. They bring Connie samples of juice which I ask her for. What is up? Why can't I get any food? We walk outside and kick dry leaves as we walk back to the hospital. it is dark now. I'm so frustrated and hungry, but no one connects to this.

Mom and I went shopping to return a light fixture and look for other options for Dana's room. We also hunted for the best crock pot, but didn't have time to go back and pick up the best one at Lowe's. I had to return for TEAM HELP or CAROL'S COVEN as Jody nick named the girls. They are planning another fundraiser with bands and silent auction for January 10th, 2010. I told them what Mom said to me, "Don't you think you've gotten about what you can get from people?" Mom pushes hard on my guilt button.

I do worry about asking for more…asking for too much…. "How much does she need?" I worry that I'm a fraud. That would be something to find out!! That I don't have stage-four cancer! I worry about the girls taking on so much with their already busy lives and goals…. I worry about being a burden. They don't want me to worry. My friends want me to be well. I want to be well and be able to help other people again.

November 25th, 2009

I dreamt of Jody and the girls buying us the gift of a new kitchen sink. The drain was especially good on this sink and a big part of the gift. I took a deep breath and gratefully accepted this expensive new sink. It was our sink exactly.

Last night Dana and I had a nice relaxing talk about graciously accepting the help of our friends who want to help us with another fundraiser. Dana felt tickets should be less expensive. She said, "We can always do another fundraiser." But I said, "No, this will probably be it. Our friends want us to have a nest egg – I will probably be in this process for a five-year period and the money will help us get through more easily." I will let them plan it and try not to whittle away their efforts with my insecurity. Our friends think about us, the severity of the disease I have, and say they want to do something to help us be, to help me stay here, help us live through this. I will graciously accept their help and their love.

I am rich with friends.

Mike took me to a 9:00 am chemo. We had a wonderful talk and a game of Scrabble. I had one of my best scores ever (in the 300's) and was glad to know chemo hadn't hurt my game. Mike's game was quicker paced and inspired me that way. I took a nap while Mike ran out for a bit. We left the office around 2:00 pm. We came home and had salad with chicken breast. Dana came home from school and joined us…family time.

Dana and I ate a delicious dinner cooked and delivered by Kate SC. We ate while watching <u>Ugly Betty</u> episodes. Fun. Now we are on break while Dana packs for her O'Brien Clan Thanksgiving trip. Oooh, I'll miss her! For four days!

Sunday, November 29th, 2009

My dreams and sleep are coming back to me; it's 8:30 am, not 3:00 or 4:00 am and I dreamt of a small factory. We made clothes. We were a team or a school class. We ate, did dishes, cleaned and sewed all as a team. There are stacks of garments, cut in piles on a table… someone was carving wild looking railings for the three stories on the outside of our building. Students were taking turns being counseled by teachers in the basement. I am older, but wanted to be counseled too. I want to know I'm on the right track.

I had my lowest post-chemo energy on Friday and Saturday. I was lazy and achy all over. My feet ached the most and I was a movie slut: four episodes of (BBC's) <u>Wives and Daughters,</u> four of <u>Daniel Deronda</u>, <u>The Commitments</u> (Irish, 1991), <u>Sissi</u> (German 1955), <u>The Sunshine Boys</u> (1975), <u>Up</u> (2009), <u>Mystic Pizza</u> (1982-ish), and I began watching <u>The Dish</u> (Australian).

I made a pink fleece hat with long braids, copying a hat that Leslie gave me, and I need to make Dana a duvet cover for her new bed that came today. Bobby helped me move furniture yesterday so her room is pulling together. The next big question is what will she wear to the Winter Ball?

Thanksgiving was very nice. Mom did a great job with Bobby assisting as the turkey lifter. The table looked lovely and the food was delicious. It was a small group this year with my son, Mike, and his girlfriend, my grandniece, Chloe, and her father, Derek, my nephew, Mike Gargano, his wife, Jamie, and step-father, Terry, along with Mom, Bobby and me. We walked after dinner and then enjoyed dessert. We were all done and packed up by 5:00 pm.

We need groceries today… Back to work tomorrow.

It's bedtime and my energy feels a bit restored. I made dinner after grocery shopping and Dana and I ate while watching Miss Congeniality. It was funny and so good to laugh. Earlier, while the dinner was cooking, I finished watching The Dish, about the 1969 moon landing; that was also very funny. Mila rested on my chest as I watched.

Monday, November 30th, 2009

I dreamt I was being spoiled and allowed to save what I wanted to save. My poetry and stories were not edited and the furniture that I saved was nursery furniture which I would never need again. But to appease me, to pamper me, I was allowed to keep it. In another part I was learning how to make boots, working on the fit of the front and thinking about zippers up the back.

Going on a subway, my friend and I kept seeing deformed or injured animals – a turtle with a half shell sticking up through its raw back. We walked through throngs of people to find a less crowded spot in the car. I hoped no more of these frightening animals were furtively scurrying about.

Tuesday, December 1st, 2009

I dreamt I was in a large church waiting in line for a breast cancer detection diagnosis. I finally made it to the woman doing the detection and I quickly told her I was stage-four metastatic. She wrapped a sheet around me and felt my breasts, enthusiastically proclaiming that things weren't so bad! I had a lot of life in them yet! It was all so quick, I wanted to hear more, but I was asked, "Do you have a surgeon yet?" Yes, I do need a surgeon.

PURGATORY

I grew up in Albany, New York, part of a "small" Irish Catholic family – we only had five children. I began parochial school in kindergarten and became a devout Catholic; I made May altars in my bedroom with my own Blessed Virgin Mary statue. I read about the saints and aspired to be like them. As a child, I ironed Dad's handkerchiefs, a task Saint Theresa would surely have done; she was the saint of household chores.

In first grade I was the Virgin Mary in our nativity play. I was transformed by a white sheet, wrapped with gold cord; a piece of blue cloth covered my head.

In second grade, pale blue mimeographed instructions, in Sister Nicholas' neat printing, inspired me to become a nun. "Where is God?" She asked our class. "God is everywhere!" we shouted back.

My best friend, Kathy, and I made a play date after school to say rosaries. We learned that for every rosary we said, we could free a "lost soul" from Purgatory. We began respectfully, saying each prayer together, but after a few rosaries we realized this was going to take a long time. We wanted to rescue those poor "trapped" souls and send them on to Heaven. Kathy had heard that even saying the Lord's name was enough to count as a prayer, so we prayed faster and faster; "Jesus, Jesus," but God was shorter so we said, "God, God, God," to free as many souls as we could before Kathy had to go home for dinner.

Wednesday, December 2nd, 2009

I had espionage dreams. In the last episode I pulled my car into an elevator and went up one level, and opened

a sliding door to exit, but it closed before I could get out. I stuck my hand in it to make it re-open. I walked in on bomb making and quickly tried to exit before I saw something I wasn't supposed to, but I was called back. It was okay for me to see the two people making or dismantling bombs. The first person was a woman whose baby slept near her, uncovered, on top of a box. The baby's skin was poisoned or unwell. The other person was a big guy pacing anxiously as the deadline drew near.

I married Charlie twenty-five years ago today. I was laughing as I texted Charlie "Happy Anniversary" and he texted a laugh back.

I stayed home today. I got all ready for work and took a long nap on the couch.

I posted on my Friends and Family of Carol Dwyer Facebook page tonight with an update of Chemo #7 & #8 dates. I asked for my friends to "Picture me well." Paulette, Robert's sister, reminded me to "Picture ME well." It was a good reminder. I have an appointment with Diane tomorrow. On the phone she asked me what else I need to do to say good bye to my breasts, to let them go, but I'm not sure and couldn't answer.

Thursday, December 4th, 2009

I dreamt my girlfriends were taking me out to celebrate my birthday, or mastectomy, or pre-mastectomy, not sure which. But was I ready? I was until everyone else was there. Then I realized I didn't have my shoes on. I put one on, tied it, and carried the other to the car, but wait, my camera! I don't need money or keys, but I need my camera. Okay I'm ready now. We are piling into two compact cars, but I run back to the house for my charger because my camera batteries are low. My house is on a block of storefronts, but I can't get into it without my key. I run back to the packed cars pulling out of a house-sized door and I move flowerpots off the stoop so they aren't run over.

Its pouring rain and windy outside today.

Work with Diane: *Taxol is the same big, yellow taxi driving through my body.*

I am picturing letting go of my breasts and being myself without them, being loved for who I am, not being afraid to say good bye. I'm sad, but not fearful, sad to let them go, sad that it has to change, but moving forward and I know I'll be okay.

My edgy spot is picturing something I'm passionate about doing a year from now. I began to picture it.... I was confident to this point, but began to feel my confidence crumble. Diane coached me through this, to picture my life moving forward after all this is over and I am again full of positive energy and creativity.

I just cried tonight watching <u>Ugly Betty</u> while the character of Daniel is told by his wife, Molly, that she has cancer and might be dying. She'd run away from him and told him not to follow and he admitted he'd been relieved, but now he'd found her and swore to stand by her and I cried at art imitating life and being the opposite all at once. This was not my life, but only an episode of entertainment that made me cry.

Saturday, December 5th, 2009

I dreamt of travel or planning to travel. I dreamt of a globe, pincushions, scissors and hemostats. I had been visiting Uncle George and he's driving me home, south in Manhattan, but I tell him several times that I need to go east and catch the bus home which isn't downtown anymore.

My home is my center, alone or with Dana, cooking, organizing, working my photos, talking to friends. There's no tugging of sexuality right now; no compromises of sexual relationships, just love. Love for me, love for Dana, love for those who choose to enter my world in person, by card or internet. Self love is remembering to drink my nettle brew, lubricating my nose so it won't bleed and choosing to have chemo, surgery and radiation to be well and live to care for and enjoy my children. Self love extends love to others. Self love is being as honest as I can.

December 9th, 2009

I dreamt I was in a large spacious apartment in Philadelphia. I'm a guest, but my port IV is used to feed the host and family. It's not the first time I fed the family with my IV, but this is a holiday celebration and I am aware of the irony of my situation.

I woke with another dream, but didn't write it down. Dana called me for a snuggle in her bed and we had a great chat. She made a Mediterranean scramble for breakfast that was excellent.

Mike and his friend picked me up late for my chemo today. The roads were unplowed and I made the mistake of suggesting that we turn up Janet Street and we got very stuck mid- block. It took the help of a man shoveling to get us out and we made it to my appointment by 10:00 am. We were the only ones that didn't cancel today. Mike stayed with me until about noon and then I napped. My friends, Carole and Bill, picked me up and drove me home. Carole stayed and made tea.

Friday, December 11, 2009

I dreamt of a large corn roast event that I was attending, and working at. When I turned to get an ear of corn there were only scraggly ones at the bottom of a pit into which someone reached to hand me one. No matter, the event was full and energetic. A young teenage boy said to his mom that his ear was swollen and I looked over and it was as big as a potato. People were looking for places to sleep. I looked out the window into a bare tree ready for winter. I dreamt of turning over and over and back into sleep. I dreamt of picking up a stripe cardigan that I'd begun knitting in 1993 and working on it.

9:00 am I got up and made Dana toast, but got back into bed, tired, listening to my body, with no judgment. I'm drinking lots of water.

Saturday, December 12th, 2009

Kate Foote sent me the best gift I could ever want: the negatives from photos I took at the age of fifteen that she found in her basement! Her brother and I had a darkroom down there and they were packed up and stored for the last thirty-nine years!

Danielle is here for the weekend. She and Dana made breakfast before we went shopping to find Dana a dress for the Winter Ball. I got exhausted, but back home, Danielle made us lunch while I napped. Later she made dinner and I listened to the story of her childhood which she shared fully for the first time in the thirty-five years we've been friends. I had time to listen.

Tuesday, December 15th, 2009

Tonight I am blue, overwhelmed by Christmas expectations and stress; drowning. I finished season three of <u>Ugly Betty</u> tonight. Daniel's wife Molly dies of cancer. He was devoting all of his energy in their last bits of time together. It's just a fucking television show, but it knocked me off kilter. That and going to a wake with my Mother for a woman that grew up in our old neighborhood. "If you can't take me, then I can't go," Mom said. I dreaded going in the best of circumstances, but today I'm tired and achy, but we went. It was nice to see our old neighbors and pay our respects to our old friends. Mom started to plan other errands, but I drew the line. Not today. I'm not my old self and the pressure of the upcoming holidays point this out "big time."

Wednesday, December 16th, 2009

I was too grumpy to get up and write my dream, but it was partly in an East Village storefront where I looked at an art exhibit. A guy did a piece using a futon bed as a canvas, showing the faint hint of a woman's body under a gauzy fabric – the hint of a woman under the covers. I was so impressed that I tried to imitate it on the piece itself, but I was heavy handed and messed it up. He was extraordinarily patient and restored his painting. Such a light hand – a whisper of femininity.

Sunday, December 20th, 2009

I'm going to bed in clean sheets. Back to work tomorrow. I'm reading <u>A Room of One's Own</u> by Virginia Wolf. She speaks of receiving a fixed income from her aunt that eases the bitterness and anger of struggling to make ends meet. My friends and family are doing that for me. They are affording me the ease to heal. I am grateful for their gift.

December 21st, 2009

I woke up to my nose bleeding. I have a spot, a mole-ish type thing under my eye, that's turned gray on chemo and yesterday half of it fell off! I hope the other half falls off too. It is very dry and scab-like.

December 22nd, 2009

I am awake being grateful. Grateful for all the kind people I have met helping me at doctor's offices. I am grateful that besides the side effects of the "cure," I have been comfortable. My body put its cancer in relatively easy to remove places. I'm grateful to not be in pain. I'm grateful to be well. I'm grateful for the days I can keep this all in perspective. I remember Uncle George commenting on being but a spec in the universe. I think about what Aunt Marg and Uncle George endured to live, mouth and prostate cancer, emphysema, Chrone's disease, the surgeries and medications; I think about the young man working in a retail store with one good hand, and I often think of our neighbor who fell off his roof and the immediate change it made in his life. I don't know why I was chosen to witness this change in my body. I trust it is for my education to be a better person. I trust that it is a gift to be explored. I believe I have the help of angels and that they protect me. I haven't been abandoned and I will be able to turn and help others at some point.

Dr. Andrade said again yesterday that he has several patients with metastases that go on to live ten, twelve, fourteen years and he has several that are still going. I trust I will live the life I have. There is no guarantee for anyone. I have always pictured myself remaining in my current age forever. I would be forever sixteen, with my Hawaiian tan and sun bleached hair, wearing 4" shorts and halter top, or nineteen stomping around the West

Village in my high- heeled boots and Vidal Sassoon haircut. I couldn't lift my head from my children (one on my hip and the other by the hand) from ever being beyond the moment-to-moment love and care of them. I could never really picture a time of independence when there were meals to be made diapers to be changed, crying comforted. I couldn't picture loving them more than I did or imagine all the wonderful people they added to my life. I didn't picture cancer either, but my life has unfolded and powerful gifts have been presented. Can I lift my head now and look outside? Beyond the edge of cancer and see the life unfolding each day that leads to the time beyond the focus of this disease? Yes. Life will go on and I can see myself and my altered body continuing beyond this time. I'm studying what I need, what I want… cancer has forced me to look up, beyond the mere acceptance of my life, to stand still and be present.

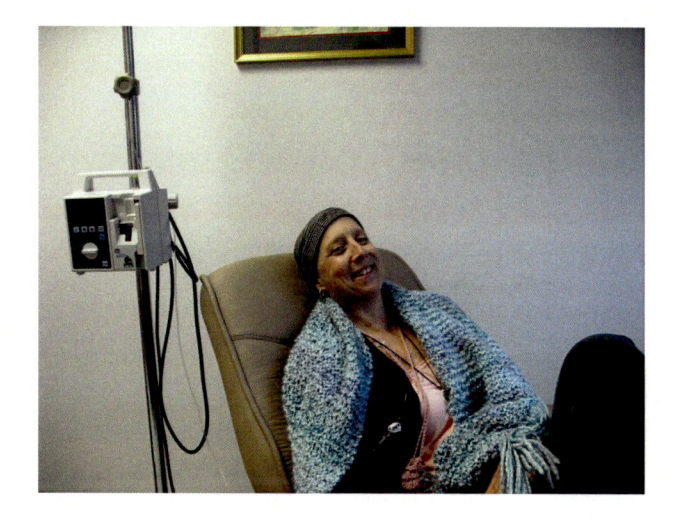

MY PERFECT BODY

December 24th, 2009

I enjoyed dressing Christmas Eve; putting on my red argyle tights, short black dress, and boots. I felt like me welcoming back my younger self who loved wearing colorful, humorous outfits. I'd spent years compromised, wearing jeans and a t-shirt to rush off to work. But tonight, I'd put on my little blonde wig, the one that Mom helped me pick out, topped off with a cute red knit cap. It was four months since my diagnosis and I'd survived the first big 'leg' of my cancer journey. I'd been very afraid and uncomfortable, but being on this side of aggressive chemotherapy swept away the litter of my complaints.

After a festive evening, Dana and I returned to our quiet house. I kissed my daughter good night and went to my closet to change into pajamas. I took off my wig, catching my reflection in the full length mirror. There I stood, bald, but still owning the breasts and nipples under my tight red sweater. With the onset of my diagnosis I abandoned the luxury of cleavage and under wire bras, so the breasts I saw were bound in a sports bra; a shield of protection after all the poking, prodding and biopsies that assaulted them. I was facing a definite mastectomy of my right breast, but would probably need both breasts surgically removed; a "bilateral mastectomy" is what that's called. I was practicing the spelling and pronunciation, trying to wrap my head around the idea.

I stood there looking at my bald self realizing that while I was preparing to let go of my breasts, that right in that moment, I still owned them. I wished I could keep them and knew that I could be satisfied now, even with lumps and a wayward nipple. I looked at myself and realized that I *am* good enough, that I had always been good enough. There were many years I was discontent with my body. I was a gawky, six-foot-tall teen with no discernible waist, hip or bust. In college my critique for being a student model included being told that my breasts were too low. I remember gazing at a fashion photo while working at Parsons and saying, "I'd like to look like *her* in that dress!" Andrew looked at me calmly and said, "Honey, you c-a-a-a-n, with the right foundation garment." I wasn't willing to undergo the discomfort of the transformation; I wanted to look like the model without the undergarments. Even as an experienced and jaded fashionista, I still bought into the fashion myth. Fashion does very little to encourage a healthy body image. I took a self portrait that night to remind me of that moment, standing in the middle of my closet, conscious of what I was leaving behind and curious about what was in front of me. I knew that I would do what I needed to do to live; breasts, or no breasts, I would *still* be good enough. That's the attitude that I needed, the old dissatisfaction was going to have to go.

I smiled in the mirror at the irony of appreciating my perfect body when it was about to change, permanently. I witnessed my perfection for a long moment and then I got ready for bed. I had to rest for my journey and prepare for the lessons ahead.

December 26th, 2009

I had a triple header today: went to Mom's for dinner with Bobby and we watched It's Complicated starring Meryl Streep and Alec Baldwin. Then with dessert and popcorn we watched George Clooney in Up In The Air. Bobby drove me home and we watched Precious. Now, to sleep

December 27th, 2009

I got up and watched What's Eating Gilbert Grape? Later I watched

Ballet Shoes and finished watching 500 Days of Summer with Dana. Then I finished Brideshead Revisited. It was my second day of serious couch potato. I almost forgot that I also watched the French film Summer Hours. I watched five movies! I have numb hands and feet even with the supplement of L-Glutamine. Bobby stayed over last night and Matt and family visited today on their way out of town.

Monday, December 28th, 2009

I dreamt this morning that Mom needed a blood test. She agreed and put on her brown wool tweed skirt from the 1960's, but she would not sign the form so when I brought it up to the desk, I forged her signature. Everyone was eating at the cafeteria — people from work, family. I was writing, but didn't have my journal so I wrote with my finger on my packaged salad, scribbling away, feelings, thoughts, before I saw that it was not leaving a mark or impression, no memory of what I wrote…a waste of time.

I watched the Dixie Chick's Shut Up and Sing with Dana today and tonight I watched four more episodes of Weeds. I even took a toke of weed to watch it. I am passing time, no judgment or guilt. I love to be a movie slut and escape through movies.

Jody stopped by with a few groceries that I needed and have a cup of tea. I told her I'm ready for my bilateral and that sometimes I forget that I still have breasts or I'm surprised by how healthy my left breast looks. I'm on the surface right now, not deep and its okay.

My hands and feet are still numb today, but less so, not as wobbly feeling. I have slightly more energy today too. I enjoyed the bloom, but needed to rest mid-day.

Charlie ran over with a "loaner" DVD player since ours stopped working and he knows how important movie watching is to me. I remember other movie hibernations I went through: watching all three episodes of The Godfather with Charlie after our miscarriage, when I broke my ankle in Washington D.C., and in the old house when Charlie and I were separating.

I'm still embarrassed by all the money requests in my name, but appreciative and grateful for all the thoughts and prayers filtering my cancer.

Tuesday, December 29th, 2009

I did have an epic entertainment dream: *a woman was singing to a large audience in a church and when she came backstage I gave her a glass of water and found her missing glasses in a pool. I watched her fix her hair to a great volume and listened to her stories of sleeping on the floor of the church in a pew with her children lined up behind her and the baby would squirm away in the night somehow and scare her half to death. Her no-good-alcoholic husband arrives in an old station wagon driven by his friend. He wants money for cigarettes. I say good bye and take a short cut over the lawn to a stone walkway on a hill over the sidewalk near the convenience store. I can hear his wagon won't start; one more problem in his problematic world. There is a small castle above the convenience store; I choose to go up and through its dark doors to the shadowy interior. Inside, I am barefoot and hop over smelly, suspicious urine rivers.*

I watched seven episodes of Weeds with the cats taking turns snuggling. I also packed gift bags of dolls and clothes for Cousin David's daughters. They are visiting tomorrow with Bobby. The day after is my PET Scan.

Thursday, December 31st, 2009

I dreamt I was with old girlfriends and I was setting up a display at the front of the room like a school, but I hadn't really thought it out and it was poorly done. We were all given a list of things to go get. I had on my list to get eight green apples. There was a shop across the street so I went there and asked for eight green apples. The clerk brought back fake apples and pears. The she went back and returned with mini-sized pears. No, I said. Then I heard her spray painting, in the back of the store; she apologized for the toxic fumes. Finally, she came back with six mini-green apples and two green pears. Fine. I accepted it as close enough. I left the store and went to go drop off the "fruit," but I don't have my keys to the loft. Where is it? Where is my jacket? In the locked loft or the closed shop? I stood holding change from the "fruit" purchase in my hand and looking bewildered. A woman asked if I needed money to make a phone call. I turned to look at a long stretch of busy telephone booths. No, thank you, I have change, but I'm not sure who to call. I will go look for the other things on my list.

Today was the MRI of my breasts.

So far it's just Dana and I for New Year's Eve and she has been tired and grumpy…I finished season two of <u>Weeds</u>.

January 1st, 2010

Dana beat me at Scrabble for the very first time. We had fun watching movies and playing games, then texting and talking on the phone to friends and family wishing all a Happy New Year.

January 2nd, 2010

I was quiet today, witnessing a restlessness inside that's mine and only mine; it's been lifelong. I cut out a shirt from vertical stripe linen, jewel toned blue, green, red and black that I've owned for about twenty-five years. Why wait any longer? I will enjoy wearing this shirt, too, but one step at a time; first I'll sew it.

I'm thinking about mastectomies and clothing, wearing clothing without my breasts, talking to doctors in my head. I'm thinking about my upcoming fundraiser concert, about exercising and getting back to a new temporary normal. I'm listening to the wind, drinking more water and wondering why I got cancer, especially as I lecture someone on "Eating Right" and I stop myself and say, "Wait a minute – I'm the one with cancer! What do I know?"

Chemo is over and my hair will start to grow back, like grass on a new grave. I will get scars and heal and still be me. Tired today – I am a witness to being present on this leg of my journey.

January 5th, 2010

Dr. Andrade and I spoke today. He reported that my PET Scan detected no visible cancer! the tumors remain, but "the hypermetabolic mass seen in both breasts have been excised or treated and are no longer seen." I still needed surgery, but the cancer was "cured" by chemo, prayer and Seinfeld! So much love and appreciation! Everyone at work was so happy and hugged me generously! My neighbor Anne jumped up and down!

January 8th, 2010

Charlie and I drove down to the city today to meet with Dr. Sheldon Feldman at Colombia Presbyterian Hospital for a second opinion. We walked into his office and he sat with us at a round table covered with papers; he didn't hide behind a desk. He reviewed the scans of my PET results and we discussed my case.

"So if you want to proceed with me, let me know soon. We'll need to schedule surgery within the thirty-day, post-chemo window. Surgery would need to be this month."

"I've already decided," I told him confidently. "I want you to do my surgery." His calm presence, and focused expertise left no doubt in my mind that he would make the best decision about removing lymph nodes or not. I knew I was in good hands.

RECONSTRUCTING MY LIFE

I watched and listened as my new breast surgeon pondered over whether my left breast could be saved with just a lumpectomy or not. My right breast was going, that was definite, "But I might be able to leave some of the left breast intact," he said. "Let me look more closely at the scans." But when he returned he told me that it was not an option. There were too many calcifications, too many risks leaving any part of my left breast behind; I was already stage-four.

"If my nipples have to go, then I am not too worried about letting go of the rest," I reassured him. "I accept what I have to do to save my life." If there'd been a way to save my nipple, a nipple with sensations left in it, then I'd be more attached to the rest of it, no matter how misshapen it might be. This was what had to happen though; the bilateral was the only safe way to go. I had to be able to live with every decision, so with each approaching treatment or surgery, I learned to prioritize my feelings about the outcome. I would lose my breasts, the sensual pleasure of my nipples, but I would live, recuperate and rejoin life without them.

My surgeon asked if I was considering reconstruction. "I've decided that I don't want reconstruction," I told him. If I had large breasts and was having one breast removed then maybe I would consider having it reconstructed, for balance, but that's not my situation. I just wanted to get this over with and get back to normal, a new normal, but back to my family, friends and work. Dr. Feldman was concerned that I was making a decision without all the facts and strongly recommended that I consult with a plastic surgeon to be fully informed.

His office staff made it easy by arranging an appointment for that same day and I ran downstairs to the plastic surgeon's office. I was called in and asked to remove my shirt and lower my pants, so the doctor could see my breasts and assess my body fat. My breasts were measured, examined, he felt their weight and then he looked at my tummy and ass. We sat on the edge of the examination table and looked through his photo album of women's torsos showing their reconstruction results. He explained that he could not use my own skin to develop new breasts because I am too thin and determined that I would have to have implants. If I decided now to have reconstruction, then my doctors could plan the first part of reconstruction during my bilateral, thereby eliminating one of the reconstruction surgeries. My breast surgeon would remove my breasts, and then the plastic surgeon would place 'expanders' under my chest wall muscles and close my incisions. Post-op, I would visit the plastic surgeon's office every few weeks. During those visits, air would be blown into the expanders, to stretch the muscles, in preparation for the permanent implants that would give me the size breasts that I wanted. I have since seen women's blogs and videos online where they illustrate this procedure in great detail, often sharing their excitement about getting larger, new and "improved" breasts. Women in support groups have told me the "other" stories – stories of radiation-melted implants, leaks and hidden tumors.

"I also tattoo nipples on after your implants are surgically placed and healed," he added.

"Do they work? Will I have sensation in them?" I asked, knowing the answer, but feeling punky about the assumption that all I wanted was to look normal again.

"No, they don't," he answered.

Personally, I did not want one more surgery or one more doctor to visit; it is surgery and things can go wrong too. I felt there was already a lot of uncertainty ahead and I chose to save my surgical time for life saving measures. Having "boobs" would make it easy to "fit in" and be normal. The other way is Amazon, rebellious, freaky… which way do I want to be every morning? Which way is "real" for me and true to my spirit? I couldn't visualize myself with blank, sensation-less bumps. Who would I be doing this for? I was fifty-four-years old, with Stage-Four Metastatic Cancer, and I had no time to worry about looking good in sweaters for strangers. My friends and family would get over their discomfort by my side.

I had wonderful breasts, I used them and enjoyed them and now I will see some other aspect of life that does not include breasts. My friend Janet said, "Remember Carol, we weren't born with them. They grew there." Mike said, "Mom, breasts are highly overrated." And Danielle said, "As a woman of the sixties, I've just never been into cleavage." I felt lucky that all I had to lose were my breasts. I would be fiercer than an Amazon; I would go back to the confidence of my youth, before the insecurity of pubescence. It took time, but that is where I live now.

January 10th, 2010

It was an incredible day. Bill and Jody Sterling organized a concert, Kate SC organized the food and Meg Clark had a team of friends help her organize a silent auction to benefit my fund. All of Team Help was on board. The church was donated for the event and I loved seeing all my friends gathered together; like a wedding and wake all wrapped in one, only I'm alive to feel it and enjoy it. The energy of the event was high from the more than one hundred friends that participated. It is ironic to feel blessed and have cancer.

January 14th, 2010

I dreamt there was a gathering and my color was enhanced like an ektachrome color print. I had been given a dye in my body to help me see what I needed to get rid of as I developed.

It was a good and full day. I finished up my projects at work and cleaned my space. I went to Thirsty Thursdays at Ann and Ray's house with Dana after dinner. It was a full house and I told every one of my next plans: NYC tomorrow to meet Dr. Chao about radiation oncology, pre-op testing, a breast cancer support group, and to see Dr. Feldman too. My fingernails look horrible from chemo. Dana had to hold them on so I could clip them.

Sunday, January 17th, 2010

Today Bobby drove Mom and me up to visit Uncle David in his new apartment in an adult facility. Afterwards we drove back to Albany and they dropped me off at my friend Susie's house for a "Girlfriend Gathering." I got there about 3:30 and there was a great turnout of friends spanning from kindergarten to high school. Of course we talked about my situation and upcoming surgery, but it was part of a larger conversation about life. We are all headed into a new stage of life, leaving the old pressures of "belonging" behind us. We all belong now. The acceptance of our individuality is prominent in our acquired wisdom. I felt such a presence of love. The girl's began dancing as I reached for my coat to leave. Linda and Susie began a "healing dance" around me and one by one my old friends joined in the spiral dance, placing me in the center. Someone called to hold hands and then "hands in the air" and "touch Carol" while Love Is King played on Susie's IPod. Bobby and Mom had arrived and Bobby got wonderful pictures of the spontaneous event. I'd never felt so much compassion and love as the send off the girls gave me.

Mom looked at me and said, "Have you been drinking?" Followed by, "You look very tired. Who was the thin girl in the beige jacket? What kind of doctor is Amy…?"

January 18th, 2010

Crying. I just thought of wearing my bra for the last time. I have been "theoretical" thinking about the "big picture" and how "it's not the hardest body part to lose" or "things could be worse," all true, but my breasts! Was I only supposed to be a woman for a short time? Oh fuck! Fuck, fuck, fuck…

January 19th, 2010

I woke sad and tense. My body curled tightly in a fetal position, dreaming of being in my grandmother's back yard.

January 20th, 2010

I dreamt of being in the audience at a Parsons student fashion show. We sat wherever we wanted in chairs placed randomly around the room. There was a two-story runway and five gowns came out in quick succession — too fast to enjoy all the work that was put into them. Then there was a crisis backstage. We waited over half an hour wondering what happened. I walked behind the curtain and found students everywhere un-doing their projects, pulling off trim, ripping seams, dissatisfied with the results.

In a pre-surgery session with Diane: *I am encouraged to give myself compassion. I want to replace my insecurities and sibling comparisons with a new compassion…I see it with iridescent colors of blue, purple and green… My breasts, as an aspect of womanhood, have been fully explored. I will grieve… I am sad already, but I know I will still be a woman. I can visualize myself a year from now, healthy with the dread of this behind me.*

Last night I received calls to wish me well before going into surgery. People I love in every part of my life called. Dana and I tag-teamed with both phones for hours.

Charlie's brother, Russell called this morning and his wishes for my health, and appreciation of being part of the family were spoken like a prayer. I'm grateful to know this. I drove Dana and Molly to school today and my neighbor, Anne, came running up my driveway to give me a hug. Maria, Charlie's sister, called too, and Dana texted from school that Joanna sent her love. Darcy texted a love message and I feel the richness of my life overriding my fear. I head out soon to catch the bus to NYC. Bobby and Cousin David will meet me and escort me to pre-op procedures at the hospital.

I feel like I am headed to the convent. The mastectomy is the ritual before entering.

Friday, January 22nd, 2010 @ 7:00 am.

I spent the night with Tommy and Danielle. I am bathed, dressed, packed and ready. I took a self portrait in their guest bathroom mirror. This last portrait of my breasts has Bandaids from yesterday's shots of radioactive dye to highlight my lymph nodes for surgery. I did not choose cancer, but I *choose* this bilateral mastectomy to save my life. I choose to be present for my children, family and friends. I choose to be ready to help someone else that finds they are walking this path.

Tommy drove us to the hospital and Danielle escorted me inside where we met Diane, found the waiting room and Charlie joined us there. Surgery was scheduled for 11:15, but the message was "Be there by 8:00 am, because we hope to go earlier." I don't remember timing because I wasn't rushing anything. I filled out the hospital release forms and my health proxy with Charlie, using the germ laden pen provided by the sick clerk. Diane went and got the Purell.

They finally called me into pre-op. Charlie, Danielle and Diane accompanied me. Charlie left when it was time for me to undress. It was a small space, crowded with our belongings. Much later, my brother Matt rushed in from the opposite direction, with motorcycle helmet and backpack in hand. He had told someone that "My sister is being operated on in fifteen minutes and I have to see her!" So a guy brings him in the back way, illustrating Matt's charismatic nature. We had some time alone together to talk. He was surprised at how calm I was. I told him, "I feel ready, Matt. It reminds me of the end of any relationship. No matter how good it's been, when it's over, or when it goes bad, you have to leave it behind."

★★★★★★★★★★

Thank you Dr. Feldman. Thank you to all in this room. I appreciate your knowledge and expertise. I want you to know I have enjoyed these breasts fully and deeply. I choose to let them go to save my life. Thank you for being here to help me.

I didn't actually read the words I had prepared to say in the operating room. Diane, in scrubs, walked me into the intensely lit operating room where everyone was fastidiously preparing for my surgery. They looked ready to pull on their masks, but let me see their faces first, most were smiling. Dr. Feldman had worked with Diane before in his OR and welcomed her. The nurses helped me onto the table and introduced themselves as they hovered above me. I did not need to delay them; the words I wrote were in my heart and Diane had my energy safely in her hands. I remembered to pull my energy inside me, deeper than my breasts, so that when they were gone, I would still have it. I breathed in and out slowly, to slow down my blood flow to assist my surgery. She sat to my side, next to the anesthesiologist, who was the last face that I remember.

Diane witnessed my surgery, while quietly reminding me of my intentions from our work together over the last four months. She remembered what else I was putting into my "numb lumps" before they were removed. Dr. Feldman looked up at Diane during surgery and asked her how I was doing. "She's doing Great," she responded.

Dr. Feldman spoke to my brothers, Bobby and Matt, when I was out of surgery and told them it went well. He felt confident that they had "clean margins." The three of them were walking down the hallway when Matt, 6'6" and 300 pounds, suddenly said, "Oh my God! That means I have the third largest breasts in the family!"

I was still out of it, but could hear the voices of my family and friends talking around me. Later, Tommy asked if I remembered him sitting to my right, massaging my hand in the recovery room. I remember Diane, Bobby, and Danielle taking turns feeding me ice chips. I will never forget waking up to those tall people standing around the foot of my bed as I slowly woke, blinking one eye open at a time. I still had tubes up my nose and I was being teased for snoring. My breasts were gone, but I was still me. I remember Robert with the large bouquet of cream colored roses and Paulette with a bag of fresh food. She pictured that I would be hungry later, but the nurse said "No" and told her not to leave it. Bobby was there taking pictures and got one of Matt on his cell phone, near my heart monitor with the sign forbidding cell phones. He was calling our family to let them know that I was out and doing well.

There were no surprises. Dr. Feldman came back to check on me and look at my bandages, which cleared the small, curtained quarters for my privacy, or their anxiety, but Matt said he didn't turn away, "And now I'm scarred for life," he told me. "I've seen my big sister with no breasts!"

June had arrived, but was told that Donovan was too young to enter the recovery room. She and Matt took turns visiting, but before they left,

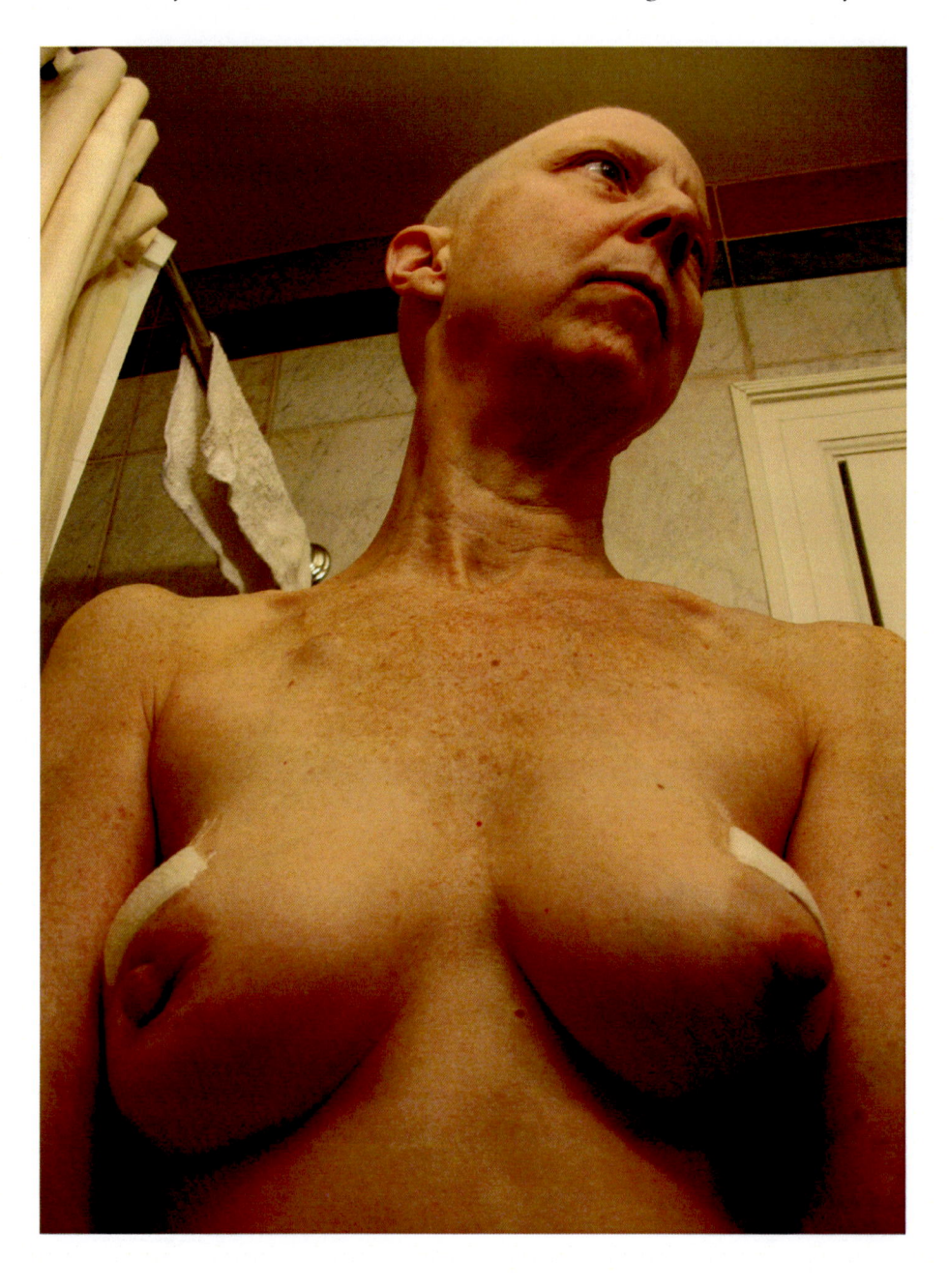

Donovan was lifted high in the doorway, across the room, and I waved to him. He was worried about me.

Diane stayed with me until I was settled into a room for the night. "Is there anything else I can do for you before I leave," she asked. "Yes," I told her. "Take a picture of my chest."

(Picture of me and my bare chest)

Saturday, January 23rd, 2010

The nurse had placed a button in my hand, connected to my IV, that I could pump if I needed more pain medication. The only time that I hit it was in the middle of the night. I was groggy and thought it would reposition the bed.

Tommy and Danielle came this morning to pick me up from the hospital. Bobby and Diane had been visiting while I waited for my discharge papers and instructions. Tommy drove Danielle and me back upstate so she can help for the week. Only a close friend could help to measure and drain the lymph juice from my four drains.

Monday, January 25th, 2010

I dreamt of Parsons again. I was outside looking through sketches, trying to find mine. I didn't find anything familiar. Students were all over campus working on their projects, when I remembered, Oh right, I hadn't decided what my sketch was going to be yet, but I am remembering from the future, knowing what I know now. Should I do the sketch I know that I worked on? Or should I do something different? I walked through back yards full of milk weed in full bloom, all milky, an opportunity to make a new choice that could guide a future outcome.

I look at my chest periodically. It is so absolute. No maybe. My breasts are gone.

EXPOSURE 1973

I stood next to Tim in life drawing class and we both flirted with the nude, male model. Tim was my best friend and most competitive rival. After class we disagreed as to who the model returned his flirts to. I thought it was me, but Tim disagreed, insisting it was him. It was 1973 in the fashion department of Parsons School of Design in Manhattan's West Village. The model probably flirted with both of us, but we made a bet: next week we'd stand on opposite ends of the room and see who'd win. That's when I borrowed Meg's adorable off white organza blouse. It had short puff sleeves, a buttoned front that ended with a bow on its high collar. Though sweet and conservative, it was sheer and I wore it braless. It was tucked into my long camel wool trousers; cuffed over my two-toned spectator platform shoes and I did look sharp with my long blonde hair swishing loosely below my waist.

Tim and I were having a friendly competition for the nude male model's attention, but there was also something else; our life drawing instructor so blatantly loathed the young women in our class that I couldn't resist the opportunity to irritate him. He was a short dark-haired man, full of passion for art and men; he was an unrepressed misogynist in a department that preferred men. It was almost bully-ish to put my six-foot frame in 4" platform shoes wearing a sheer blouse; my breasts were unavoidable. I spent the day humorously noting the levels of distraction that baring my breasts achieved, the life drawing teacher had already ignored me, but this week he couldn't

CAROL DWYER

help notice. I watched everyone either look at them or try not to; even my conservative gay teachers were blushing. I won the attention of our bisexual model that day. Tim said I was cheating, but he agreed to pay his debt, to buy me a drink at the Oak Room in the Plaza Hotel.

★★★★★★★★★★★★★★

We took the subway up to the Plaza after school and walked through the doors of the prestigious establishment. Entering into the elegant Oak Room, I requested a table for two. I followed the maitre d', with Tim trailing, hidden behind my broad shouldered vintage fur coat which I casually slipped off as I neared the table. As I sat, I realized Tim was gone! "That bastard!" I thought. "He's dumped me!" He had a reputation amongst his friends, for "disappearing". I was furious to think he'd get picked up and leave me like this, but decided to wait for a few minutes before I ordered; give him a chance to join me, but he didn't. There were two business men sitting at a table to my right that had been watching me. "Are you waiting for someone?" they asked.

"Yes, a friend," I replied.

"Would you like to join us for drink? While you're waiting?" they inquired. I was only there because Tim was paying his "debt." "Thank you," I replied. I chatted about school and my ambitions of being a fashion designer.

The drink, a White Russian, loosened my tongue and I talked about the apartment that Tim, John, Laurie, Meg and I aspired to rent on the top floor of the Fred Leighton building on MacDougal and Eighth Street, "But our parents won't give their approval or financial assistance, so we have to stay in the 'awful' dorm. We love this apartment!" I told them enthusiastically. "On the wall outside the building is a large painted advertisement for Bolton's. Under the window of my chosen bedroom, it says "Fashion Designer Clothing." The advertisement feels like a premonition of my career. We're 'dying' to get this place!"

They bought me another drink and we, or I, chatted some more. They laughed and over a third drink asked if my friend was wearing a pink, plaid flannel shirt tied at the waist and denim bell bottoms? "Yes!" I exclaimed. "Did you see him? Where is he?"

"I'm *s-o-o s-o-o-rry*. I should have asked you *before*," said the higher ranking businessman, "because they asked him to leave. He was inappropriately attired. It doesn't look like he'll be joining you. Would you like to join us for dinner? As our guest, please, to make it up to you?"

I was embarrassed to think that I had not gone to look for Tim. That I had sat there waiting for him, instead. I had been distracted by the men buying me drinks, but Tim was surely long gone by now, so I would let the men buy me dinner before I went back to the dorm. The cafeteria was closed by then, I justified, and it was the least they could do after withholding that information.

"Okay," I replied and ordered the most expensive thing on the menu: Surf and Turf. That was what my high school boyfriend, Randye, and I ordered when, just a few months ago, we used to go out together for a nice dinner. We'd dress up and order a bottle of red wine. Only I was safe then and not being misread as a young whore in a sheer blouse.

★★★★★★★★★★★★★★

I could gloss over this. Stop the story here, but it was a huge life lesson. In our table discussion the "big" business man acted outraged that I would be made to take a bus home for Thanksgiving. "No, I insist, please. Let me buy you a plane ticket to go home to Albany for your holiday. It won't take long, just come up to my room and I'll use the phone there to order you a ticket. We could have another drink." The other man said he'd wait downstairs and offered to drive me home.

I wasn't totally comfortable with this, but followed him up to his room. He placed the call to the airline, reserving the ticket in my name. It would be at the desk in the airport when I arrived. The man was my father's age and began to seduce me.

"Just a little sex, you'd do that for me wouldn't you? I reserved you a ticket home didn't I? Maybe we could work out an arrangement to rent that apartment you want. I come into town once a month or so."

Wow! Get the apartment for my friends and me? That would be a coup! What's the big deal? I got into his bed for the five minutes that it took him to cum with my eighteen-year-old ass on top. That was easy enough, I thought.

As he relaxed afterwards, I asked. "Do you have a family, a wife?" I'm thinking I should get to know this man that would rent our apartment, but he was uncomfortable with that line of questioning and got up. He called the other man to meet me and drive me home. He'd contact me about our arrangement.

I met the other man downstairs and he gregariously insisted on driving me home. But he pulled over on the West Side Highway, onto the dark, empty pier and begged me for a blow job. "That's all I want. Why shouldn't I get anything out of this?" He implored; begging me to feel sorry for him. When that didn't work he threatened to make me, or leave me stranded in this desolate place. I was still new to the city, unsure of where I was. I told him he was disgusting and I didn't want to. I leaned as far away from him as I could get and insisted on going home. But I don't remember the rest. I honestly don't; I can picture both possible scenarios. I did get home though and told Meg, in the bathroom, about the plan I was brewing to get our apartment. She seemed to understand, better than I did the cost of the deal and was worried that I was willing to pay it. I wanted the apartment and saw only the freedom it offered, not the price. I washed the blue eye shadow and mascara off my eyes as Meg looked at this stranger in the mirror. "I was worried about you, Carol, and I *still* am."

I spent my bus fare to get to the airport. The ticket lines were long, but my turn came. I walked up to the ticket counter and asked for my ticket.

"Here it is. Here's your reservation, Miss Dwyer. That will be $64." She looked at me. I looked at her.

"There must be some mistake. I have a paid ticket, could you check again? Please?"

"I'm sorry, miss, you have a reservation." I remembered the scene clearly now. What a rube. He made me a free reservation and I had no money to get home. I called Meg, who loaned me the money for the bus. She was happy I learned my lesson.

I went home on the bus, later than expected, but my parents never learned about my diversion or how close I came to making the wrong turn. I never contemplated a "sugar daddy" as an option, or life choice again. I understood all too well, how other girls could. I had just been lucky that I only been ripped off, and pissed off, before it began.

Tuesday, January 26th, 2010

Epic dream of a Renaissance dress I was supposed to make. I am in a long bedroom with twin beds (like in an orphanage). There are two women and two men. One of the guys is supposed to supply us with lonhjohns. I have my dress laid out on my bed. The long john guy shows us a commercial for them, but does not supply us. Teri is not ready for her part in this. I put on the dress, but the spell is not complete without the other components. I go in the medieval chapel, but do not transcend. It is okay. I will do it eventually without the other actors. I am not ready for the full power of being sacrificed. I'll help others that are ready to play the next scene.

January 28th, 2010

Yesterday Dr. Feldman said everything looked really well. He quickly pulled out two of the drains, one from each side. Danielle held my hand and Dana held my booted foot. It felt awful – like a tree root being extracted from my chest! I can go next week to have the nurse pull out the remaining two.

We had taken the bus into NYC and Tommy had picked us up at Port Authority and driven us to the hospital. He picked us up when we were finished and drove us back up to Kingston. Danielle decided to stay with us a few more days, until Friday. We sat and watched <u>Weeds</u>, Season 3, disc two, all episodes.

One of my drains is clogged and clearing it is disgusting, but preoccupying.

January 30th, 2010

I dreamt I was walking on the beach waiting for my turn to fly in the air with someone. Did I know a guy to fly with? Or did I have to wait to be asked? I walked up and down the beach looking and waiting. I caught a spider to hold while I flew. Eventually I flew, but with no memory of who I flew with, but I looked down on the busy waters below and saw dangerously sunken boats just under the surface. They could cause more shipwrecks, and I thought the waters were polluted with them.

January 31st, 2010

My underarm felt fat and puffy earlier, but tonight it drained suddenly, filling up with two and a half ounces of lymph juice. I guess the drain is working.

I had so much company today. Danielle's been feeling ill for a few days now and no better this morning. Bobby took me to the store where I realized I was not as hot-to-trot as I thought. I got tired carrying my hip pack. I napped when I returned home. Connie and Richard came, then their friend Barb, and Charlie. Tommy came to help Danielle with her "chores" and took Bobby with them back to NYC. Dana and I watched <u>Seinfeld</u> episodes while eating Connie's homemade chicken soup. Then, Katie SC came for a visit. I spoke to Mom, Dad and Mary, Shaindl and Diane. I laid down and watched all of season 3, disc 3 of <u>Weeds</u>, my current vice.

I'm a bit grumpy, itchy, bitchy and tired of being asked, "But how are you *emotionally?*" I just am. Day by day, hour by hour, I'm just grateful for the love and rest. I feel like the world has stopped so I could step off.

February 1st, 2010

My underarms and the side of my chest are sore. I need to stretch gracefully today.

I turned over and dreamt Charlie and I had another baby. We downsized to an apartment and I was not sure why. Why did I have to leave the washer and dryer? I woke the baby up and nursed him, but he was frustrated. I was basking in the voluptuous richness of nursing, but the baby flipped over me and practically fell out of bed! I put him in the middle of the bed and went out for a walk. Then I remembered that I had no breasts. A man tried to get my attention to tell me my fly was open. I scurried away back to the apartment. Poor baby! Was I delusional to have another baby? I had to feed the baby! I was going to start the oatmeal. I lay the baby down, but he pulled himself up, walked holding on to things and reached to the top of the dresser and put pins in his mouth! I quickly scooped them out. Charlie came home to talk about his play and I had to feed the baby and I was sad to lose my house. Why did I have to give up my house? Charlie was happier to move on to a new space, but I was at home more, so it was more of a loss.

Tuesday, February 2nd, 2010

I am still itchy and achy, I was moaning in my sleep and had to jump up to kill a spider in the shower for Dana. Her eye is irritated today and I am letting her stay home from school.

I turned over and dreamt that I could not find Connie or my cell phone to call her. I was at a friend's house and she was caring for older women. I looked all over for Connie, self- conscious of taking off my coat. Then I walked out of the neighborhood and into the city and took pictures of the colors. I went into a building and found myself in a relationship, snuggling and then he's inviting another woman to join us and I leave and exit through the city again and into a museum, where art work from Parsons 1975 is hung up. It all looks so familiar and I walk past a guy and follow the trail of art down the spiral stairs into the dead end of a bright white, shrunken staircase. I'm scared of being trapped there. It's hard to turn and climb up and out, but slowly I do. Back in the city I am again looking for a cell phone and Connie.

Dana and I ate breakfast and watched the movie Ice Age. Dana and her boyfriend broke up tonight. It's been coming on. It seemed to end well, but is still sad. Our friends, his parents, brought us a delicious dinner before heading out to celebrate their anniversary. They didn't know about the split between our children. Dana and I watched four episodes of 30 Rock, season three.

February 4th, 2010

Work with Diane: *today, I want to be settled. I had a blue day, just wanting to be done.*

THE SHORT STORY OF MY BREASTS

As a child I was bruised by the womanliness of my Mother and older sisters. I was a female, too, but of a sub-class: girl with no breasts. When I finally grew breasts I wanted to join their sorority. My breasts were from the genes of my father; small and perky. My sisters had breasts of the matriarch: very large and heavy. I envied their voluptuousness, yet bragged that my smaller breasts freed me from bras.

In college I'd worn the see-through blouse to life-drawing class, to see if the nude male model was straight or gay. I walked topless on Jones Beach, Fire Island and the beach in Penzance. I have nude self portraits, like the one I photographed in my Grandmother's Victorian mirror.

I began wearing bras at 35 when I was pregnant with my first child. With pregnancy *my* breasts became voluptuous, full of nourishment for my babies who were happy and content drinking the velvety milk pulsating from my nipples. Was anything ever more satisfying than that? I don't think so. Nursing was the pinnacle of my breasts' *career*, winning them their olympic gold medal.

One breast was a little larger than the other and sat lower on my chest. I had prominent nipples that responded visibly to cold. Seven-years ago, my right nipple began looking like it had a stroke. It was disturbing to catch a glimpse of myself in the mirror with chilled nipples aimed in opposite directions; I succumbed to wearing a bra with molded foam cups.

I was diagnosed with Stage-Four Metastatic

Breast Cancer and had both breasts removed to save my life.

I recall the day I read my surgical pathology. I sat by the window in Danielle and Tommy's apartment. We had just returned from visiting my surgeon. I was healing well. The scars looked remarkably well for just two weeks post-op. I held my breath as I read:

"An underlying firm mass is palpable in the central portion…
The nipple is mobile and everted.
A long suture indicates lateral aspect of the specimen…"

Danielle was concerned and said, "You don't have to read this, you know."

But I did. I needed to read this *other* story of my breasts. I cried to hear they left my body on a steel tray labeled with my name, those breasts I longed for as a girl; that I grew and shared pleasure with. I could no longer push them up in a bustier at a costume ball, or rub them on a lover's chest, but my flat chest still holds these memories

RADIATION BEGINS

The radiation months began prior to surgery with the scariest part first: taking the elevator down into the thick-walled bowels of Colombia Presbyterian Hospital, Level T, the Department of Radiation Oncology.

I went there to meet Dr. Clifford Chao, the head of the department, who I was referred to by my breast surgeon, the head of Breast Oncology at the same hospital. I was an interesting case, I was told; a prognosis perfect for attracting the expertise of these prestigious physicians.

On that first visit, just a few weeks before, I still had breasts. One of the many, friendly oncology nurses, took my weight and basic stats before being joined by a frail Asian resident doctor that made notes about my diagnosis and story. He signaled to open my hospital gown. His latex-gloved hands probed my breasts while he held his eyes squeezed shut, holding his head as far away as he could. I watched in disbelief, wondering if I scared him or he was petrified of breasts, in general. He turned from me to write his notes silently. The chief doctor entered the room friendly and spirited, feeling my breasts while talking to me, looking me in the eyes. I felt human again, removed from the resident's Petri dish.

February 20th, 2010

I worked on the gray vest today, but instead of participating in the PROCESS, I see every flaw as a failure and slow down instead of forging ahead for the experience of perfecting the pattern.

MY PERFECT BODY - part two

It's taking some time to adjust to having no breasts. First, it was the physical discomfort and recuperation from surgery, the exercises of physical therapy. I've felt a self consciousness that I haven't felt since pubescence, like I'm going backwards and will be considered third class: a woman without breasts. I have worried traveling the subway that I will be stared at, but as the days wear on, I realize that people aren't looking at me anymore than they had when I was a paranoid thirteen-year old.

I've been wearing scarves all this time, looped around my neck so that the ends fall on either side of my chest, covering where my breasts used to be. It's been a month since my surgery, but tonight a vicious hot flash made me loosen my scarf quickly. I was so warm that I had to take off my polar fleece camouflage. I hesitated, slowly peeling it off knowing that I was "coming out" as a flat-chested woman. It was a casual unveiling of the new me. My close co-ed friends didn't seem to notice the unwavering stripes of my gray and orange cardigan. No one stuttered or stared and I realized, in that moment, that my relationship to these friends never did revolve around my breasts.

Sunday, February 21st, 2010

Sometimes when I look in the mirror I see a centaur, but mostly now, I just see me, the lean me, having been through a reverse pubescence.

I made cookies today. I brought Mom some when Dana and I went to her house for dinner. She made grass-fed burgers with homemade steak fries and salad.

After dinner, Mom made a comment about spoiling Dana for her birthday – that the "money,"(from the fundraiser) was not to spend on a laptop for Dana's birthday, or boots, or – I reminded Mom that I still had my paycheck, that I only "chipped in" for my daughter's sixteenth birthday present and she accused me of being defensive. "You don't really think I'd say something serious like that?! I'm just joking!" then Mom commented that I have been responding to her like that a lot lately. She had a sad face. I thought, "Drop it, Carol, or its going to be a *huge*, upsetting argument." I apologized. *that* is Mom.

Dana loves her Gramma and later said, "Gramma gets her unedited thought out there and then calls it a joke so that you shouldn't be able to justify being offended." Meanwhile the thought that escaped into the room is an elephant. I deserve to be happy and I still need to take care of my daughter. I cannot internalize my Mother's restrictions and fears. They do not belong to me. I am molting. I love you Mom. I appreciate all the good that you do.

February 23rd, 2010

Radiation round #1 of 5 is done: 40 minutes total of lying on a hard table – 20 minutes of scans to test all the angles, and then 20 minutes of the real treatment. I ached. My arms ached, I was tired, but the radiation was an opportunity to deepen the knowledge of my mind. Restricted by a mask, I began to panic, but I was able to calm myself with thoughts of my Adirondak lake. I pictured swimming in it, out into the open water, beyond the lifeguard ropes. I love looking out over the vast expanse of reflective water as it mirrors the sky. Still, I was tired and achey.

We didn't get out of there until 7 pm. The weather and roads sucked, but, luckily, Charlie was driving; he is a great driver. When I got home Dana and I watched Coco Before Chanel with Audrey Tattou – fantastic film. For dinner, I ate some of Charlotte and Tony's delicious chili and cornbread.

February 25th, 2010

I texted my siblings yesterday about the death of Mary Jane Gunther, Mom's great friend, and our neighbor, growing up. She was 86-years-old and glamorous to the end.

My upper back was in spasm last night – all night. The shadow of it is still dominant. I still can't lie on my side post-surgery. My body is bored.

I watched <u>Auntie Mame</u> last night, starring <u>Rosalind Russell</u>. Cousin David gave it to me saying, "Carol, you're going to need this some day!" and last night was it. Dana was very consoling and sweet last night. Relax. Let go.

My body was in spasm for a good part of the day. I've been so uncomfortable. It is easy to be "sick" when you're comfortable. The real test is being in pain. My back did not ease up until after 8:00 pm. I got up and worked on photo pages of Christmas. Dana made her garlic pasta for our main meal at 4:00 and we watched two episodes of <u>30 Rock</u>. There's a lot of snow outside today and now it's raining. The basement has water. Dana has been working on her school project up to the last minute, feels sick and she's *not* done. She'd be lucky with another snow day.

February 27th, 2010

Radiation was cancelled yesterday. There was so much snow in NYC that the department closed at noon. I couldn't possibly make it in before that, so I squeezed in a physical therapy appointment and was able to join Dana, Mom and Bobby for the drive upstate to Mary Jane's wake. I was glad to be able to make it, to be part of it. She was my mentor and an inspiration for me to choose fashion as a career. She had me modeling as a kid, and later she used to buy clothing from my East Village shop in New York City. She was a fan at my fashion shows.

Mary Jane's daughter, Kate, told us that when she visited her mother in the hospital, a few days before she died, Mary Jane said, "I'm going out of business, Kate." Kate's cousin and I reminisced about the time he chased me playing tag and I chipped my front tooth on the church's stone wall. One of Mary Jane's other daughters had breast cancer a few years ago and she held my hands and said, "Carol, you look so good for…" and then stopped herself, remembering how much she hated people telling her that when she was ill. Dana met one of Mary Jane's cute grandsons and was suddenly willing to go back the next day for Mary Jane's funeral.

I got to visit with all of Mary Jane's children who hadn't gathered together in awhile, also friends from the lake. This was my first public outing to see them post-surgery and I joked, "Now I'll really be under-endowed this year at the lake!" in reference to the many buxom women friends there. Al said, "Carol, you're still hot!" and hugged me.

Matt, June and Donovan met us for dinner in Albany. Matt said I have a slim "fashion figure" now and I should play it up. "This side of anorexic," was my snarky reply.

I was exhausted the next morning and could not turn around quickly enough to make the funeral. I wanted to, but couldn't physically do it. I tried, but I had to ask myself the question: what was I trying to prove? That I'm a super hero doing cancer so well! I can't be overtired and I was. Dana would have liked to flirt with Mary Jane's grandson, but not without me. We both went back to bed and slept late.

March 1st, 2010

There was a Full moon last night. I slept poorly; woke up after dozing off and finally turned the light back on and finished reading Willa Cather's My Antonia. I tried to rouse myself, but my libido is so dull. Smokebomb came and lay right next to me and tightened the blankets and I cried to be so far away from myself.

March 2nd, 2010

I took the bus to NYC today. The woman selling the tickets asked if I wanted a senior discount. I should have said yes, but don't like to lie.

I got to the hospital with time for lunch. I made it to radiation by

2:00 pm (appt @ 2:30). They called me to change at 3:30. I had the chest wall simulation with Miguel and Raul. They created the form for my body to lie in and then two hours of laying still with my arms up over my head while we waited for Dr. Chao to work out the fine details of my treatment plan. I finally had to move my arms. My right arm and shoulder blade felt smashed, aching. Raul was uncomfortable giving me permission. I was supposed to lie perfectly still, but he was torn between his compassion for my desperation and his job. When I was done, Miguel tattooed me. He had to do double dots to differentiate from the spinal treatment tattoos. He added 12 more. I had asked Chao if they couldn't just use the same tattoos as the last treatment, but he smiled and said, "No, they have to be very exact." "It was worth asking," I replied, and we all chuckled. Some spots are still numb from my bilateral surgery so I didn't feel it, but most of them I felt and a few felt hyper-sensitive in comparison. They are all very nice and understanding, but "It has to be this way". Simulation ended at 6:00 pm and I waited for almost an hour with Danielle before my spinal treatment began. I was less upset because I knew what it would be, but it was just as fucking uncomfortable. "No way out, but through" – breathe. Be here now. Spinal radiation #2 is finished.

Saturday, March 6th, 2010

I am having a moment outside in the sun. I pulled a chair out from the garage. A bird, small, gray and smooth with a floof of a crest is singing for me.

I watched it climb each branch of the red maple tree, until at the top, it flew off singing in every direction. The kitchen window is cracked open and Sinead O'Connor is singing from my IPod. I am showered. I massaged Emu oil on my scars. I feel low-key today. No batch of errands compelling me to rush off. I meditated in my room, my healing space; light warming the room through lace curtains made on East Ninth Street over thirty years ago.

Dana is home from singing with her chorus group, the BlueBelles. Her guy friends dropped by and helped us pick up pine cones in the back yard. I am feeling more comfortable in my body. This is my form now. I have had other shapes and other habits in this life.

Work with Diane: <u>High Heart Chakra:</u> *corresponding to the T-1 vertebrae – it's about serving from your heart. Doing my Soul's work on the planet. I have a right to serve from my heart. I have an obligation to be as "Carol" as I can be.*

March 7th, 2010

Dreamt of being at Gramma Tugie's house with Dana. We were doing hand laundry and hanging it to dry. We were traveling somewhere…not staying… Gram had questions. She was unsettled by a choice I was making.

My cancer is being transformed into a lotus. I am transforming too; my unspoken darkness walking in the garden, in sunlight, on my path.

March 8th, 2010   Dana's 16th birthday!

Wednesday, March 10th, 2010

Yesterday, I had spinal radiation #4. Charlie drove me down, and drove around, and around looking for his magic parking space – no $3 valet parking voucher for him!

Set up went more smoothly and quickly. Errol highlighted my

"spinal tattoos with a marker. I did not remember that I had one under my chin! Miguel and Lamia set me up. I lay perfectly still. *The lights went dark and then gold light and the shimmering shape of Jesus was there, kindly, patiently leaning over me and removing the thin shards of gold leaf cancer from my spine. They came out so cleanly, they were very fragile, but pulled out intact. Thank you, Jesus. I appreciate your help in regaining my health.*

Nurse Brenda took my weight (145 lbs.) and blood pressure. The doctors asked if I had any side effects. "No, I'm fine, just tired…" I forgot to mention the itchy neck that drove me nuts in the car on the way home, like a sunburn and tightened throat. I am in a hurry to be well.

I can't have blood drawn from my arms because of the lymph nodes that were removed. I can get swollen arms from overworking, irritation or infection since I have fewer nodes to circulate the juices. I need to see my oncologist for the blood-draw from my port, as requested by my nutritionist.

Ellie, my physical therapist, was amazing as usual today. She fully and deeply massaged both arms. It is deep work to regain full mobility of both arms after the surgery.

Friday, March 12th, 2010

Kate SC and I had a nice ride down talking and listening to a Dharma talk from the Zen Monastery. I feel at peace. Everything is as it should be. I am grateful for this knowledge.

I had my last spinal radiation today. *Suddenly I was looking at Gramma Tugie's African violets in the window of her dining room. I knew she was with me, feeling love and calm, I felt her presence; I did not see her or need to. I felt done, like this treatment was a follow-up, but the big work was finished on Tuesday.* I am not quite as tired today as I was on Tuesday.

Tonight I ate Charlotte's left-over turkey chili from the freezer and watched <u>Snow Fallen on Cedars</u> starring Ethan Hawke, Robert Jenkins and Max Von Sydow. It's raining outside and Dana has gone to Molly's for her official birthday sleepover, just the two of them, with pizza and cake.

March 13th, 2010

I dreamt of new friends going in a store and making acquaintances. Then going to lunch and sitting in a booth with all new women, except for Mom, Connie and Dana. I dreamt that Dana had a picture of a little bird nestled into a small milk carton with a wash cloth. We looked down the street and saw the carton on top of a car and watched her run to me standing by the car. The carton was whole and full of milk.

I got up at 8:00 am. Alone. Its quiet except for the furnace and Smokebomb's clickety-clack toenails. I have begun to read <u>A Thousand Splendid Suns</u> by Khaled Hosseini. I watched <u>The Secret of Words</u> with Tim Robbins and added Shaindl's movie recommendations to my queue on NetFlix.

Monday, March 15th, 2010

Dreamt of my family in the basement with a main room, but back by the stairway there was a labyrinth that led to the inner room. I felt claustrophobic to enter with my winter coat on. I removed my coat and walked easily into the inner sanctum. Sometimes there was a stream flowing and earth with small twigs of trees, but I brought my friend, Arlen, in to show her and it was low water and the wiring showed, like a damp basement. Back in the main room the family gathered and Mom raised her questions behind my back, speculating with the others. "Do you

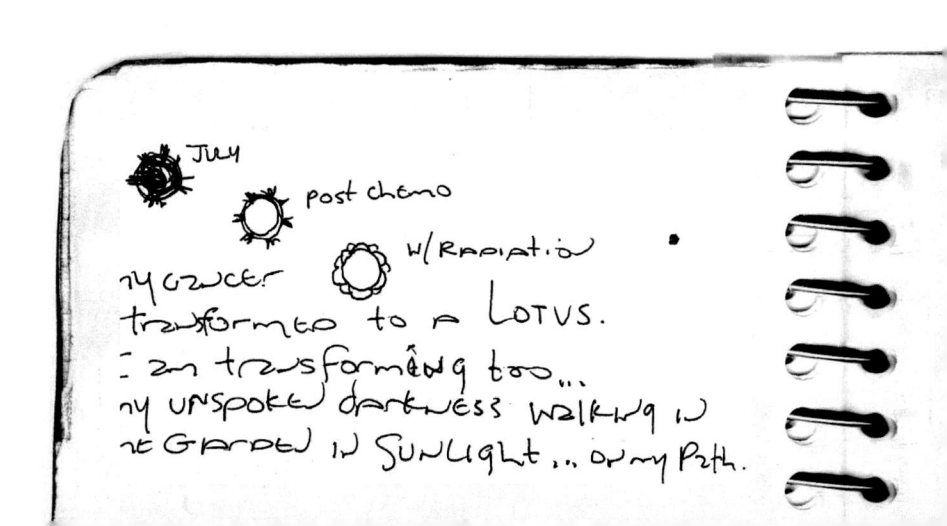

really think Carol's treatment is working if she isn't suffering from the side effects?" What could I say to that? Full of doubt, she was like Mrs. Bennett in Pride and Prejudice…worrying. I felt my teenage self reacting minimally and believing what I believed. Then I was on stage – The Family Show! We were eating cake on stage to celebrate a birthday, not usually done, but the audience had complained about a performance in England, so Mother felt we could torture them by eating in front of them, I was not sure of my lines.

I went into the City with Charlie this morning. He drove me to Annie and Jim's on East 10th Street where I'll be staying until my room is available at Hope Lodge, a "hotel" run by the American Cancer Society for cancer patients to live in while receiving treatments at New York City hospitals.

We unloaded my stuff and he took me up to the hospital for lunch and the test run of my chest wall radiation. There wasn't any real radiation today, but I was drained afterwards and came back to East 10th Street to read and rest.

EXCAVATION

For one-and-a-half months I had chest wall radiation in New York City, five days a week, always in the late afternoon. I spent a lot of time getting there, and waiting there, and then on the weekends I went home to be with my daughter, Dana. I didn't restrict her normal high school weekend activities. She already had enough changes to cope with, but the time we got to share was sweet and cozy as we snuggled, watching funny movies together.

But there was more; I was seeing this time in New York as a special opportunity to visit all the old friends that I hadn't had time to see during my parenting years. I used to commute to teach at Parsons and stayed overnight with Annie and Jim, until I bumped into my old friend Robert, began dating, and stayed over at his loft. In the spring of 1999, I left the city to work at the Tonner Doll Company. I no longer had to commute and I'd only pop in for quick visits.

I stayed for a week at Annie and Jim's apartment while I waited for my Hope Lodge reservation to open. I'd met Annie in Washington Square Park when our boys were babies sharing the sandbox. We hadn't talked in ten years, but when I emailed that I had "Health Issues" she responded seamlessly, inviting me to stay for the whole six-weeks of treatment. I enjoyed my dinners with Annie, Jim and their daughter Sara. It is amazing to have friends that pick up wherever we left off years ago. They made me feel so welcome.

There was something to look forward to in this time living there again, something beyond radiation and getting through the hours of waiting. Each day revolved around who I got to visit that day for lunch, a walk or a trip to the museum. I visited Sandy, my East Village friend and mentor who taught me to love healthy, organic, whole foods. I visited with Janet who worked in my East Village shop with me for seven years, Tom, whose coffee shop was my breakfast nook for a decade, and Leslie, whose restaurant was the Mecca for healthy eating from way back in the day when we were both young entrepreneurs. Joe, a colleague and friend, invited me to the Parsons Fashion Show and I visited with many of the faculty I had worked with for years. We got to visit and talk about the old days and new.

Cousin David was my first date. We were buddies from my early days of living in NYC when we went for the cheap seats to all the Broadway shows. He and Bobby always helped at my fashion shows, and more recently helped me to clean my house for the winter of chemo hibernation. I went to Barbara's sandal shop to have her re-strap the leather sandals she made for me in 1983. I also enjoyed many more nights with Danielle and Tommy and their dog, Pucci. They opened their home to me, drove me to treatments and fed me. Danielle and I go back to the East Village days, too, when I met her on Ninth Street and she became a muse for my clothing designs. She was my maid of honor at Charlie's and my wedding in 1984.

I hated to leave my daughter behind, though I knew she would be fine at Charlie's house. I knew there was something special about these radiation days. There was a personal journey, an exploration of my past and all the past selves that had splintered off in the ensuing years of parenting, teaching at Parsons and Marist Colleges and working at the Tonner Doll Company.

I was searching for those missing parts of myself that each friend held for me to reclaim. I was bald and breast-less now, but was the same person that they had known and it helped to feel that. I had been here, living, breathing and part of the fabric of a neighborhood. I began here and made clothes for women in this city. I cleaned and swept my block, and part of me was still in these streets. Nothing is like it was then, though, except in my dreams where I still own that shop and apartment, and I go to it to sort through what I left behind.

I was in New York to excavate myself, the self that had spread too thin, the self that let go of aspirations and fit in wherever I went. I had rounded too many corners and I came to get them back, to feel sharp again, edgy, and full. My East Village self was not insecure and I needed her to help me be breast-less and still provocative.

Tuesday, March 16th, 2010

Today was my first chest wall treatment. I sat in the inner waiting area chatting with the two Turkish sisters escorting their brother for his brain radiation. I spoke to Dr. Chao and his resident prior to treatment and weighed in at 143 pounds. My skin will be affected more today because they put on a rubber mat called a "bolus," and gave me a higher, saturating, but superficial dose of radiation. The mat added some protection to my lungs. Radiation went pretty quickly – about 10-15 minutes per side. Then again, after the spinal treatment, this is not so hard.

I remembered my visualization that came to me during a session with Diane, of pulling down my old storefront gate under my skin to protect my insides and reflect the radiation back through my skin for maximum effect. I was worried about the heat on the metal gate though, and added a stream of water running over it to cool it down and moisten my skin. I am well.

Dana sounded exhausted and upset tonight. I love you Dana. Mike called me today as I was walking with my cousin David. He said he was going to ride his bike to meet Dana at the high school. She doesn't feel comfortable walking home alone to Charlie's house. I hope that he met her.

Wednesday, St. Patrick's Day.

I'm feeling so cold. Cancer has brought a connection to solitude. Cancer has brought me to a sexual standstill; brought me to a place to stop and stand back and ask, "What do I really need to be doing?" Cancer asks,

"What brings you joy? What is your life's work?" I have not answered, but I am not blindly sleep walking through my days either. I am awake. I am shifting tracks for my life's new direction.

Treatment is so much quicker now and everyone is so sweet, so respectful. I am very appreciative of how they care for me.

Thursday, March 18th, 2010

I seem to be accepting less than a deep sleep, although I did dream this morning. It slipped away, but I knew it had been there. I finished my book last night. I preferred it to his last book, <u>The Kite Runner</u>.

Friday, March 19th, 2010

I am now living at Hope Lodge. The name feels dramatic, for me. I am not fond of stranger's condescending statements about HOPE for my CASE. I, luckily at this point, supply my own hope, but I don't even think in terms of hope – I know I will be well. I have this gauntlet to pass. I HOPE I am this positive if my skin gets crusty.

I listened to "Dauow's Sickness," a Dharma talk, on my IPod today. My illness is part of the world's illness. My health is part of the world's health. There is no difference between them.

Saturday, March 20th, 2010

I dreamt I was listening to my phone messages in my head. I wrote down "John and Bruce Wainright." I needed to separate from them. They would hold me to how things were, but I needed to change. Food was what I most needed to change. I was in a deli with Charlie. We needed to grab something quick to eat. We were looking at macaroni salad, mac & cheese and Italian bread...one of the dishes tipped over and I wasn't going to leave it there. I tried to scoop it back in the dish. What a mess. We left without buying anything, but we were still hungry. So we went back in the store, but it had been cleared out for a Frank Sinatra dinner theatre concert. We walked across the front of the store. The deli owner's son's bike was blocking the fridge and we could see the food we rejected before, but needed now. Charlie moved the sardine bait hanging off the bike and it was dripping and making a mess and I told him to stop! The owner called his son to move the bike. I was trying to reach around it to get the container out of a fridge. It was not arranged professionally. The front of the store was a messy, small town, dry goods store.

It's 7:03 am and I can hear the birds outside. I slept well, home in my bed and remembered a dream! The first one all week!

It's a beautiful day doing my errands, mail, signing taxes and then a visit to Therese for acupuncture. I'm communicating with Ellen from the Metastatic Breast Cancer website. It organizes, informs, and connects people with metastatic breast cancer (MBC). We've been emailing and will speak Monday night or Wednesday morning, before she goes away for two weeks.

I spoke with my friend Joe today and we will meet at Parsons at 2:15 Monday for tea. I am looking forward to seeing him. Thursday night I am seeing [Wonderland in 3-D](#) with Bobby and Danielle. My dance card is filling up.

Sunday, March 21st, 2010

I dreamt that there was a very large spider in the room — tarantula legs and a fat tiger print body. It is the circumference of a coffee cup! Bobby swatted it off the table or someone's leg and it went right in the waist of my shirt and scurried up my chest to my shoulder! Bobby loosely grabbed my shoulder as I whipped off my shirt! I was so spooked that I really took off my shirt and finished sleeping topless.

Then I was at a costume party in "drag," dressed as a big drag queen. I had a big blonde wig, a long red sequin dress that was slit up the thigh, big boobs, and lots of foundation for a tan color. Then the party was wrapping up and packing up. We had to get back to our buses and some of us had another performance to do. I realized at the party that I forgot to finish my makeup — no eyeliner or mascara, I was a half-assed drag queen! Would I make it to the bus? I wanted out of my costume, but I had no time to change and where were my clothes anyway?

Thank you Artemisia for my dreams.

Work with Diane today: *Visualizing a poultice on my chest. Brought to me by my guides, who today are impish little fairies that have much energy; energy enough to share with me. They brought tropical leaves, with medicinal properties and had woven three layers of them for the protection of my chest. A chest plate of healing and protection…layered as feathers on the chest of a bird…layered to be a little thicker where my breasts were. The leaves are a healing poultice. They nourish the radiated skin and protect my chest from the burning and drying effects of radiation. Radiation is the treatment I choose to protect my life. The poultice is a gift from my guides to assist my continued healing.*

Monday, March 22nd, 2010

Big day tomorrow: I'll be seeing Dr. Cigler to begin a "TARGETED therapy drug" called Herceptin. It suppresses the "Her2Neu+" proteins in my cancer cells that encourage rapid cancer growth in my body. I will get infusions of it for one year. The chemotherapy I had in the fall and winter was an aggressive, heavy-duty chemo for breast cancer: Adriamycin, Cytoxan and Taxol. Herceptin, along with Tamoxifen, are specific suppressing the variety of cancer puzzle pieces that I have. Targeted drugs are part of the new strain of treatments to help fight specific aspects of my cancer and, I'm learning, have the potential to extend my life.

Tuesday, March 23rd, 2010

I did a 17-minute, silent morning meditation. I want to be open to the creative abundance of the universe. I want to be open to all abundance. I want health, peace and energy today. I had my supplements. I will shower and then make a smoothie.

I have been very sad all day. I still am. I sat in the infusion chair for the first time since December reading Olive Kitteridge by Elizabeth

Strout. I was laughing, but when I finished with my Herceptin infusion and went to the bathroom, I could have sat on the floor and cried. I felt flashed back to feelings of vulnerability and sadness surrounding my previous chemo infusion days. The day itself was cold, windy and wet. It had been a trek to get to the Weill-Cornell Hospital on the Upper East Side and it felt exhausting to approach my return. I was underdressed so I splurged on a cab to rush back to Hope Lodge and redress, eat and zap back out to the A train for a ride to Colombia Presbyterian Hospital on the Upper West Side. I was right on time for treatment.

I lay down on the radiation table with Marguerite helping to set me up. I visualized the gate being drawn down under my skin, to protect my vital organs. The projector passed over me for the first round of pretreatment scans and I saw my reflection, naked with arms stretched provocatively over my head. I saw my eyes looking at me, then my scars. I imagined the cooling water over my gate, but today, in this reflection of great sadness, the water became tears, one connected to the next, spilling, pooling in my ears and spilling again. I tried to picture Dana and Mike but that made me cry more. Marguerite thought they took too long with the films and said that next time they would split it over two days. I said, "No, it's just me today. If I had hormones, I would swear I was premenstrual!" She gave me a big hug.

I am tired of people's cancer stories. I am not at home and I'm homesick. This is not fun or special – me either.

I ate dinner at Whole Foods. But first, when I came up from the subway, I was lightheaded and had to quick sit down to regain my composure. I felt better after I ate and read. Robert came and picked me up. When he greeted me, and looked me in the eyes, he suggested that we don't go to see <u>The Girl with The Dragon Tattoo</u>. "Maybe that's too violent for tonight." I agreed. I told him it was the worst day of life, thus far. We decided to see <u>City Island</u> starring Andy Garcia and Julianna Margulies. It was a great choice – so funny. We laughed like old times and held hands. We enjoyed our time together. He walked me to the subway entrance and we said another goodbye.

Back here at the Lodge, I called Ellen and we finally spoke. Jeff Rubin had put me in contact with her as a source of metastatic breast cancer information. She gave me all the information that I never wanted to know about this illness. I will have this for the rest of my life. I am eligible for Social Security Disability because of this diagnosis, but I want to go back to work! It was a crushing end to this low-down day.

Wednesday, March 24th, 2010

Dreamt I was taken in by a couple. They were letting me stay for dinner like I was a stray cat. I was asked to set the table, but when it was served, I was told by the wife to take my plate down to an empty apartment on the 4th floor. I felt deflated. "Sure. Which one?" I asked. But my deflation was so complete, my apology for my existence so apparent in my posture, that she relented and said I could sit at the table.

I woke at 6:30 am, but turned over. Fuck my regimen of supplement consumption. I need sleep. I need food too. I lost a pound yesterday on the scale at the doctor's. I don't want to lose weight. I wanted so badly for Robert to comfort me last night. I could picture his arm sweep around my shoulders like it did that rainy night near the lilacs in 1998, our first date. I grieved for the loss of us while riding on the subway alone.

Thursday March 25th, 2010

Cinemaplex dreams that drifted away without me…multiple hot flashes prying my fingers from each one all night. The first hot flash was only an hour after going to sleep. I woke so completely that I thought it was morning. I had to sleep without PJs.

Now I have done my yoga and 16 minutes of meditation. I'm sipping green tea from my Superman mug…looking out the bedroom window of room 1004 at the faded vertical sign for Gimble's peeling off a brick wall.

Abstract shapes, created by sunlight reflecting off windows onto the other building…a church cross…people walking…another hot flash as I sit perched on my windowsill writing.

I enjoyed my time with Matt yesterday. He arrived on his motorcycle, at 1:00 pm to pick me up at Hope Lodge. I dressed warmly with my winter coat, leather gloves, scarf and sneakers. We put my hip pack in the trunk on the back of the bike. Matt slipped the helmet on my head and buckled it. FVVvvvvROOM!!!! Off we went! It took quite a few blocks of ferocious gripping before I could relax into it. I knew the tension would be unhealthy, like shoveling with your back; my arms are still regaining mobility after surgery. I began to use my legs to grip Matt as we stopped so I wouldn't slide into him each time. I worked on loosely holding on.

I remembered Matt's trust of me when I rode him on "*our* bike"— the green Schwinn that we got for my fifteenth birthday. I say we, because I also got a black framed child's seat with green plaid vinyl cushions, for the back of Our bike. I have a vivid memory of stopping at a crosswalk and losing balance of the bike. "Hold on Matt!" I yelled and turned to see my three-and-a-half-year-old brother just holding on. He had no seat belt or helmet. No protection except his trust. The bike was just about perpendicular to the ground before I got it balanced again. My baby brother held on. No screams; no exposed fear. I felt trusted.

Now it's my turn.

Matt came into the radiation oncology department and met just about everyone. I spoke to Marguerite at length. Dennis and Bernard wear white coats over their street clothes. They do the same job as Lamia, Miguel and Marguerite, who choose to wear colorful scrubs; mystery solved.

After my chest wall treatment Matt called in reservations and I guessed we were going to Matt's favorite steakhouse. An adrenaline rushing motorcycle ride down there – people kept jumping out of nowhere and everywhere! "A live Frogger game," Matt called it. We shared a big dinner of steak, tuna (both rare), garlic mashed potatoes, grilled asparagus, red wine and mixed berries for dessert. We laughed at the statement on the menu of "Grain-Fed Beef" when we know the real specialty should be "Grass-Fed Beef." Matt introduced me to everyone; he was in his glory at a place where everyone knows him. We talked deeply and we opened to each other like we hadn't in a long time. He shared his frustrations and disappointments. Back on the bike, he drove us to Colony Records, but first stopped at the Brill building so Matt could say "Hi" to the guys he used to work with in his early days in Manhattan. One guy said, "You want records? Go take mine on the 5th floor!" And so we did: Jimi Hendrix, The Who, and Bruce Springsteen – a cache of albums. I took the Procol Harem duplicate when he offered me one.

March 26th, 2010

Radiation was smooth today. Easy. Out by 3:30!

Saturday, March 27th, 2010

Work with Diane: *Laying on the table, but not the radiation table. Diane massaging…clearing energy; so different from a week of fingers poking and prodding. I am in the middle of my family again. I am in the middle radiating love and compassion, connection. My old middle tried to move mountains, but my new middle is a seed of love. We cannot cut each other off. We need to know and accept each other in order to heal. I need to imagine my tropical poultice wrapping around and under my arms to protect my skin.*

Sunday, March 28th, 2010

Dreamt of dreaming and tried to slip out of the dream, but No! I had to run alongside the dream until I could jump out. It wasn't easy! My best sleep seems to be going back to sleep in the morning.

Monday, March 29th, 2010

Epic dreaming: Sandy trying to guard an ill seal in a tub for the vet to look at. I was looking for an apartment in NYC with composite boyfriend/husband. Nice place – empty when we kind of snuck in, but filled up fast with interested tenants. It had two bathrooms on either side of the apartment marked men and women. In fact they looked like the rounded doors on a navy vessel. I tried to go in, but got stuck in the women's door! That's when the broker and other people began coming in. How could a door be so small that I could get stuck going in sideways? The bathroom itself is pleasant; a nice size and design, but I could not live with the dread of being stuck every time I needed to use it! The kitchen had a huge island/table with all the cabinets underneath. It was a great efficient space. I tried to talk to the broker, but she snubbed me. We had snuck in and were not on the official list. Other people followed the male broker through a door to a wine tasting. Um…this wasn't working out too well.

Then, walking back through the city, with each of us holding part of a mannequin. I reach for my camera to take our picture but I don't have my bag! I think back and realize that I haven't had it all day! We re-trace our steps back to the disgruntled female realtor that had my film analyzed to determine my financial status and was holding the camera for a bankruptcy hearing! My composite and I stood around waiting. For what, I'm not sure. I did not want to steal it back, but I wanted it back. That is all I cared about for the moment! Some guys in a band were rehearsing and offered sympathy till the broker zipped that shut. They were camping out in the office and we still stood there. The cancer was making me even

CAROL DWYER **122**

more tired than my composite. Limbo. He was looking for an acting job and might have even slipped out for an audition. I waited for my camera.

Back from chest wall radiation treatment #9. Restless. Feeling to call – plan – go, but too tired. Hot flashes. Mood lowered. Marguerite said they would only film one side tomorrow. I said, "If the machine works tomorrow, do both sides and be done!" She said we will see what the schedule is tomorrow.

Radiation…scarred chest…not home…Be Here Now…stop moving…stay put…the sign in the Lodge lobby invites *us* to join *them* for dinner on the 6th floor tonight. Watch a movie…Meditate.

Not in that order. Tea, now. Read. Settle in. It is messy outside.

I feel unmoored.

Carole said the rain is negative ions and it's good for us.

I need to vacuum out my mind. I stopped and meditated for 15 minutes.

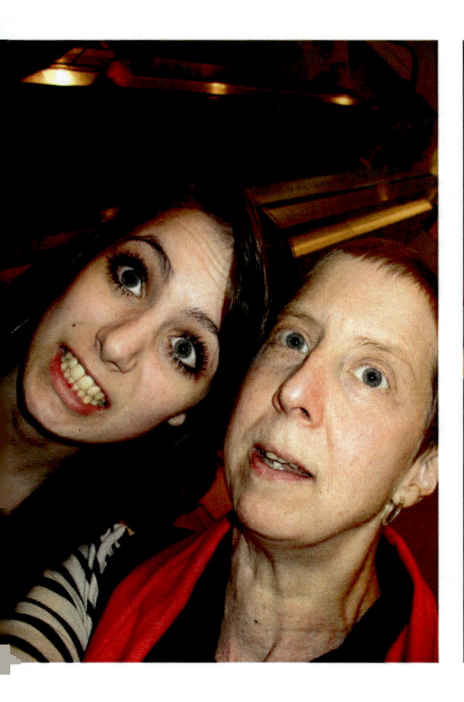

I spoke to Therese today, briefly, but confirmed that I am keeping my pledge to establish a daily, 15-minute meditation.

I just watched <u>Gran Torino</u>, starring Clint Eastwood. Eh.

I am receiving a Herceptin infusion tomorrow. I am grateful to be able to take this drug. I welcome it to help me.

Tuesday, March 30th, 2010

Dreamt of a ferocious wind blowing through my old North Main Avenue home. Doors whipping shut. There were very few cars on the street. A sturdy cyclone fence in the basement, the house was a dirty mess inside. Dirty dishes. Broken dishes. I began to wash some big bowls and almost dropped them, they were so greasy.

Sopping day! Sopping rain every time I went out. First, I went to Dr. Cigler's for a second Herceptin treatment. I asked my doctor about my current assessment of metastatic breast cancer: that I have about the same chance of reoccurrence as anyone else. It seems like I could be well for a long time. She smiled and seemed to agree.

Friday, April 2nd, 2010

Still thinking of yesterday morning's dream: *climbing a tree to my studio in a "tree house" with a deck around it. I was trying to hoist myself up to the deck, but I couldn't get a spot to throw my leg up. I finally succeeded in standing on the deck, but there were so many things clogging the low, narrow opening to the studio that I couldn't get in. One of the things was an unpacked tent. I looked around for ideas and saw a vertical post with a perpendicular bar attached. The post had varying lengths of chains hanging off it and I realized that I had nothing to lose by grabbing one of the chains to see if I could swing on it and slide into the studio opening. To my surprise the chain extended itself slowly and I gracefully swung in a large arc, around to the back of the structure and gently touched down on the larger deck and found a taller entrance to the studio! All the problems of congestion were solved. I found the better way to enter.*

Dana and I went to radiation today. It was her first time escorting me to an appointment.

Saturday, April 3rd, 2010

I ran errands all morning for pre-Easter grocery shopping. I got to Diane's at 1:00 pm and had another incredible session. I talked of my important desire to be connected and to connect…to be impeccable with my word and to connect to the creative abundance of the universe. I told Diane of my dream on Thursday morning, of trying to hoist myself into the studio. I remembered the graceful arc I made flying on the self-extending chain, the perspective it allowed me while flying around the studio…the fear I threw away in order to grab the chain…the trust I had that I should go exactly as I should and land in a better place than where I began. There were so many positive images.

Work with Diane: about choosing and welcoming Herceptin this week. I had asked my nurse to let me hold it before it was infused through my port. I am grateful that it is available to help me. I am grateful to have Diane working with me and teaching me how to be empowered instead of being a victim to my illness. I am walking the path, not crawling.

I have been reflecting this week about Easter. I surprise myself with how powerfully I feel about celebrating the holiday at my house, with my family, pulling everyone together; that I am here to pull everyone together. Practicing peace, love and tolerance begins Right Here, Right Now. We pull together for the holidays to share food and love and be together as a family. We have to keep practicing being together, practicing loving each other.

I am joyous that it's spring and that I have made it through the toughest winter of my life. I am grateful to feel the abundance of spring. Thank you for coming together today. Thank you for being part of my life.

Sunday, April 4th, 2010

I dreamt of being hired to help with "criminals." The person was sitting in a chair and I was told to put on latex gloves and be one of two people that would cautiously, but firmly, handcuff the "criminal." I was instructed by a man dressed as a doctor prepped for surgery. I ask a question of him saying, "Doctor?" and he corrected me saying, "Father." I asked, "Father, are you a priest?"

Bobby was downstairs at 7:30 am to help with the ham.

I began Tamoxifen on Easter morning.

We had an incredible day! Perfect weather, food and company! I got to see everyone in my family that is within driving radius. Chloe helped me get her Mom and Uncle (my niece and nephew) to be here though they don't seem to be getting along right now. Jessica came with her ex-husband, Derek, and Chloe brought her new boyfriend that she'd been texting about; he seemed like a nice guy. We celebrated Chloe's sixteenth birthday. We did a lot of hanging out on the front lawn watching the boys skateboard in the street. A particular highlight for me was seeing my niece Meaghan talking with Mike and Dana at the dining room table like the young adults that they've become. So many frictions put aside for the day. The floral arrangements were also particularly beautiful, pleasing. I just posted pictures on Facebook. My stomach is unsettled. Was it the ham? Just too much rich food? I want to eat brown rice tomorrow!

Tuesday, April 5th, 2010

I had many dreams, many hot flashes too. Sometimes the heat is so violent! Sleeping naked and throwing the blankets off for a quick fix is the only way to cope. I am also sleeping on my back with my

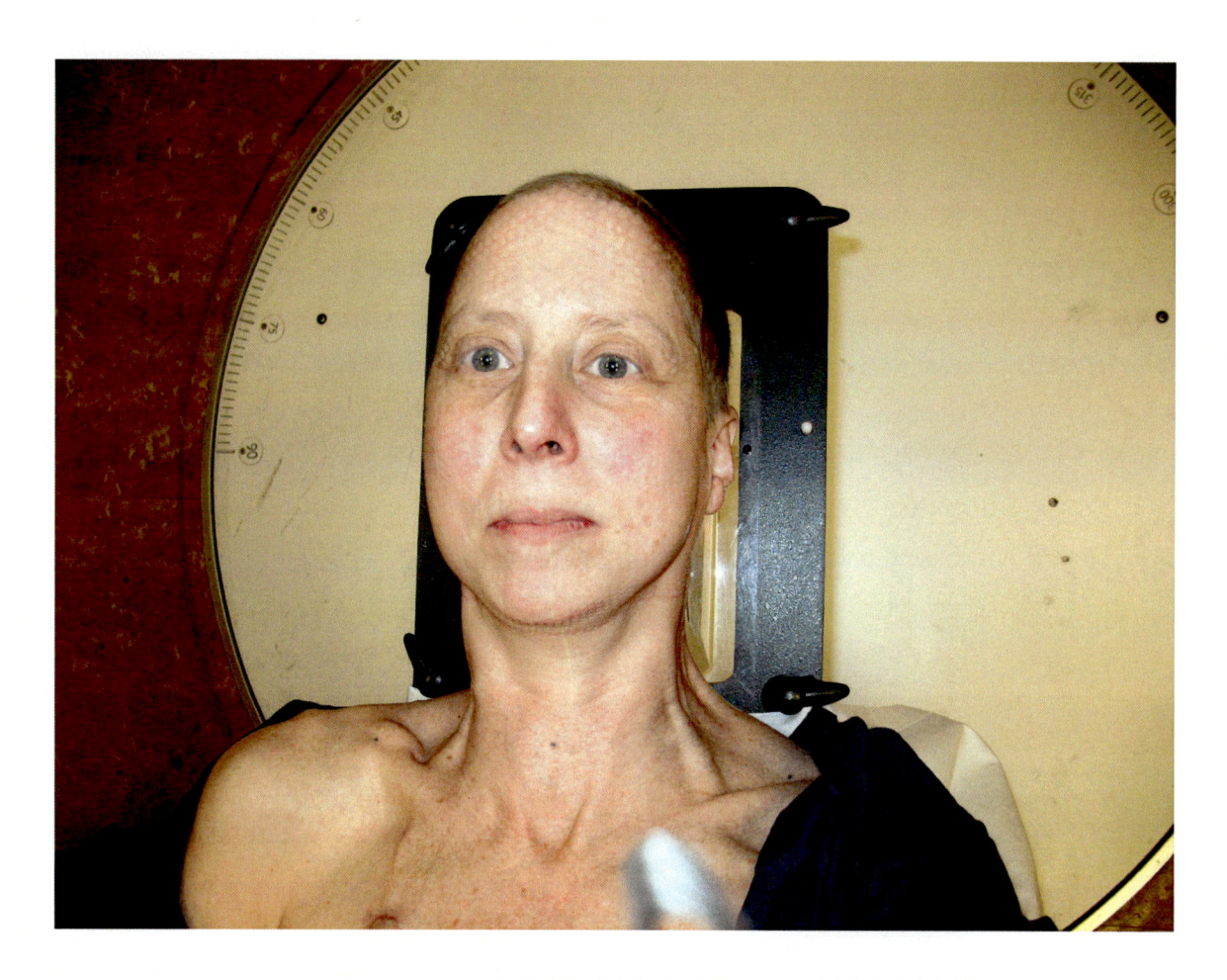

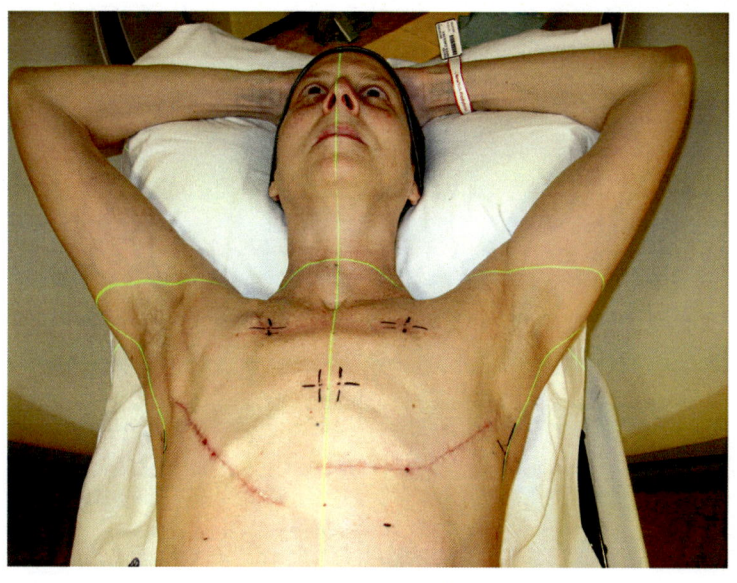

ENOUGH 127

arms stretched overhead to open my chest. My upper chest and collarbone are getting red and itchy from radiation.

Yesterday I fell asleep at the end of radiation and Miguel scared me when he woke me up!

I dreamt of waiting in line at the bank, a long line. The tellers knew me by name because of the fundraisers. Then one called me over to cut the line. I was getting $100 cash. She said the bank would give me $45 and take the rest from my account.

In another dream there were Chinese people working, assembling cheap trinkets. They were trying to find the right glue to put together miniature, vinyl, webbed umbrellas. The glue was oozing out and should be clear. I wasn't working with them, but present and worried about the odor of the glue. I went in the basement and found a big gap in the stone around the window and was thinking that I should plug it up.

I'm sitting here topless, literally. I got so warm today that I stripped to a tank top with a white sweatshirt tied around my neck. I am on the subway two to six times day, watching people and know people are watching me too. I am working on maintaining self-confidence…maintaining breast energy.

Thursday, April 8th, 2010

Many layered dreams between peaceful "power surges." I sleep topless and when the heat rises, I throw the blanket back an arm's length and easily, happily, pull it back over me when I feel chilled. I am grateful for the relief both ways. No panic or anger, just relief, with dreams layered in between: a fast food lunch served thinly melted on a metal tray – why would I eat this? I was living in a shack on Catholic grade school property with Mike and Dana when they were little.

April 9th, 2010

No treatment yesterday, the machine was broken. I called today before going there.

I had treatment #17, #11more to go.

Saturday April 10th, 2010

Work with Diane: Opening. Very conscious of deep breaths that came from my very core...

I saw my pods of white blood cells incubating and when she worked my chest and shoulders, the pods ripened and burst, like the pollination of a flower. I saw all my visits with old friends this week as revisiting with "old me's" that they knew in our early relationships...I felt part of my mission was to call them back home to the Mother Ship - back to my core — then, un-splintered, I can go forward.

I am ready. I plan to add five more minutes of separate meditation for white blood cells.

Monday, April 12th, 2010

JUST FOR TODAY I WILL LET GO OF WORRY. I am up and fed Dana a good breakfast.

I'm sitting outside in the sun, listening to birds as I wait for Andrea to drive me to the bus. It is so warm and spring-like today! Green! The tulips are just beginning to bloom and the daffodils are expiring.

I am listening again to "Daowu's Sickness," the dharma talk about the sick and the not sick, the Human condition, Spiritual illness, Disappointment, dissatisfaction, a grasping and clinging mind. It points out how my illness has brought me to the knowledge of my well being. To be sick, I no longer need to live in fear of being sick. In that way my health and spirit are healthier than before.

I returned to Hope Lodge for lunch. I had an early treatment at 2:30 and finished at 5:45. It is depressing down there. I'm fine for a little while and then I slide down…

They were questioning my "Bracelet" mark on my burnt chest today. It is a bracelet looking pattern on the right side of my chest, pale marks compared to the burned skin surrounding it. Errol and Lamia said to talk to my nurses. Brenda looked at it and called in Christine. "Show Chao tomorrow," was the consensus. Everyone wondered what it was from. The resident took pictures of it with a digital camera.

Robert texted back a suggestion to solving a problem I was having on Photoshop over the weekend and told me he's painting his bedroom.

Wednesday, April 14th, 2010

I slept in this morning. I relished every moment of it as purposeful for healing. I had to pass a few pushy, unproductive thoughts of "wasting time." Hell no! This is what I'm supposed to do! Let my body recover from radiation and I *am* getting *red*. I have nine more treatments to go. Dr. Chao has a new resident now, who enthusiastically stated after inspecting me for the first time, "You're doing great! You look just like you should! But ALL my patients do great!" I was livid to think this snot nosed doctor could claim my success as his own!

Work with Diane: I'm feeling underneath all the treatments and feel like whining, but then I open a window and get a better perspective. I'll pack my bag for the transition putting in a large robe of FAITH to wrap around myself and then pack my Self confidence that I've put somewhere where I won't forget it. Then I decide it was **suitcase of self confidence** *that I could pack the other things into and maybe I didn't need to repack, as much as I needed to remove the things I don't want to carry any longer. It is a new day, a brand new day.*

Diane planted a seed of EASE in my jaw to relieve my tension there.

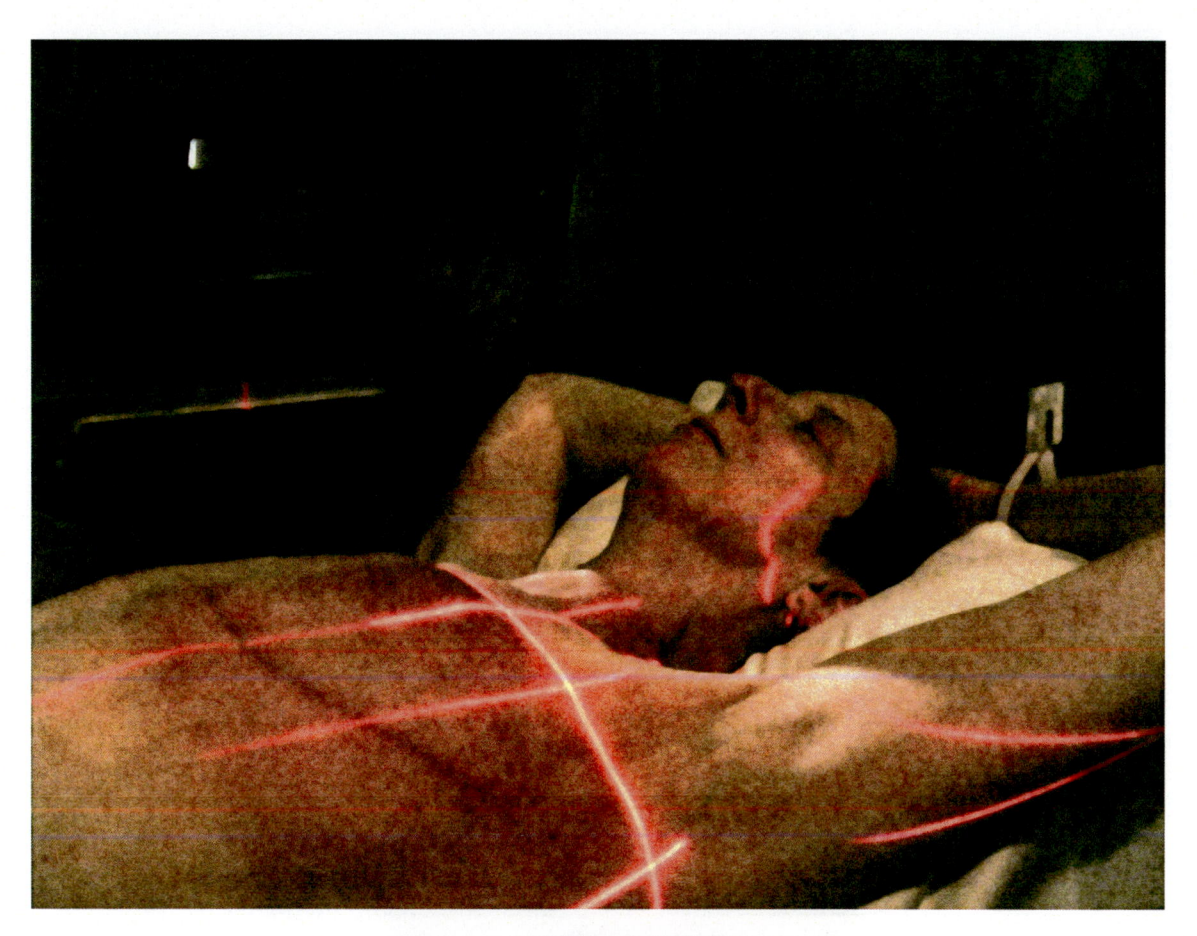

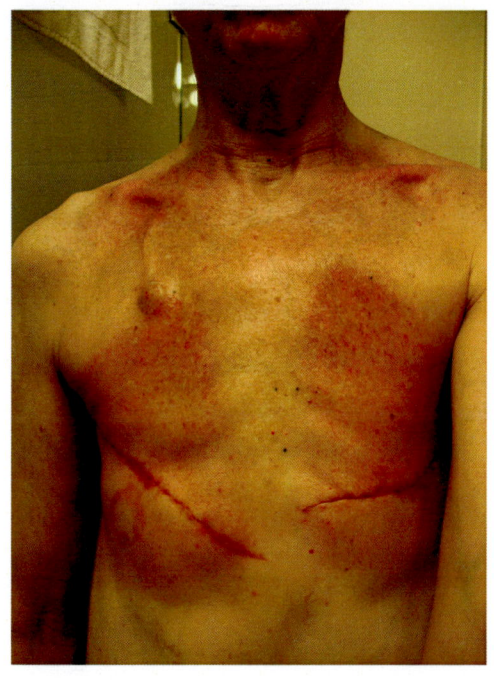

ENOUGH **131**

THE BIKINI 1971

My HOT little sixteen year old ass, in the briefest of bikinis, stood on the porch of the rented cottage overlooking a beach on the Pacific Ocean. We were somewhere on the island of Oahu. My Aunt Alberta and Uncle Tom had rented the unfinished cottage that looked to be part of a new development right on the ocean. Uncle Tom had just returned from a month long trip overseas working for US Naval intelligence. I was recovering from mononucleosis that had been transmitted by my oldest cousin's friend, a surfer and former Navy guy named Topper. He knew it too and gave me a coral bouquet, the size of a large grapefruit, as an apology before he disappeared.

The adults left after a few days, but my cousins DeDe, Maeve and I were to stay for the rest of the week. They might have been distancing me from the reach of my older cousin's friend, but Maeve was also very busy that summer dating several young sailors. There were a few good reasons to isolate us from the Ford Island Naval base.

I walked off the porch in DeDe's tiny string bikini and faced the broad expanse of ocean. The beach was bleached white in the sun; as bleached as my long blonde hair that stretched beyond my thin waist. The water was calm, but a strong, continuous breeze blew off it. From the porch I could easily see the path through the long coral reef that accessed the deeper water. I walked in, looking to either side at the intricate reef that had been ruthlessly sawed through. I walked until I got beyond it and swam, buoyed on the waves.

Then I began to notice a change in the water; I was feeling pulled out to sea. The water seemed to be sucking at the edge of the reef. I became tired swimming against the pull and looked to swim back to shore, but I had no perspective as to the precise location of the path through the coral. I swam back and forth looking for passage, but I was beginning to panic. The word "undertow" came to mind; this is what an undertow feels like. I tried to stay at the surface and waved to Maeve on the porch as I yelled, *"WHERE IS THE PATH??"* She waved back. She couldn't hear my distant voice over the waves. To miss the path put me in danger of being dragged over the sharp coral reef as the waves crashed in, which I had painfully experienced on a short reef, when Topper took me snorkeling. I was panicking now, almost flailing in the water, but I had to find the way myself, no one was coming to help me. I persisted and found the dark edge of the path through the pale coral reef and swam back to shore, exhausted. I had never faced such real fears before; never had I been in such close proximity to death. I told my cousins, but they had not seen the danger I was in. I was alone in knowing the face of that terror.

Wednesday, April 21st, 2010

I had fussier sleep last night. It's too crispy to lie on my left side, but my right side is actually worse with raised bumps and redness.

I just met up with my new Hope Lodge friend, Yulinda, in the kitchen and talked about her problems. She had a bad sleep last night with lots of fear. I talked about witnessing how our minds work. I shared about my MRI and radiation thought experiments, what I've been studying with Diane about welcoming the process. I said, "I'm not a preacher and I hope I don't sound like one!" She thanked me for the help and said it was stuff for her to think about. I'm glad my morning was free. I'm realizing that she hasn't been talking about her illness because she is so afraid, not because she is cavalier.

Treatment was on time today and then I waited for Dr. Chao to tell me "Everything looks good." I requested his resident to take a picture of Dr. Chao and me together. Then Brenda told me to pretty much never expose these burnt areas to sun again. In the waiting area was an eleven year-old boy waiting for simulation. Two social workers were explaining about the mask and the mother looked near her breaking point. I told him that I had a mask too and told the mother how compassionate everyone is…it is all creeping in my pores today…so many people with much bigger problems than mine. "I am but a spec in the universe," Uncle George had said to me when I wished him a happy birthday years ago.

I feel alone today. I am alone today. I walked through Macy's on my way to treatment and picked through the sales rack again and found two little tops and some tights. Shopping to feel good and to have "enough."

THANKSGIVING 1971

Thanksgiving, 1971, we arrived at Gramma Tugas' house, on the corner of Walnut and Wall Streets, at the top of the hill in Hudson Falls. Mom always said she lived 'up the hill' and various cousins, 'lived under the hill', a comment that I understood to insinuate my mother's unspoken superiority.

The sky was heavy with an impending storm, thick clouds hung low, oppressively so. Dad let us out of the car before he pulled up beside the old stone wall that supports Gramma's side yard and parked his car facing down, with the emergency brake on. A light snow began to fall. It was freezing out; we ran the short distance to the green storm door that Gramma held open for us. It was going to be a simple Feast with our family shrinking by the moment. Matthew was born in 1967, the youngest, making us a family of five children, but within a year our big sister, Chrissy, left home after an incomplete semester of junior college. She ran away, across the country with a boy. Mom said he was a 'bad influence.' Then Aunt Betty, Uncle Al's wife, died of ovarian cancer. In 1969, it was Connie's turn to take off for college and skip out of classes to live with her boyfriend, in a commune.

I became the big sister then, and Matt was my adorable baby brother; Bobby shifted to the middle child position, left to fend for himself without Connie to protect or favor him. Mom helped him finish his sentences, just like Gram finished Uncle Al's.

We entered Gram's house, hugging her thick corseted body, and sat in front of the television to watch the big Macy's parade. The smell of Gramma's house, the Thanksgiving feast, and the pies she cooked yesterday, seeped quickly into my spirit, mingling there with all things comforting and safe.

Mom, Dad, Bobby, Matt and I were a subdued bunch compared to the old days of raucously taking over Gramma's house for the Holiday. To top it off, Mom and Dad were tense, the stress of my sisters' choices taking a toll on their marriage. At home, Mom was unsuppressed and Dad was absent. I was also beginning to check out. I didn't know what the hell their problem was, but from not knowing, I took the next step, which was not caring. I began that spring to anesthetize myself with marijuana and began my studies in sex. That summer I'd taken an advanced course while visiting my cousins in Hawaii. I was prepared to be the oldest sibling at home now; no more innuendo would pass over my head.

Mom was helping Gram fix dinner while I set the table. Gram's dining table was solid mahogany, covered with a pressed linen tablecloth in an old shade of pink. I helped as I was asked, but not with the old joy. I placed the "good" china, with the old floral pattern on the dusty rose border, at each place around the table followed by well-used, matching napkins.

My mind wandered with the boredom of being with my family as I gazed out Gram's three dining room windows. The snow outside blended with the ruffled, white organza curtains and accentuated the bright purple African violets and minor knick-knacks that sat on shelves. The snow was falling thickly now; turning into the predicted blizzard. I asked again if my boyfriend, Sarge, could come over after dinner to visit. He lived nearby in Glens Falls. Mom said, "No," as Gram said, "Yes." "What's the harm, Mary?" She asked her frustrated daughter. "They can visit in the dining room, while we sit in the living room. We'll be right here," she offered calmly. Mom did not trust my short boyfriend and said I was being rebellious dating someone that much shorter than I was. That only added to his fragile attraction. Finally, Mom gave in; he could come after we ate. The snowfall increased as I called Sarge to give him a time to pop over and visit. He was not worried about driving his antique 1940's car in the thick snow; the car was a tank.

Mom, Gram and I cleared the table and prepared for dessert and coffee. The dirty dishes were stacked on the counter as the pies were pulled from the warm oven. Bobby got the vanilla ice cream from the freezer, while Gramma made homemade whipped cream for the pumpkin pie. After dessert, Uncle Al and Dad retired to the football game on the television, the only thing that they shared in common, that and falling asleep after dinner. Sarge's visit happened when it was dusk outside. The snow was so deep that he could not stay long. I was not in love, just enjoying the company of his testosterone. We sat briefly on Gram's single bed in the dining room with the family in the adjoining room. Matt and Bobby cut through to go to the kitchen, just to pester me. Nothing seemed to alleviate the weight of my dissatisfaction.

EARTHDAY, April 22nd, 2010

Even though I've been looking forward to being through radiation, I am feeling panic ending it. I have a split personality of emotions. My back is wrenched between past and future, ending and beginning, resting and socializing. I have a long wait today; a "complicated patient" is ahead of me. It's been rare for a complicated procedure to not be planned for time. I suspect that the patient ahead of me is suffering from anxiety and they had to stop the treatment. I feel for him. I sit waiting, thinking, napping, breathing, and listening to my back.

Friday, April 23rd, 2010

I am good until I'm not good. My back is still bothering me today. I was anxious about my appointment with the new doctor today, an endocrinologist and woke repeatedly, at 2:00 am, 3:00, 4:00, poor sleep. There are two new couples in the Hope Lodge kitchen this morning. There seems to be a new turnover of guests. I am cautious about getting to 'know' new people and new diagnosis and new treatment plans. I am getting ready to leave soon too.

My endocrinologist, Dr. Sinha charted my TSH chronologically on the computer. We suspect that I had a spiking incident in my thyroid from spinal radiation. I had to go to Dr. Cigler's office for a blood draw from my port. I don't want to risk *lymphedema (a swelling of the arm and hands after lymph nodes have been removed during surgery)* from an arm draw if I don't have to. I have an appointment on Tuesday for an ultrasound of my thyroid.

Sunday, April 25th, 2010

I'm off to Breast Cancer Options Health conference with Barbara Sarah today. I met Barbara yesterday. She's my new neighbor! I saw Anne, Kathy and Marge talking to the "New Neighbor" and walked over to introduce myself.

"I'm Barbara, Barbara Sarah," she said.

"Barbara Sarah!" I exclaimed.

"Why? You know me?" she asked.

"*Nobody* has breast cancer in Kingston without hearing of *BARBARA SARAH*," I replied. Then we made the date to carpool today to the BCO Conference. It's a rainy spring day.

April 27th, 2010

Yesterday was my last radiation treatment. I got my thank-you cards finished. My cards had individual or group pictures of all the people that have helped me through this period of my life, written with personal notes. I handed them out and everyone seemed to appreciate them. It was so cute at one point, Marguerite walked out to see me sitting with Bernard, Errol, and Raul, chatting. I am so grateful that they were so good to me.

Wednesday, April 28th, 2010

Dreamt of being at Penn Station/Times Square on an escalator looking at the big boards of information — trying to pinpoint my disabilities before I crossed over the bridge to the other building.

I am home. Charlie picked me up after a brief visit to Dr. Feldman's office, which is always warm and friendly. I asked about being concerned about my daughter's birth control pills and the link to BC, but he assured me that she was fine. Today's pills are such low doses of hormones. I'll come for my next appointment in three months. I finally got a photo of us together and another of the nurses that have been so kind, Sylvia too, who does the manic scheduling of the office.

Charlie drove me downtown to visit Barbara Shaum who is fixing the sandals she made for me in 1983. I dropped off books I borrowed from Sandy and Robert and we headed home. When Charlie dropped me off, and was leaving, I cried. I thanked him and I cried to feel plunked down on the other side of it all, all I have experienced over the last six months. It was shocking to land. We shared a big hug and then I lay down on the couch, in my house, with the blanket. Smokebomb joined me there. I slept like a rock.

I peeled myself up to attend the Board of Education's award ceremony for Sue Foss's photography students, including Dana! We returned home and made a pasta dish with practically nothing in the fridge. We read the newspaper and funnies. I snuggled into bed with Smokebomb and Netflix and watched Audrey Tattou in Priceless. Cute. Just right.

Thursday, April 29th, 2010

I can feel myself over the years – half in, half out – whining or complaining out of the side of my mouth, but not approaching my discomfort or unhappiness head on; not deciding what I want or what I need, just sitting in my discontent. I worried about confrontation. Discomfort was better than having to fight. That is no longer the way. I want to be clearer, more conscious of my needs, dreams and goals. It's narrowed down mostly to wanting to be well.

Work with Diane: *The rest on her table is as deep as resting after a long journey. Diane took me to a deep restful place. I swung in the hammock of my* *filter. The filter is no longer the glowing, fiery gold that was needed to filter out the cancer from my body. It's cooler now, peaceful, and helping to filter and prioritize the many creative endeavors that are inspiring me now.*

I also saw myself amongst my friends and family, mingling back into the group. I don't need the elevation of support that was a gift to me during the crisis of my diagnosis and treatment. I am so grateful for the shared energy of the many groups of friends helping me.

THE RETURN TO WORK
May – June 2010

I reflect back to this transitional time from active cancer treatment, to re-entering "Normal Life." I was home from radiation in NYC and feeling a little better every day. I began to feel guilty about not being at work, about people thinking maybe I wasn't as sick as they thought. I liked being off work and regaining more energy, but the guilt was weighing me down. I went into work to visit and spoke to Joe. I asked when he wanted me back. He said, "I told everyone you'd be back in June, so enjoy recuperating! Relax and we'll see you June 1st." I was relieved. I went home and enjoyed working in the garden, napping, beginning some clothing projects.

Then POOF! I was back at work. When I was diagnosed just less than a year ago, it seemed like an impossible amount of time to be out of commission. Diane had helped me work at picturing this time; a time to connect to a new stage of my life post-chemo, post-op, post-radiation and suddenly POOF! I'm back at the sewing machine working on tiny doll hats and beautiful doll gowns. It was hard at first, hard to get used to the fast pace, the pressure to complete projects, but I was happy to be back. I was a WINNER! I beat cancer! I was well again and enjoying the friendships of my co-workers and our jokes and dedication. I was excused for my infusions and doctor appointments; I just gave Joe a list of the dates ahead of time so he could plan the workload.

July 4th, 2010

I'm aware for the last few days, since my last work with Diane, that my chest is beginning to feel like it belongs to me. She put pressure on my scars during our session and used the image that she could feel the rift and was pushing the plates back together, like the plates of the earth after an earthquake needing to be reconnected. My chest feels more connected, unified, whole, as it should be. There is no other way for it to be.

Monday August 16th, 2010

I swam around the island today with Irene. Half way up the first side of the island we saw four loons straight ahead of us doing their loon calls! It was overcast and chilly when we began, but a big blue sky opened up for us. Half way around the far side of the island, the loons flew overhead, close to us, circling the outer rim of the lake. It's another special, hour long swim on our third day at camp. I am swimming without breasts, in a bathing suit that doesn't pretend I have them. I look like a tall ten year-old.

Tuesday, August 17th, 2010

I got up early for kitchen duty today, early enough to see the mist swirling on the lake…a prayer of nature speaking to me. I'm so grateful each year to come back and renew my personal quest to be a better person. Camp gives me practice, practice, practice at listening, not judging or witnessing when I do, having more compassion, sharing a communal experience.

Every year we come back if we are lucky, we try again; someone gets embroiled in drama, children have civility lessons, we are a microcosm of the universe.

August 23rd, 2010

I had a good day today, I got my echocardiogram, took Dana to the dentist and went to physical therapy, which I needed more than I knew. I felt stiff on both sides, tense muscles needing to be massaged. I went back to work and finished the project I was working on.

How bizarre that I lost my breasts. Lost. A funny word, like I misplaced them. I wake flat chested every day. It's only been seven months, not long. I wore the striped vest I made and felt comfortable and confident at work.

Tuesday, September 14th, 2010

I'm sitting having a Herceptin infusion. I've been back to work since June 1st and I'm still trying to be "Back to Normal." Why? What is normal? And why is old normal still something that I aspire to? The unknown is not comfortable. I'm standing on the edge, but I haven't jumped.

Sunday, September 19th, 2010

I read through some of the notes I wrote in the little orange notebook after working with Diane during the treatment period and they were inspiring to me. I need to be re-inspired, to rise above the day-to-day and be reminded of the life lessons I've learned. Why did I need to be altered? Alerted? I'm inspired to put notes of that experience to pictures of that experience, even if it's just for me, my art, because as time goes on, it feels like a potent dream that's slipping away from my consciousness, leaving me standing here asking, "What the fuck now?"

Tuesday, September 28th, 2010

I heard great results from Dr. Andrade today! My PET Scan results were clear – no hypermetabolic activity on my spine, chest wall or lymph nodes. My lungs were clear too. I drove over to share the good news with Mom.

I feel relieved by this news – a burden was lifted from my shoulders. I can be well now.

Work with Diane: *we worked on my immune system today, visualizing my white blood cells being sat on by loons; nurtured and kept warm. I visualized giving* *my WBC rest and joy when I go to bed at night…the simple joy of relaxation. They burble up out of their pods and spread throughout my body. Knowing I am well takes the pressure off them, making it easier for them to procreate and work for our well-being.*

October 10th, 2010

I dreamt of slipping into a meeting going on in the assessor's office. I kept low to the floor and opened my suitcase to get ready to speak. Everyone at the table is busy with papers and negotiations. I look at the top of my pile and see a magazine of soft porn photos! Why did I pack this? It's of no use to my case! I don't look any deeper in my briefcase for clues or purpose. I'm embarrassed. The meeting adjourns and everyone files out. Someone I know on the board asks, "Are you really alright?" "Yes, I am," I told him.

October 19th, 2010

I asked Dr. Andrade if the Herceptin could be making me tired and he said yes. "Is it accumulative?" I asked, because I seem to feel progressively more tired. He said "Yes" to that too. It's a relief to know what it is.

October 20th, 2010

It's a whirlwind day getting ready for Dad and Mary's visit at home and the Tonner Doll Company Halloween Convention at work. I'm looking forward to being part of the convention next weekend; I missed going to the big one in the spring. I have my costumes almost done.

I was expecting Dad and Mary at 5:00 pm after work, but they called from my driveway at 2:00! I hadn't put the cats in the attic yet and Dad is allergic to them! Dana got home and called to tell me that Smokebomb threw up on her bed and Mila pooped in my studio. Dad and Mary went to the diner for a snack and I ran home to help Dana get the cats into the attic. We got Mila upstairs, but the elusive Smokebomb would not cooperate! We ended up chasing him all over the house, laughing so much and having a great time together. We finally got him up there, but he's sitting at the door scratching and meowing.

Saturday, October 23rd, 2010

Mary and I made two Dutch apple pies before breakfast this morning, and then headed to the Farmer's Market. I gave them a tour of the Tonner Doll Company and introduced them to Robert Tonner. We returned home with groceries and prepared a feast. Connie and Richard arrived, then Danielle and Tommy, and Matt came with Donovan and surprised us. We got to introduce Mary and Dad to the fun of playing Jenga with our family and it felt like a holiday.

THANKSGIVING 2010

I was growing hair, tight curly post-chemo hair, that had never belonged to me before. I was happy to have hair again; I left the display of it up to "Nature" and didn't worry about it. I looked in the mirror and had to laugh. It reminded me I was on the other side; it made me giddy and feeling so much like my old self that I took on Thanksgiving with a vengeance. I could do it all again, even without Robert who helped me for over a decade of Holidays. I invited Diane, Marc and Katie to join Mom, Mike, Dana, Charlie and me.

Mom brought over the turkey, stuffing and cranberry sauce the night before. Dana made the apple sauce when she woke up. I made a pumpkin pie from my health food cook book with an oat-almond crust, pumpkin, maple syrup and spices, no dairy. It was good, but next to Diane's flourless chocolate cake "It tastes like ass!" my son commented and we all laughed. It would have been tastier to make the real thing, but I'm trying to reel in my sweets and not fall off the wagon. The holidays are a hard time to maintain good habits. I made a gluten-free crust for the apple pie which turned out well. I made the pies the night before and ate all the crumbs.

Mom brought over horseradish dip and Dana put out the cheese and crackers. Diane brought Indian meatballs that were delicious. I made roasted vegetables: baby turnips, carrots, Brussels sprouts, beets, and fennel, all from the last Farmer's Market of the season. I tossed them in olive oil and garlic. I cooked the 20 pound turkey from 11:00 am to 5:30 pm basting every half hour with garlic and sage in melted butter, lifting the big bird in and out of the oven myself. I set the table with an ironed tablecloth and fancy dishes. I was beaming. Diane jumped up and did dishes with Dana and Katie. Diane was worried I was doing too much, but I was unstoppable, until the next day when swelling appeared in my right hand and arm, the discomfort was not minor. Now I know what lymphedema feels like and why I was advised not to do heavy lifting or continuous strenuous movements after lymph node removal. I had a major "A-HA" moment and the 'Woods' I thought I was clear of came back into view. I found a woman who does lymph massage and I made an appointment to be fitted for compression sleeves and gloves. I remembered the woman I saw wearing them on the day of my diagnosis more than a year ago, and I'd thought how unattractive they were, but understood now that if they help me, then I welcome them.

It was very disturbing to watch my arm swell from overuse. I put my compression sleeve and gauntlet on my right arm and slid into post-holiday-post-partum, holding my arm in the air over my head while resting on the couch. Diane called to check in and reminded me that it's not life threatening, but I feel vulnerable and thrown off course; I thought I was *all* better.

December 1st, 2010

I went to work and tried using my left handed scissors to give my right arm a rest. It was slow going, very frustrating even though I write left handed; I am a right handed scissor user.

Work with Diane: *I need to open a space of awareness for my shortcomings, make choices knowing my limitations. I need to ask for help. Plan ahead. I can't go back to the old me and her habits of DOING IT ALL MYSELF*

Saturday December 4th, 2010

I love my bed, my room. I am so grateful for my warm comfort. I visualize the lymph juices pooled, swelling my arm, but by elevating my arm on the fort of pillows surrounding me, I have tipped the pools and they are streaming and trickling away, flowing into the remaining lymph nodes to be processed. I have learned about doing too much and the repercussions. I need to make choices, delegate, hire. Panic is stagnating and acceptance is freeing. My arm is healing.

Writing and then reading what I wrote brings me close to the edge of what is next for me…I sense the edge like in a dream, feeling for the ledge to hoist myself up on, but I can't see it, the next step, the next level, moving forward, always in a life-lesson-learning trajectory.

December 11th, 2010

Yikes! I set my alarm for 5:15 am, but forgot to save it and woke at 6:15 to be at the Holiday Inn at 7:00 for a Tonner Doll Company sale. I arrived only 7 minutes late, but hadn't eaten, taken supplements or my blender drink. I did wear my makeup and earrings and holiday snowman sweater; Mom would be proud.

The sale was very busy as usual, with lots of old friends and collectors waiting in line for the doors to open. I stood cheerily handing out numbers to keep the line organized, and prevented people from peeking in the banquet salesroom. I kept checking my time and the crowd, not wanting to ask to be dismissed too soon, knowing all my co-workers would be working their butts off for hours yet. At 11:00 I asked Shauna and she said, "Go!" I grabbed something to eat on my way to Sky Lake Lodge for my second Unconditional Healing Retreat with Jeff Rubin. I got there in time for the end of people talking about why they are attending this weekend. I spoke about trying to keep up, but today, for instance, I needed to ask for a special task because of my lymphedema in my right arm; I couldn't do the lifting that we all usually have to do. I backtracked a few minutes later, to share about my chemotherapy-bilateral-mastectomy-two-rounds-of-radiation-stage-four-breast-cancer status. I also shared that my Mom has been badgering me with her thinking I need prosthetic breasts, which I have no interest in getting. I don't ever have to wear a bra again. There has to be an up-side.

After lunch there was more meditation and tea. I sat and spoke to Ellen, who first introduced me to everything I never wanted to know about Metastatic Cancer. She depresses me, but I tried harder to open to her. I realize her experience has been very different from mine, difficult in different ways. I shared about how I'd looked in the mirror last Christmas, when I still had breasts, and realized that I still owned them, but in a month they'd be gone. I witnessed my transformation, my impermanence. "Carol, how did you do that in one moment?" she asked. "I've been trying for nine years to accept this." Jeff asked me if there was a secret, but I was just there, in that moment, conscious of what was to be.

It reminded me of being in the third grade. I was a young girl very good at kicking the boys when we played on the school yard at recess. When the boys chased the squealing girls, I could turn and kick to defend myself from being grabbed. I placed my school shoes by my bed at night, so if burglars attacked my family I could put on my shoes and protect them. I remember laying in that same bed when I realized one night, that my Grandmother Tugas would die one day, and I cried then at what a huge loss that would be for me. Later, in my twenties, I took a lot of pictures of the last two years of her life, appreciating everything about her in photos, her in her kitchen, her plants and house. I documented her simple life and when she died in 1983, I sat up all night looking at my pictures of her. I had been present all along and it helped me to accept her death.

December 13th, 2010

I'm very tired today, falling asleep on my feet. I rallied for Dana's jazz chorus concert and pot-luck. I enjoyed seeing all our friends that she and I share, but my fears were very present too: worrying about being sick again, keeping up my pace at work, and projects at home. Fear creeps in whispering, "Is this as good as it gets?" How does one plan a career? My swollen hand is still limiting my activities. The darkness of Ellen's statement haunts me and her statistics pool in my spirit. I need to detox and visualize. Be me now and moving forward.

I read in the newspaper that Elizabeth Edwards, former wife of presidential hopeful John Edwards, just died of breast cancer after six years. She was sixty-one years-old. Peace be with you, Elizabeth, and thank you for asking for better services for people without funds to live with cancer.

FLAWS

My son posted me on Facebook today that he's getting modeling photos taken in NYC with his friend. I am reminded of Ann Keagy, chairperson of the fashion design department when I studied there in 1973-1976. She had all the potential students that could model Junior student's garments stand in a line as she listed our FLAWS out loud. Her assistant, Ed, took notes. I spent all the years since that day saddled with the *flaw* of having breasts that hung too low. I am free of that *flaw* now, but I wonder how my perfect children will be saddled with flaws. Dana said I told her she was too short to be a professional model, which is a fact, not a flaw. Mike will find out on his own whether this is his career or not.

Last night I went to the Kingston High School choral concert and listened to the beautiful voices coming from every size and shape of person. I listened to the sound of their harmony. I listened deeper for a harmony of thoughts; peaceful and non-judgmental, mental harmony. I do not need to list anyone's imperfections. I seek to accept myself and gently buff my edges. Christmas brings out my barbs and the jagged edges of expectations, pressure and guilt. My lymphedema is a measure of my humanity, my limitations, as I strive for a happy medium of me.

CRISTMAS CAROLING 2010

It was a lovely evening with my favorite holiday back at my house because of all the help from friends contributing to the pot luck feast. It is a miracle how we arrived with the perfect mix of food without any stress of organization. We sang, and Dana noticed again that the songs are too high and next year we will transpose the keys! Everyone joined in the chorus and it made me so happy; a real Christmas spiritual sharing. This is church at its best. My favorite part of Christmas mass growing up was singing the Christmas songs in church next to my sister Connie.

December 25th, 2010

I dreamt of showing up when a man in the village happened to be getting married and I got in line to throw rice at the bride and groom. We lined a small lane and I could see the back of the groom, but we were waiting for the bride. Then we waited quietly in the rooms of their house. Then she arrived and I got to congratulate her, and hug her. She was such a kind and mellow woman. I said I'd read her book; such a traumatic, tragic story, exposing her to poverty and death. She was humble about it, warm and grateful to be on the other side. She was grateful to have found a kind man to share life with and to set up a home.

Our celebration of Christmas Eve was lovely. Carole, Bill and daughter Faith joined us and helped to make dinner. I made garlic bread to go with Mom's lasagna. I was able to fit the ten of us around the table. Other friends joined us for dessert, Diane and Katie couldn't stay, but Darcy, Sean and daughter Molly added much to our merry eve.

Dana and I waited until all of our guests were gone, even our family, before we opened our small gifts. She was happy with the small trinkets I had picked up for her: Chapstick, concealer, mascara, an IPod charger for the car, and earrings. She gave me my beautiful handmade scarf and a pair of Thinsulate mittens for walking to work. I am so grateful for these heartfelt gifts. This is my idea of Christmas. Peace on Earth.

On Christmas day Dana and I drove to New Jersey to visit with all of Charlie's family: the Pistones and Martoranas. It was a wonderful day, just like old times only better, Dana and her cousins are growing up enough to appreciate each other and talk. I hadn't seen Mom-Mom for awhile, she looked frail and walked with a cane. She told the story about when she was a young girl and her father told her in Italian to put "two strands" of pasta in the boiling water. She put two strands in the water, but realized that the expression must have meant something different because of how angry her father was when he saw what she did. I love to hear her old stories and we laughed and laughed. It was a sweet day.

March 16th, 2011

Work with Diane: *a feeling of deep lightness poured into me. I sucked air like the first breath at birth. I am coming into ME – the ME beyond cancer. I am well.*

"Inspiration," Diane said.

NOT THE BEST TIME

April 2nd, 2011

I realize that I am lying awake, listening to the rain outside. I have floated ashore from sleep. I have been dreaming vividly of the desolate waiting for the end of the world. I was in my car with someone else driving and more people crowded into the backseat. I was trying to keep all the windows shut to avoid radiation poisoning. Later in the dream we are in a high rise apartment that has a large terrace off the living room. I am focused on trying to keep the sliding glass doors shut for the same purpose, but we all keep going outside on the terrace anxiously searching the colorful horizon for the final destructive mushroom cloud. It is 3:30 am, not the best time to be beached from the ocean of sub-consciousness. I sit up and journal my dreams. At 5:30 am, I am still awake. My daughter's alarm goes off for the first time: beep, beep, beep, until it stops on its own. She often sleeps through the first three times or so until the big guns come out and her phone screams the first stanza of the Best Coast song: "I WISH HE WAS MY BOYFRIEND! CAUSE IF HE WAS MY BOYFRIEND". Its very hard to sleep through, I know.

Dana is seventeen. Last night she didn't have any homework and we sat together at the kitchen table and ate dinner while watching an episode of Glee on her laptop. It has been two weeks since we had time to relax and eat together. We finished and began to clear the table. Dana suddenly states, "Oh! The application and essay for the National Honor Society is due tomorrow!" I stare. I vaguely remember it being mentioned around two weeks ago.

"Do I really even qualify? I mean, they ask for all this shit about school clubs and activities," she complained. I can see the "why bother" thoughts running through her brain.

"Get the application and show me," I replied, as I started to load the dishwasher. She ran and got it from her room and brought it down. We sat and discussed her possible answers.

"Listen to this," she asked periodically as she wrote the essay.

"Gladly," I replied.

We are in the last quarter of her junior year. I am well aware that we are sliding off the edge of our life together and into the whirlpool of senior year and college prep. I am basking in this special connection that I still have with her, but aware that we have already begun to move in a slow spiral and soon I will release her into the larger world.

There goes Dana's alarm for the third time and it is still raining outside. I feel sleep once again behind my eyes, but now is not the best time. It is time to begin another day together.

SAFETY

May 14, 2011

My seventeen year old daughter informs me that she is going out tonight. I walk into her room, sit on her bed and watch her looking in the mirror. "Do you like this outfit?" she asks. It's 10:30 pm and she got home from her job a half hour ago. "Brent will be by soon to pick me up." "Where are you going?" I ask. "Over to Billy's. He's having a few friends over," she replies. "Where does Billy live?" I inquire. "Hurley," she answers. "Brent will be the designated driver and get me home safely," she adds quickly. "Reliable, is he?" I ask. "Oh yes," she says with a slight hint of hesitation. She is on shaky ground here and we both know it. I saw Brent's Faceook page and it only has pictures of him partying: pictures with smoke and pictures with beer. Also a paragraph on how his earlobes are *stretched*, *not* gauged. My son has warned her of Brent's reputation for stupidity, while drunk in particular. Dana gets ready for her evening out. About 10 minutes pass, quietly, they are texting back and forth. "Mom? she calls from her room. I go to her. "Can I just stay over at Billy's? It would just be so much easier for Brent not to have to drive me back and forth and all." "No," I reply. I am not about making it easier for Brent. It seems to me he needs to choose tonight: Dana or partying." I stand firm. She undresses, washes her face and goes to bed. "Good night Mom." "Good night Dana. I love you." One more night I know that she is home safe in bed.

AWAKENING
July 25, 2011

There was a physical comfort of contact all day, touches that overcame our distance and differences. A touch to the waist in the photography exhibit; arms casually draped on his shoulders while walking, shared coffee and popcorn foreplay. Then I sat at his kitchen table, my toothbrush secretly stowed in my bag, and missed the last bus home. He watched me do it and did not mention the hour, though he too knew it was passing by. We broke up two years ago almost exactly. The imperfections of our arrangement screamed for change as I dealt with my imminent cancer diagnosis. He left as I asked him to. We had broken up several times before, but he would come back and I would accept him; he was my most intimate friend. This time was too serious to test me. I went in survival mode and my other friends rallied around me.

Now, I feel an awakening from the triathlon of cancer treatments that hid my libido under a rock. I feel an awakening of passion and longing. I feel a gravitational pull back to the known; back to us.

"Do you want to show me?" he asked. He has not seen my chest since my breasts were removed. He was the last lover to touch them and that will always be special between us. I lifted my shirt and slid it over my head. I stood before him and watched as he kissed both sides where my breasts had been. Then he kissed my lips and we fell to the bed beside us and made love. He did not forget and grope the memories of my breasts; I would have noticed and missed them even more. We shared pleasure after a solid two year hiatus from each other or anyone else. We joined for shared healing.

August 18th, 2011

This time period is a cauldron of feelings, sweet, but fraught with anxiety. My daughter is beginning her senior year in high school and beginning her college search. I'm so grateful to have one more year living with her and so anxious about letting her go. Looking at colleges with her makes me want to go back to school and study model drawing, painting, animation and digital photography. I'm completing my college course on cancer; a two year program with no degree, but a renewed life is its own reward. I look back at my work getting well as effortless. I took the time to visualize my healing along with western medicine's chemicals, surgery and radiation. It was a luxury of time that I basked in, but now I'm up to bat again working at my job, stretching my money and preparing to let go of my lovely daughter.

August 28th, 2011

It's pouring rain outside. The basement is flooding. I was able to use my sump pump for 2 hours before the power went out. I'm sitting with Mila in my chair waiting for the fire department to pump us out, but there are bigger emergencies than ours I guess. Darcy has two feet and Faith reported that their house has three feet. The fire truck just blasted past our house with sirens blaring. The rain is normal now, but the ground is saturated.

Dana got her shower in before the power went out, but I didn't. I went outside in my pajamas to clean the back deck gutters, empty the rain barrels and dig trenches. I looked up to see Anne and Ray on their porch watching me get soaked. I told them I needed a shower, but forgot my soap! Ray had already called to see if we needed help and I was grateful for his call.

There is more traffic going by: joggers in ponchos, boys on bicycles, cars. The worst is past. It would be so nice to have the power back on so I could pump out the basement myself.

GRAMMA'S COOKIES
August 31st, 2011

I made cookies on Saturday night in anticipation of Hurricane Irene. It was a summer evening, but cool enough to turn the oven on and I experimented with my ever evolving cookie recipe. This time I used a half cup of raw sugar and one *tablespoon* of Stevia, a natural sweetener. The cookies were not green, like last time when I used a half cup of Stevia, but they were a slightly odd color. I made my cookie dough and tasted it with my finger.

I step back in time, to my Grandmother Tugas' kitchen; a summer day, early in the morning. The kitchen door is open, sharing a lazy breeze from the shade of the maple tree. Feeling the breeze makes me turn and look outside over the shaded grass, slate path and stone stairs that lead to the road down the hill. I look back across the enamel tabletop at my Grandmother holding the big wooden spoon, stirring the thick cookie dough that we've made. I've had my turn, a brief turn, and I admire my Gran's stamina and strong arm that doesn't shy away from the hard work. What I do love comes next: making the cookies on the trays and licking my fingers and sneaking extra lumps of the classic "Tollhouse" recipe. "Carol!" she scolds. "You are going to get a stomach ache if you keep eating that dough!" Maybe I will. I think I kind of remember that happening before, but it tastes so good now, that it is worth the risk: the soft butter, sugar and chocolate chips on my fingers! Then the fresh cookies, warm from the oven.

When we made cookies especially for my visit, Gram would buy butterscotch chips because those were my favorite. The cooled cookies were always placed in the clown pottery cookie jar with a piece of bread to keep them from getting stale. That cookie jar, a gift from my mother when she worked at the Five & Dime in high school, called to me whenever I entered the kitchen. It was the first thing to see, prominently placed on the corner of Gran's kitchen counter and it was rare for one batch of cookies to last the whole week of my visit.

September 1st, 2011

I got my spinal biopsy two years ago today. I was just beginning my study of cancer. I accept my Associates Degree.

ALL CLEAR
September 17th, 2011

My appointment for my yearly PET scan was on Tuesday, the same day Dana needed my car to go to work, which meant I needed to borrow Mom's car. I didn't want to worry her so I hadn't mentioned why. I figured that I can tell her the results; the good news.

Monday night Dana dropped me off to pick up the car and Mom asked, "Why did you need to borrow my car tomorrow?"

"I have a PET scan," I replied.

"Which one is that?" she asked.

"It's the one that let's everyone know that I don't have cancer!" I told her cheerfully. That went well, I thought.

The journalist that Diane spoke to about healing imagery called to interview me Tuesday night after the scan. She is writing a piece on the topic in preparation of Bernie Siegel's visit to the area for the Breast Cancer Options conference-fundraiser. I love talking about my experience with healing imagery and how I studied it with Diane in preparation for cancer treatments. I also gave examples of how I use it daily, at the dentist, or for my PET scan.

On Tuesday I had my PET scan. I called the oncologist on Thursday for the results. "I'll have the nurse call you back," the receptionist told me. All week and last I was not worried. I went to the scan and I was not worried; hungry, but not worried. But waiting for the results for one hour, then two hours, then three before the nurse got back to me, made me worry. I began to pace and get distracted from my work. I stopped at one point though and saw myself winding up. What's different from 3 hours ago? What's different from last week? I asked myself: nothing except verification. I saw how easily I can lose faith, to doubt what I know.

SEIZURE

January 31st, 2012

I am in the hospital, too dark to write.

I spent the deepest part of the night in this hospital bed with Charlie and Andrea sleeping bookends on either side of me. I hit a pocket of sadness which held me awake and I cried with Jesus on his crucifix hanging on the wall across from my bed. If I'm chosen for this human experience, I'm resigned to be here. It is shocking, unthought, unplanned, unexpected; plucked from a perfect day, full of playful spirit at work and at home. I made dinner and cookies and was doing dishes when my right hand went tingly numb and then my arm. My hearing suddenly picked up the sound of the radio in full circle instead of from one direction. I sat and tried to find the description of a "stroke" on the internet at my kitchen table laptop. It was a strong possibility from the pictures that I had the symptoms. I looked at the newspaper and read with no comprehension. I called Diane and left a message. I went upstairs and changed into knit pants that didn't have robots on them. I texted Melanie from work, she knows everything, and she texted back: "GO TO E.R." I called Charlie and he drove over and picked me up. I texted Dana to "call Dad before you drive home." I packed the baked cookies into tins and walked outside as Charlie pulled up.

The tingly numbness pulsed down my arm and hand, lasted for a few minutes and receded. We checked in and were told to sit in the waiting area, my head in a bubble of too much sound, only comprehending brief segments. I told Charlie we had to call Kate Brandt. He said, "Later." I said "No, now," and dialed her number. I hadn't contacted her the last time I came to the hospital with Mom and she was mad. I didn't want to make Kate mad. I handed Charlie the phone. They spoke while he went up to the office again and told them I was having a STROKE NOW and they shifted gears into emergency mode, including an IV into my right arm. I protested because of lymphedema possibilities, but emergency trumped.

They ran me for a quick CT Scan and then a chest x-ray and back to consult with a doctor in charge, "It's not a stroke. You have a small tumor on the left lobe of your brain." The steroids they put in the IV relieved the swelling and the numb tingling and comprehension problems receded. I understood what he was saying. It was shocking. I reflected on any signs over the past few weeks, but nothing stood out. POOF! Tumor!

Charlie, Mike, Andrea and Dana rotated through the room visiting. Dana was freaked out at first. Charlie had warned her that I was in a state of confusion and she was afraid to see me like that. Andrea popped her head in to see that the drugs were kicking in and reported, "Dana get your butt in there to see your Mom!" it was so good to look over and see both of my sweet kids. We ascertained that Mike will shave his head in solidarity with me, if I need to. We laughed about letting go of his ¼" of hair will not be stressful for him and he'll be guilt free!

So I am adjusting, adding a new chapter to my experience. I will be off work and go home to rest, but I will also go home and see what I can accomplish! I haven't lost my ambition and the projects pile in front of me.

I came home after three days in the hospital to phone calls and visits. I still hear the loud "clock" in my right ear. Dr. Andrade told me it's my pulse and to take four of these pills a day with food. Charlie stayed on guard so I could shower and have someone to yell to if I fell and then he took me for a walk up Loundsbury. It was almost 60 degrees and gorgeous out. Then he set me up with a bigger monitor to watch movies on. Mila sat on my chest while I caught up on <u>Downton Abbey</u>.

I have a brain tumor and it has gathered the love around me. I look in the mirror and see confidence in my face while I feel gratitude in my heart.

February 2nd, 2012

This morning I dreamt of making small suits of armor; short, broad shouldered suits of armor, some arranged right-side-up and others upside-down, in a design, like wall paper.

I turned on the prayer chain today and felt the amazing energy lift me. I also got to meet Mike's new girlfriend, Sara, and I liked her very much. Tomorrow is PET Scan day.

Wednesday, February 8, 2012

Yesterday was an amazing day; an adventure of spirit. Everyone's love and concern carried me through, above the fear and worry. Chas picked me up at 8:00 am. He gassed up and drove me to Colombia-Presbyterian for my visit with Dr. Chao at Radiation Oncology. It was so nice to see Miguel, Raul, Janet, Brenda and Lisette. I was grateful to not have to undress and redress; they were just looking at my brain scans. Dr. Chao and his resident were so clear and positive in their interview before sending us on our way to the neurosurgeon for my consultation. We needed to hear from him whether he would choose surgery or Gamma Knife radiation therapy.

We entered Dr. Jeffrey Bruce's office. I sat facing his big desk, two med students observing from the couch to our right, and his nurse to his left. Dr. Bruce stood about 6'4" and shook our hands. He is perfectly, confidently, cast as my doctor. He turned his large monitor towards us with a view of my brain MRI. I am in luck – it's only one tumor. I could see the contained edges, unlike the ultrasound of my breast cancer, whose angry roots infiltrated my breasts. He rotated the image and we could see its odd, but clean shape.

His plan will be to slit my scalp, cut out a circle of bone, and the *good news* he pointed out was the dark line next to the tumor. That's a fold in my brain tissue. That will make it easier to unfold that area of my brain, remove the tumor and put me back together. It will be approximately three hours of surgery, three days of recovery in the hospital and an assessment of any possible need for rehabilitation; vocal or motor. Dr. Bruce will discuss with his associate about the possibility of doing the surgery with me awake to determine any nerve harm during the surgery, but the fold in the brain tissue makes it an easier determination for them to make.

I talked to Dr. Bruce's assistant, Aileen, who will tackle the operating room schedule. After talking to Danielle the other night and being reminded that schedules would need to be made, I thought, "Monday would be a good day for it." Aileen turned and said, "I am looking at Monday." I didn't hesitate. I didn't need time to decide.

The love and support I feel continues to hold me above the lower energy of fear and worry, for the most part. When we were done, Chas drove us down to meet Danielle for lunch and Robert met us with his homemade poppy seed cookies (with lemon zest this time). I grabbed the arm of his friendship as we walked to the car. Danielle and Charlie embraced. What great fortune I have on a beautiful sunny day in February.

February 9, 2012

Today was exhausting but successful. Chas escorted me to all my pre-op testing. I succeeded in falling asleep during a claustrophobic MRI and they had to do it twice. Back home, Thirsty Thursday toasted their wine to my nettle infusion, Mila found me in the big chair watching a movie, got up on me, looked me straight on, licked my chin and nestled while Dana made me a big bowl of popcorn. Natural healing.

February 10, 2012

I received and email from a friend last night including a report on cancer from John Hopkins University. It spoke of eating right, environmental causes, emotional and spiritual causes. I skimmed the article and was familiar with most of it. It was good information, progressive and good to be public, but not useful to read days before brain surgery. The question of "Why me?" reared its ugly head. How the fuck did I get a metastasis to the fucking brain? My "beautiful day in February" thoughts lay melted in a pool at my feet.

I stood in my kitchen, doing dishes, not knowing what any of this will really feel like. It is easy to be asymptomatic, pain free. Today I am checking out my safe deposit box and getting Charlie access too. I need to get things accessible. There are no secrets, nothing to prevent him from doing the best for our children if the need arises. So I take a little trip to the darker side of my thoughts.

Work with Diane Before Surgery: *magnetized negative thoughts have collected into my tumor. Regrets, disappointments, expectations and resentments are drawn together to be removed by Dr. Bruce on Monday. The tumor is white, calcified, and dull, with rounded, bulbous edges, no roots. I am prepared to release this tumor from the voluptuous fold of brain tissue that nestles it, contains it. I am grateful for the opportunity to release what is no longer useful to me.*

Diane asked, "Where are you? Is your healing place different this time?"

"I'm at the lake," I replied. It came to me immediately. I stand on the shore, near the life guard chair, in my black bathing suit. It's late afternoon, a breeze ripples light green through the darker water of the lake. I am standing there, about to enter, and it is quiet. I turn and you are all there for me, sharing your love and prayers, witnesses to my transformation as I touch the chill of the water, shiver with the breeze on my damp skin. I feel peace and power, nature and love.

WILL
February 11, 2012

I awoke this morning making a will in my head to write out for my friend, Charles Pistone, our children and my siblings. Maybe clarity would be a good idea at this time, as I spoke of it at length yesterday with Charlie, Jody and Diane, and later in the hospital with Charlie and Kate Brandt.

I do not plan on letting go on Monday. I look forward to rejoining life next week as I return home, post surgery, but I accept that the portal might open and say, "It's time to go." If my body dies, please let my spirit follow. I think of my presence at the birth of my children; my wanting them to come at their own chosen time with no intervention. I am very proud of our shared experience; each child choosing their own time, massaged in my birth canal and fed through my breasts. In that process, through both of you, Mike and Dana, I hold as the greatest personal achievement I ever accomplished. I am so proud of you both, and grateful, not only for the many personal talents that you each choose to explore, but your commitment and loyalties to those you love in your lives: your morality. I feel you walk in your lives with God and you will come to know it, eventually, even though I did not guide or indoctrinate you into a formal religion.

I also believe that we each have a time when we are supposed to be ready to let go of this life. If this is my time, please let me go without major medical interference. If my body can be of use to another human, I give permission to sustain it until my organs can be shared for that purpose. Cancer has just recurred in my body, however, which might limit the usefulness of my sharing. I choose the least polluting burial or cremation procedure possible, within affordability. If it is my time, let my energy join the larger energy of the universe.

That all being said, I do plan on returning home next week! I would like to be back at work in two months time, if possible. I do love my life! The richness of my family and friends holds me to this wonderful life! The prayers and energy sent to me during my cancer journey has been another of the greatest gifts of this lifetime. To come home to see everyone is such a lovely lure to recuperate. I miss "group therapy" at work and being part of the colorfully detailed creativity that we get to share everyday in that small cathedral of a design room.

I love the bonds of my children and am so grateful for the evolved relationship between their father and myself. To have risen above the petty details that we offended and challenged each other with during our stressful marriage is also a shining achievement. Charlie's friendship shines like gold, so much bigger than the rings that restrained us. I am so grateful to have his trust and love and know he will continue to be there for our children. It brings me much peace.

There was a moment, at the Benedictine Hospital, about 3:30 am or so, after the discovery of my brain tumor, that I looked across the room and saw Jesus on his Crucifix. We spoke and I cried for the suffering of his human experience. I felt an understanding of the cross he carried as I lay there, surprised by my new development. I am human and am challenged by mortality, but even more so by living, being truly present and grateful.

While talking to Jesus that night, I had an epiphany. I realized that if I died now, I would win the brass ring of sibling competition as I am the only one that talks to all the others! But I do not want to win that contest! "100% forgiveness is necessary for an awakened life…" (Dr. Wayne Dyer) and I would prefer to share the prize. Charlie and I have blazed a trail of forgiveness that allows me to know the healing power of it. I wish *that* for the pain of our familial bonds; the pain of damaged, mistreated, misguided bonds that press to this day on the spinal cord of our family. Only forgiveness can bring the light back into the dark caves of anger and resentment. I cannot fix anyone but myself. Breast cancer has brought me face to face with that understanding. We are each responsible to work on releasing our own suppression. I release my siblings from their responsibility for my childhood tortures and sneaky abuses. I hope you will forgive me my jealousies, rivalries and cruelties. In adulthood, our bonds are so unique, so deep, that I wish for you to share them fully too. We can only do our best to evolve during the limited time we have bound to earth.

February 18, 2012

I walked into brain surgery last Monday, more prepared than I have ever been for anything in my life. I was completely and totally open to the love that walked into surgery with me; open and fully trusting my body to the neurosurgeons there, with the clarity of vision to do what they saw to do. I was as big as the sky or the universe even. Diane was my energetic guide and witness and saw the highly skilled surgeon's remove from my brain what I did not need. My joy post-op, at feeling like me, was contagious. Go ahead and test me again!!! I felt so freakin' happy to have my faculties!

I didn't get a room until early Tuesday morning. My roommate joined me the next day, Wednesday, at 5:30 am. My head had just had its snug, gauze cap peeled away, exposing my 17 head staples and goopy comb over. My roommate, 41 years old, with 17 month old child at home and a ten year marriage, lay in bed with her swollen head and immobile left side. She suffered her third and most serious stroke this past September. Infection was swelling her brain as we spoke that early morning about her re-hospitalization. We shared our vulnerability and spoke of the unfairness of life and the unanswerable question: Why me? Why does God challenge us each in this unique way? Talking to her made me feel so much, in such a short moment of sharing, that I came home to my nest to cry for us; the two of us, but also for all of us, because we all face a variety of challenges and every day we have to choose how to live and breathe through them.

March 16th, 2012

Today, I had my blender drink, then made my healthy cookies and granola, ate some of each and then a salad and fried egg for lunch. I did not eat after dinner, but flossed as an eating prevention, before sitting down at the computer and working on pictures in Photoshop. I waited up for Dana to return from her friend's where they were baking cookies. I am trying, trying to eat less and feel less awful looking at myself in the mirror. Being bloated on steroids post-brain surgery is shaking me to my roots. I am still me, if I don't look in the mirror.

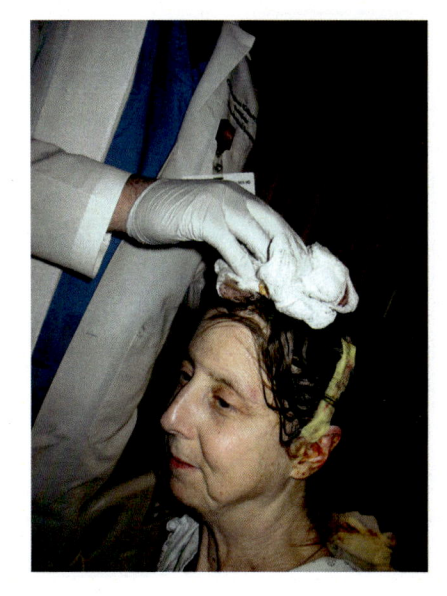

March 17th, 2012 Saint Patrick's Day.

Work with Diane: *I am feeling hideously vain and bloated, but I opened my can of worms with Diane and let her know I'm feeling down and worried about keeping up at work on the new drug, Tykerb. I am concerned about diarrhea and nausea, thinning hair, etc… and then waiting two months before the next MRI to see if tumor is growing.*

The garden is growing. I just pulled out two chairs from the garage, put them on the deck and sat down to write for a minute. I see big fat buds on the hydrangea bush. I can see my neighbor's chickens scratching through big dusty tufts of something. They look so healthy. I have mosquitoes swarming around me.

Dana is off with Charlie today, painting at Mike and Sarah's house. Dana will be off to college in a few months. I joined Charlie and Dana for a few minutes after work at the coffee shop while they split a chai latte. The two of them were joking that Chas could be my roommate when Dana moves out.

Tonight I went to Kingston High School to see their production of <u>Sweeney Todd</u>. I saw parents of Dana's friend. They have obviously *heard* that my cancer went to the brain. "You doing okay?" she asks. I forgot about bumping into people I hadn't seen recently, I felt awkward and squirmed with vanity about my fat cheeks. I felt like bad news and was conscious about being bad news. I bought a ticket from Diane, whose daughter Katie is starring in the show as Mrs. Lovett, and then stood off to the side talking to her husband Marc, stepmom and niece. We entered the theatre. The red velvet curtains look so rich, so new. I sat to the right, row N, seat 8.

A lovely acquaintance found me for a big hug. "I am so sorry to hear your news! I was shocked!" she said. I feel like I have let people down. During intermission, Kate SC came and sat next to me, leaving Rennie and Elias three rows ahead. I talked to Rennie after the show, as we waited for the kids to bask in their post-show glory. I had a hard time looking him in the eye. I felt like hiding under a rock. Lillian came up and asked Rennie to take her cello so she could go to the diner with friends. "Oh, I didn't recognize you!" she said to me when she realized who I was. We saw Carole and she rushed over for a hug and said, "But Carol, we think your cheeks are so cute!"

Diane gave me a lift home. We began our exit and there were several old friends who I hugged quickly and glossed over all my feelings and health issues with a broad stroke of "I am well!"

At home I finished Dana's sushi that she texted was in the fridge. I made popcorn and watched two more episodes of <u>Lillie</u>, a series based on the life of Lillie Langtry; which goes with the exhibit that David and I saw at Bard College's New York City campus called "Staging Beauty." I was lost in another time, someone else's life; a respite from my own.

Then I was answering emails when Dana came home drunk from a bonfire in Hurley. She'd been drinking whiskey on St. Patrick's Day. I let her in the front door, "I am drunk," she said. "I don't feel good". She went upstairs with a big bottle of water. I finished writing emails as I heard Dana puking in the toilet. Yuck. "Could you bring me a bucket, Mom?" she asked. "Yes, that I can do, Dana-girl. I'll bring it right up."

MY PICTURES

When I was a very little girl, my mother showed me a piece of black construction paper, that had chalk scribbles on it and the letters that spelled out her name. I looked up at her, amazed; she was showing me an artifact of pre-history; a time before I existed, a time before my mother knew me. Mom was showing me that she had been a little girl once too. It was a moment that fed one of my passions; a passion of documenting my history and the history of the times I lived in with the people that I loved. I began in kindergarten and all through high school; I saved catechism tests, spelling book pages, and stories that I wrote. I began taking pictures on a Brownie camera I was given at Christmas when I was about ten. I wanted to remember what it was like to be me as a child. I wanted my children to see what my life was about. I was grabbing bits of time and holding them for as long as I could.

I took pictures more seriously at the age of fifteen on my Yashica and developed them in a darkroom. I could see the power of truth in the un-posed faces that I captured, my mother not smiling, and my baby brother's dirty face. Then there was college, and after that my clothing store in the East Village. I took pictures of my shop windows, my neighbors and friends. I documented the evolution of my style and confidence, the gentrification of our neighborhood. I got married and documented the life I shared with my husband and his early career, then our children, and later my new neighborhood, and friends, when I was on my own again.

CAROL DWYER **176**

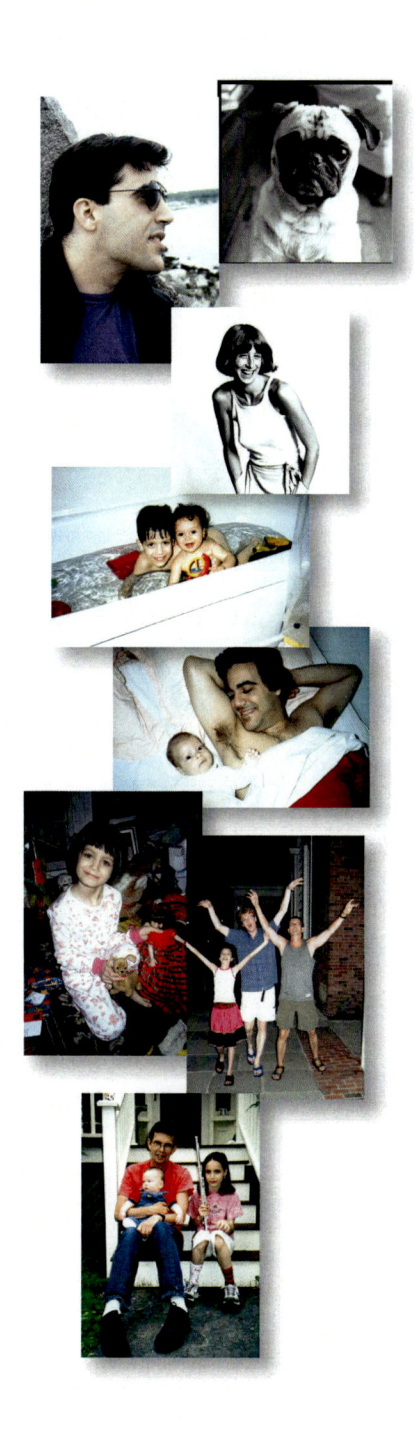

So it's not a total surprise that when I was diagnosed with cancer, that I documented my journey with the disease. I took pictures of my breasts before they left me and my hair as it fell out in the drain, I had someone take pictures of my son shaving my head. After surgery I was in the bathroom and called to my daughter to grab my camera. "Mom, what are you doing?" she asked. I was laughing at the sight of me in the mirror, wearing only pink underpants, with a striped cap on my bald head, and a bandaged chest. I had four lymph drains coming out of my sides, resting on the sink as my friend and I measured the liquid inside them. I was laughing that my inside was color coordinated with the outside and documented it with my camera. Then Dana took a full length picture of me *laughing* at what was a difficult moment.

I was also taking pictures of my son's new tattoos and my daughter going to the prom, our pot luck Christmas Caroling parties and all the other sweet things that I could grab hold of. You never know when you might forget how special every day is. People that are so important to you are here and then gone. A picture can't replace them; it only holds a moment that you shared or something that you didn't know about them, except that there they are, in the picture, there, in the stroller, at their wedding, or on their last trip.

So it feels odd now, as I witness the nearness of mortality in my own life that I should slow down on the documentation of it. I look at all the moments that I have collected and I realize that these are my moments and someday I won't be here to share them.

I am less and less behind the camera, but more and more just breathing in this brief moment that we call life. I can't hold it, it can't be held, just lived and breathed and it is not always easy, but can be enjoyed nonetheless. I have pictures to prove it.

May 6th, 2012

I enjoyed my visit with Robert. He met me at the door with dinner ready to pop in the oven. I'd just had another MRI of my brain in preparation for a visit with the neurosurgeon next week. Away from home all afternoon, I was easily knocked off my schedule of prescriptions, enzymes, supplements. I threw caution to the wind and allowed myself to be off my routine.

We chatted over dinner about our lives, present and past, the time we'd shared and movies we'd watched together. I filled him in on my understanding of my current prognosis. I have to be careful on this topic, when I feel my needle catch on the groove of my well-played record. He listened, as Danielle had earlier, and Charlie did during our car ride down. They're all aware of my morbid leaning, as I shared my anxiety of a shortened future. I say it, let it out, and then rejoin the living temporarily. I'm grateful for their compassion and leniency that lets me speak my truth; share my process.

We chose our film by its start time, as much as by interest. We decided on [Monsieur Lahzar](#) at Angelika's at 9:45 pm. We bought bottles of water to sneak into the theatre in our pockets. The empty cinema allowed us to choose perfect seats. Robert left to purchase our large popcorn and ran back for our free refill before the actual movie even started. Thoughtfully, he only got it partially filled to save us from ourselves. The film was compassionate; a perfect film for our date. We walked back to his home hand in hand, enjoying our company.

We arrived at Robert's and after quickly brushing our teeth, we entered his bedroom. He lit a candle and turned off the bright overhead light. Kissing and talking followed, both of us aware that the last two times we shared his bed were less than perfect; one confused and sad, the other as platonic friends that were baking cookies at midnight instead of making love. We have years of experienced lovemaking between us and my recent dance with mortality helped me decide not to restrict, or resist, sharing passion with him that night. The approaching full moon assisted a voluptuous night of mature passion and orgasms without breasts. I couldn't have imagined better than what it was. We talked about it afterwards, which only enriched and confirmed our shared pleasure.

The next day we went back to the new Veselka Restaurant for brunch. We sat at a window table and ordered from the menu. Robert brought up the movie called French Film, that we watched on "Break Up Eve," as he called it. The movie was like watching a version of our life together. Between that, and my looming health crisis in 2009, I acquired the clarity to break us up. He wasn't surprised by our break up, but still, he didn't want it either. Robert said, "Maybe I should've walked away from NYC years ago and moved in with you. Maybe I should've….."

"But you didn't," I interjected, "You live here."

Robert said, "But we live so separately."

"We always lived so separately. That was why I needed to end it."

May 7th, 2012

Nervous? No. Anxious? Yes, but is it a good reason? What's there or not there is already that way. I try to remain in the present moment. That is the biggest challenge of my life right now, not living with cancer, but being present. I constantly leave it, often projecting myself on my deathbed, or near death, or terminally ill dying on chemo. My mind falls into large pockets of worry and need. Sometimes I catch myself being depressed by my morbidity or is it the drugs I'm on? Yet sometimes I feel relieved too: maybe I don't need to clean out my garage and attic. Who'll care if it all gets tossed out? I won't be here! But then I remember that I can't spend the rest of my life dying and thinking about death. There's a job I was put on this earth to do. Did I figure out what that job is yet? Is it organizing my attic? Finishing another journal or photo album? Is it my job at Tonner making doll clothes? Those are all *doing* and that is how I have measured myself during this lifetime, by the measure of my accomplishments. Cancer has taught me that all these things fall away and that my greatest accomplishment, which I never felt the measure of before, is all the love that surrounds me.

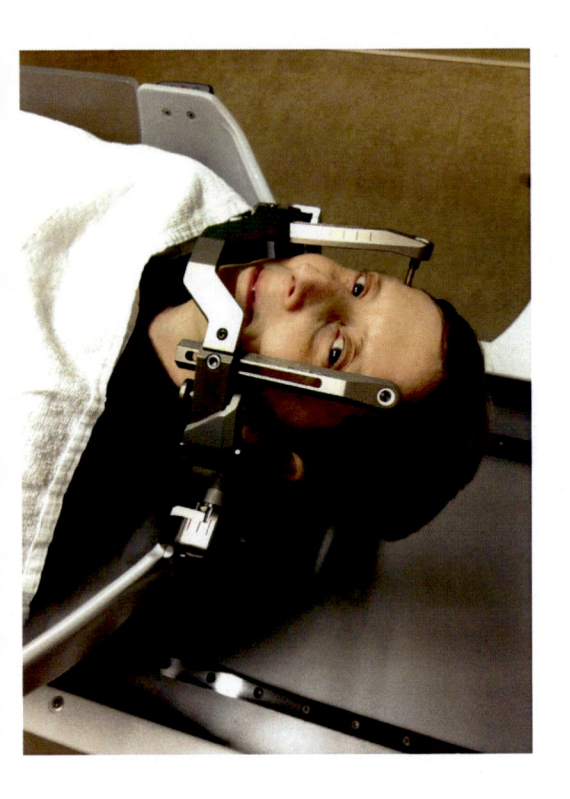

May 8th, 2012

Fear is debilitating. It does nothing to strengthen me. *This*, whatever this is, is my experience. Love will carry me further. Stop this whining and drama. Stop hiding! Find that place you found before; a place of love and meditation. But don't forget your deodorant! Dressed and sweating, I need to start over and add that. I am using the Tom's deodorant from my Hope Lodge gift bag. I never thought I would, but I never thought I would have cancer again either.

May 9th, 2012

I dreamt of making Dana's red silk prom dress over and over again. Twisting this and seaming it that way; then adding red satin.

I posted my Facebook update late. I wanted to tell Joe in the morning before everyone heard. I woke up with my back muscles in spasm. There was no way I could walk to work like this carrying my back pack and pocketbook, so I hitched a ride with my neighbor and friend, Anne. She exited her back door and said, "Good morning! How're you doing?" I gave it to her straight, "I have another small tumor growing in the same cavity of my brain as the previous one that was removed. The doctor also saw another spot developing. He said it is time for the Gamma Knife radiation and soon, before they grow too much bigger. It's only been two months since surgery. But worse, at this moment, are the spasms in my back because I'm so stressed out!"

"Oh shit." She said and drove me to work.

I went in our building, signed in and walked slowly up the stairs to the design room to shed my coat and backpack. I walked to Joe's office and filled him in on my current prognosis for Gamma Knife brain surgery and spastic back muscles.

"I know its stress Joe, and I think it's happened to make me cry, like I need an excuse to cry." Joe looked up at me surprised.

"Carol, you can cry anytime!"

"But I don't, Joe. I don't cry, so now I have a reason." He stood up from his desk as I continued, "I am stressed, but you want to know what's stressing me out the most, Joe? It is making Dana's prom dress! There are only a few weeks before prom, no solid design idea from my daughter who is "proud" of me making the dress, but living in fear that she won't like it and I might have Gamma Knife surgery sometime between here and the prom! We are almost out of time and it might be the last dress I make her…." I could not say more. My voice cracked and tears bulged in my eyes. This is not a state I normally choose to share, especially at work with Joe.

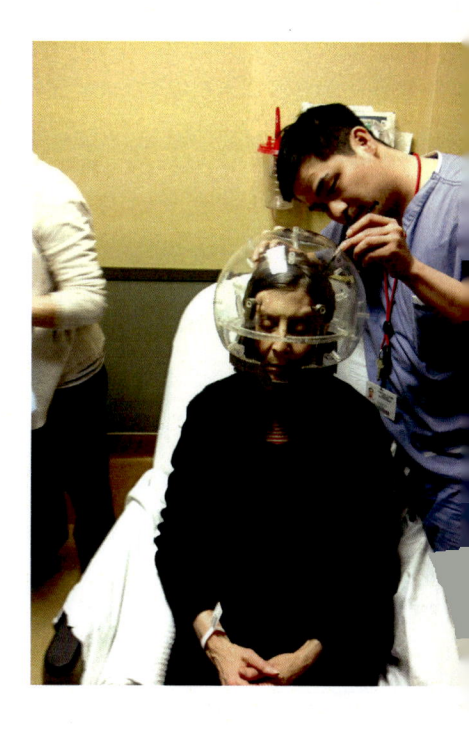

SOCIAL SECURITY DISABILITY
June 12th, 2012

I was told three years ago that I could apply, but finally, in early June, I made the call to Social Security Disability. I took the step because though I made it through Round One optimistically, Round Two was taking a serious toll on my body and spirit. I was tired to the bone. I ran back to work at a job I enjoyed with people that I love, but I was trying to keep up with the fast pace of everyone around me, the pace that I used to be part of, but wasn't any more. Stage Four, Round Two; "How much closer," I wondered, "do I need to get to death before I take time to breathe and prepare?" I cried leaving my friends at work. I cried to face the real fear of my changing life. The other side of me though, simply looked forward to having the summer off. "I can pretend I am retiring," I thought. "I'll sell off part of my doll collection to supplement my depleted income." Cancer has brought me to a new level of detachment.

I had been "dying" for months. There were steroids, anti-seizure medication, brain surgery and Gamma Knife brain radiation. Then the additions of a Tykerb, a "targeted drug" in pill form that could help prevent more brain tumors by crossing the "blood brain barrier." and Femera, a stronger estrogen blocker too. I want to pop back up and jump back into my life, but I am tired and impatient.

The weight of radiation slowly peels away; I begin to adjust to a new drug ritual. I am relived to feel alive again. I learn to pace myself and enjoy the window of time before I get the next round of tests. My daughter is preparing to leave for college. I am living consciously during our transitional time, present now, relishing these last bits of our old life together. Come fall, life will be different, but focused on Dana's departure, not mine.

THE SABBATICAL BEGINS
July 3rd, 2012

Today is the second full day of my Sabbatical or Medical Leave of Absence, or Retirement, depending on who you ask. I am approaching it with my most optimistic attitude. I learned a big lesson last Friday after I ran out of work close to tears, unsure of when I would return, if ever. My mind ran downhill as I walked home on Main Street. It was suddenly full of fear and worry about my health and finances until suddenly, SQUISH and BAM! I was on the ground. The begonia I carried from work in a bag over my arm had swung safely aside as I fell on my right arm. That was actually quite graceful, I thought. It jerked me out of my pessimism. I looked up at the big, blue sky and heard, "be HERE now," loud and clear. I rolled over looking at the sidewalk as I stood back up and saw chunks of banana that caught my heel, causing my crash to the ground. I recaptured my optimism and looked around me at this beautiful day and the summer vacation before me. That is how I will begin, by enjoying time off this summer.

Metastatic Support Group #1
July 3rd, 2012

Today I went to visit the Oncology Support Program's Metastatic Cancer Support Group near Benedictine Hospital. I've had unsatisfactory results attending a previous breast cancer support group in New York City. I sat amongst women who had had lumpectomies and chemo or lumpectomies and radiation, but I was at the end of aggressive chemotherapy, bald, headed towards my bilateral mastectomy in a few weeks and radiation to my spine and chest wall after that. I was absolutely the worst nightmare of everyone present. Recently though, my neighbor, Barbara Sarah, recommended that I try this local support group that she helped establish. "You'll love the facilitator, Rosie," she told me only yesterday. I'd met Rosie briefly when I resided in the oncology ward of Benedictine Hospital last January. It helped to have a face to go with the name, the idea.

I showed up five minutes early. It gave Rosie and me time to chat before anyone else came in. She is a special person, I can tell already; she is someone I could be friends with. The first woman walked in the room slowly, turning her whole body to pull the light door closed. She's underweight and frail. She asks Rosie for a glass of water. She is feeling very dehydrated. It has been three months since she last attended a group meeting and Rosie fills her in on the whereabouts of several other absent members.

The next woman walks towards the door and opens it, pulling her oxygen tank behind her. She wears a short blonde wig, similar to the wig I adopted during chemo. She has a full face and body; her pale, swollen legs exposed in shorts. We begin. I find myself clutching to the idea that I have more in common with Rosie, than I do with the other women. I know better, my fear makes me judgmental, and I become conscious of creating a mental division of us and them. I made that mistake before, with Ellen, who just passed away from brain Mets.

We met on the phone back in 2010 and she told me everything I never wanted to know about metastatic breast cancer. The second time I met Ellen, I went to her lecture at a breast cancer conference. There she was, talking to a room full of women with metastatic disease, telling all the lousy statistics. At the end she said, "But remember, we are not statistics." I was very upset by the upside down delivery of her presentation.

It was six months later that I bumped into Ellen at an Unconditional Healing Retreat led by Jeff Rubin. He was the person who first connected me to Ellen. He creates a healing space in these retreats and it afforded me the opportunity to communicate my frustration with Ellen's presentation of The Facts about Metastatic Breast Cancer. She was on a new chemo for another layer of her illness and was depressed about it. I thought I was successfully through cancer, stage four, round one. Last January, however, when I entered round two, I realized I had not had enough compassion for Ellen who had been through layer after layer of cancer discoveries for so many years, similar to the two women in the group today. I realized this year that I do have a chronic disease; the breast cancer has spread to my brain. It was around then that I heard Ellen was in hospice. I understand better now Ellen's feelings of the weight of cancer and I hope she is at peace. I'm grateful now for how she tried to share how it was for her, but I wasn't ready for the information. Maybe now though, and God bless her.

August 2nd, 2012

I dreamt of being ill. The cracks throughout my body were wedged open, exposed, vulnerable to more disease through the open fissures. Healing plasters were wedged in the open wounds. Then I couldn't talk on the phone for fear of opening the wounds again.

Metastatic Support Group #3
August 7th, 2012

Yesterday's Metastatic Support Group was "Ju-u-ust Right" as Goldilocks would say. Thin Nancy, Suzanne, Tom, Rosie and I were joined by red-haired Nancy. Her husband Dean carried her wheelchair in, put the leg supports in place for Nancy's comfort during our session. She was able to walk into the room to sit in it. Rosie was guiding us to introduce ourselves. Nancy and I needed to say more because we had never met before. She told her story and how she was in so much pain this past spring that she wanted to give up. "I saw the grief in my husband's face, his pain and helplessness, and I lived for him, for Dean. I continued for him until my own will to live kicked back in. I had been so depressed, in so much pain."

Rosie posed some questions to us, one of them being "How do you cope with NOW if you are not OK, or in pain?" We talked about medications, meditations and distractions, wandered off topic and Rosie brought us back to the point. The others got into a discussion about not liking being doped up on drugs, disliking the lethargy of not really being alive. I realized my good fortune, I disliked the steroids suppression of my dreams and the fat face I evolved on them, but they were talking opiates.

We were almost out of time when Tom told us about his family going away for two weeks on vacation. He lives in the basement of his daughter and son-in-law's and he woke in the middle of the night with a pain in his stomach, he sat on the floor, leaning against his bed, hugging the bucket for five hours, in constant pain and fear, until he threw up. At the doctor's the next day, nothing was found, but Tom believes it is the scar tissue formed from everything he's had removed from his abdomen.

We also touched on the larger journey with cancer. I again pointed out that I am not "fighting" cancer. "Fighting" is a logo. I am on a journey. We all live different lengths of time because we all have things we are supposed to learn in life, or teach others, and when we are done, we can die. None of us knows when we will die, or what we will die of, but my journey with cancer brings me closer to consciousness, closer to my priorities. I am more knowledgeable of being human and strive to be more compassionate for our human frailness. I want to enjoy this life while I can. I want to explore my creativity and walk confidently on my path. What a mortal wish. My detachment of this life holds me outside; my understanding that I will be leaving the party sooner than the shelf life of my lifelong frustration or angst. I've had to become a mellower person, a human, constantly measuring the value of that particular confrontation; I can only fix myself and love others as they are.

    I was explaining to Dana the other day in the car about how separate my life used to be; sectioned groups with no overlapping. My life is the opposite now with all of my groups meeting at my fundraisers. I get to enjoy all these people that I love, meeting, even the most barbed people softening a little at each event. We all expand, open, if only to see that we have further to go, to let go of our ego, of being right, of arguing. My detachment is positive then, in that light it is expansion, a letting go of the minor choices, allowing others to be on their path. I don't have to change anyone to my way of thinking. My family gives me an incredible opportunity to love, love unconditionally, not owning or bending or competing, but just learning our lessons from each other. My daughter listened, not knowing what to say.

DANA'S DEPARTURE
September 2012

Is it time to begin writing about Dana's departure? I have been walking towards this her whole life, growing with her, raising her to go off and further prepare to stand on her own two feet. Just like her birth story, this story too, is so personal for both of us. This is my second day waking up at home with her living in Chicago. Over the summer there were days I woke and thought, "Is she home?" or "Where is she off to today?" This morning though it hit me that she will not be home later today; it will be three and a half months until I hug her again.

Dana called last night while enjoying the view from her dorm window overlooking the neon Chicago Theatre sign on busy State Street. I loved hearing her voice; her happiness. It feels right, so I am not home weeping, yet. I am looking around, washing sheets and beginning to vacuum. That is my orientation process.

The day before she left, Dana felt sick with a sore throat, congestion, earache and mild fever. She had been having "good bye" breakfast, lunch and dinners for days with all her friends. Who knows what combination of stress and health issues had her lying on the couch. "Maybe I just need some last minute 'Mama-care' before I go off to college," she joked softly. I helped her to bed and made my way back to the kitchen table, called the airline and got the information on the cost and procedures of rescheduling flights. I knew we might have to.

The next morning I rose early, showered, fed our

cat, and got my suitcase stuffed with some of Dana's last minute clothes, loaded into the car. I amazed myself with the "Mama- energy" pulsing through my system, urging me on to accomplish the huge task before us. The situation demanded that I be in charge. I ran upstairs to check on Dana and she had showered, but went back into bed feeling lightheaded. I served her eggs and toast in bed. She ate them tentatively. It was now 8:15 am and I had planned our departure time to be 8:30 to get to Albany airport comfortably. I sat on the edge of Dana's bed and asked, "Can you make this flight, or do I need to cancel? It is time to decide."

"NO! We have to GO!" she yells. Panic made her sit up.

"OK, then you have 15 minutes to get ready." I went downstairs finished the dishes, watered the plants and she was downstairs, ready to go. She looked beautiful, mature and casual wearing yoga pants and her eyeglasses without make-up.

I drove us, parked, and we shuttled to the terminal, checked our bags. I snapped random photos along the way, including where I parked. I'd be returning to this parking space alone.

I'd last been in Chicago twenty-three years ago with Charlie, and our friend, Kurt; both were performing in the First National Tour of <u>Les Miserables.</u> I gave birth to our son Michael here. Kurt picked us up at the airport and let us stay with him until Saturday when Dana moved into her dorm.

Kurt's neighbors from downstairs, Maria and Larry, ran up to meet us when we arrived. They had already adopted Dana as their new "granddaughter" in March, when she and Charlie visited the School of the Art Institute of Chicago. She met them, saw the college and bought the whole package. They invited us down to breakfast the following morning. Maria made us all homemade waffles and pancakes with maple syrup, jam, crisp bacon and coffee. We ate and talked. Maria shared a few amazing stories about growing up in Germany during the war. It made me feel better to know that Dana has a home base and support when, and if, my health became unstable.

After she ate, Dana excused herself and returned upstairs to bed where she slept all day. I needed to take it easy too. I cleaned off Kurt's recliner, opened windows for cross ventilation and adopted my spot for the day; a day of adjustment, acclamation, transition. I was reading a book called <u>The Book Thief</u>, about a young girl in Germany during the WWII and I kept confusing the book's main character, with the stories that Maria had shared.

I took my Tykerb for the first day of the sixth month and by evening I experienced the side effect of severe diarrhea. It reminded me of when I had the runs when my son was a crawling infant and I couldn't stay off the toilet; Charlie was out of town in his next show, we lived on the sixth floor of an old walkup building on Prince St. My life felt completely out of my control and my bowels were in unison with the rest of my life. I felt like that night could also be symbolic of the endless flow, the unstoppable flow of life; Dana going off to her dorm room in the morning. Or perhaps it was the Vietnamese food we had for dinner, along with the Tykerb, that were exacerbating my emotional bowels. I took an extra dose of my homeopathic remedy for diarrhea. I entered month six of this life saving drug; who knew I would be on this journey to Chicago with my daughter when I began it in March. I began again to notice people around me making long range plans. My plans are short term, soft and insecure around the edges. The next day I would be with my daughter as she moved into her new life.

We rose early and loaded Dana's bags into Kurt's car. He dropped us in front of the building with Dana's luggage and said good bye to her. We proceeded to the elevator, circumventing the line of families waiting to unload carloads of essentials. We had already shipped the bulk of her things. They were scheduled to arrive next week.

When we arrived at her dorm room, one of her roommates was there with her parents unpacking. Dana and I looked over the long, tall, sunny room and she chose the bed nearest the window. I looked towards the window and then brought my eyes closer noticing the stack of boxes that read Tonner Doll Company and realized that Dana's possessions were already here! It was wonderful to be able to help my girl unpack and move in.

The third roommate arrived with her mother and her boxes seemed to explode as she quickly and roughly hung things up. The girls decided to all go shopping together, with parents in tow, for the rest of the things they could think of to set up their new home. We walked blocks and blocks to the stores they needed and I stopped frequently to snap photos of the Chicago skyline. At the next store, they put their focus on food and Dana and I both noticed that they probably won't be able to share food as the girls picked up Kraft's Mac n' Cheese, white bread and Jif Peanut Butter.

In the evening we all went to the lobby and were suddenly corralled into parent and student formations for the forgotten evening "Orientation". The girls fell in their clump and I in mine, waving good bye to the other parents who were determined to get their dinner. I didn't want to miss anything important and hoped that there were some important appetizers at the function. The event for parents was held in an old theatre across from the Art Institute. We entered the building and ascended an elegant, broad, carpeted staircase that split in two and spiraled backwards. I ran to the buffet with other starving parents and fixed a plate of hummus, guacamole, corn chips, cheese, crackers and pineapple to take to a seat nearby. Faculty and administrators began lengthy speeches about this fabulous school, the great opportunities for our children and the wonderful staff here to guide them. I bolted at the finale and called Kurt to say I was headed uptown on the Red Line. I was in an exhausted daze as I exited the platform. I had to call him again to ask which way I should turn. I began to follow his direction when I saw him running towards me, huffing and puffing, to guide me back to his place. I already knew I wouldn't make the 8:00 am invitation for parents to tour the Modern Wing of the museum with a buffet breakfast.

I caught the El back to the Loop in the morning, picking up an egg salad sandwich and tea as I headed to the next parent orientation activity. I was the last of the group and was personally escorted through the museum to the correct auditorium. At first I leaned on the short wall overlooking the balcony stairway that descended to the stage, but eventually I sat on it, cross legged, with a bird's eye view, rebelliously not sitting in a seat with the rest of the parents. At this point I was getting annoyed with the speakers' common references to "having plenty of Kleenex on hand," but I was standing firm with my daughter's readiness and need to leave our small town; to bust out of our small house and step away from my illness. It was pouring rain outside when it was time to cross the street for lunch. The school provided free umbrellas and ponchos for parents.

Finally I got to see my girl again. She was also fed up with organized activities. She confided in me that all she had to eat so far was a slice of white bread with Nutella on it. "I won't last long eating this way, Mom!"

"Come on Dana-Girl." I said. "You have the address for the health food store. Let's go get you some of your food; things you like to eat," We put on our SAIC ponchos and headed out into the rain. On the Red Line I told her, "We'll get you some food and then grab a bite to eat near your dorm." I enjoyed watching her excitement picking out her provisions, her bread and tea, granola, nuts, juice, enjoying the connection to home and the job at the health food store she left behind. We took the groceries back to her new home and unpacked them.

We had spent the last of our time together settling her in. It was pouring rain outside, so we decided to make dinner in her dorm room. She was happy. These were her groceries and she was making salad when her roommates came home. They put on their pajamas to settle in and I immediately felt out of place. "I will go grab a sandwich," I told her.

"Really Mom?" she asked looking at me.

"Good bye girls", I said to her roommates. They didn't protest.

One roommate said, "See you again soon, I'm sure, maybe on parent's weekend in October."

I'm not so sure. It shifts the tectonic plates beneath me, of not knowing. Will I be well? Will I be back? Dana escorted me downstairs to the lobby and it hit us. She cried on my shoulder. We've been good family, good roommates, and I felt the rip in my side as we separated. I hoped her roommates would be kind and bond to my daughter's open heart. I will heal with the love of friends and time, but right then, I felt a wrenching pain. The warm and sunny room of the day before was gray and sterile when I left my daughter straining to negotiate with new strangers, new friends. I know she will. They needed to adjust to each other, not to me too.

ANNE'S MADONNA

Maria unearthed her mother's trunk and opened it. It holds the last random things the siblings cleared out of my late mother-in-law's house. "Carol, do you want one of these? You could use this…" she says handing me one of Anne's vintage hem markers with a red metal base and tall, darkened wood ruler. "Sure," I replied, unable to resist this sewing artifact, a token of our common bond.

Blue and ivory caught my eye; I reached in the trunk to pick up a plastic statue of the Blessed Virgin Mary. I stared at her elongated, ivory form, the blue paint of her robe worn off the shoulders and back from Anne's daily cleaning. I am trying to remember where she lived in Anne's house. "In Mom's bedroom," Maria tells me. "Do you want her? You can have it." I can picture her there now, sitting on Mom's mahogany dresser in her spotless room. I hold the statue realizing that she is always portrayed as a young mother, calm, patient, loving, with open arms; exemplifying the preferred aspirations of real mothers. The Virgin Mary doesn't show the frustration of unkempt rooms, the pain of losing a child, the grief of letting them go, even just to grow up.

UPDATES

September 18, 2012

It's only my fifth Metastatic Cancer Support Group on this rainy Tuesday. I park and run to the building in the pouring rain to meet Rosie and Suzanne in the sun room. Rosie, who facilitates our meetings, warns us that we have two tough updates, two no-shows and one car problem.

Rosie gave Suzanne and me updates for the members not present; we knew Nancy had joined hospice, but yesterday she had slipped into her first unresponsive state, the first of what could be a practice for dying. I'd only met her once, but felt much closer. It felt shocking to hear and felt like practice for all of us.

Another update was about Tom, who'd been away in Cincinnati, visiting family and working at a car show in his home town. I've missed his jovial presence at group. Rosie said he drove himself home, non-stop, and was in such pain when he got there, that his daughter had an ambulance take him to the hospital. He found out that the metastases had gone to his spine, lumbar 2 and 3, with fractures. Rosie had visited him in the morning and thought since it was a small group, we could go for a visit. Suzanne and I were eager to go. I updated them about my strained liver, the doctor had taken me off my pill chemo and my blood would be retested on Friday. We grabbed our raincoats and umbrellas. I took Suzanne's picture as she stood there looking like the Morton's Salt girl in her yellow slicker and rain hat. We ran across the street in the continuing down pour, to Benedictine Hospital, on the fourth floor, to #4113, Tom's "room with a view."

Rosie knocked on the closed door. "Tom? Are you up for company?" she asked as she peeked in the door to make sure it was okay. We all heard the strained whisper of Tom's voice saying, "Okay." We followed Rosie into the room. He laid in his hospital bed with the chemo tube secured to his chest port, and his bangs sticking up from the week spent there in pain. He was happy to see us, though the pain meds might not let him remember. We complimented his boxers and laughed like this was normal.

I see this man in his hospital bed, this man I have known for three group meetings and I'm surprised to realize how close I feel to him. This could be any one of us in this bed, in pain. Tom's eyes are half closed, his breath is the breath of sleeping, but he stubbornly keeps trying to text his daughter. He is sure the solution is to plug the lamp cord into his phone to charge it. Rosie finds the cord he means to use and hands it to him. "What drug are you on, Tom?" she asks twice; her question remains unanswered. It is obviously strong. Rosie's patience and compassion are so large that I could cry. Her path is with us as we all learn and teach, share and benefit.

Before we leave, I ask Tom's permission to take a group photo. We laugh, squeezing in around our shirtless friend in his bed. I will turn this photo into a "Get Well" card; even if it's only "Get Well for *Now.*"

GOOD NEWS AGAIN
September 18, 2012

I've heard that you do not "beat" Metastatic Cancer. I've heard the statistics aren't "good". I've heard that every one of us living today will die, so I wonder to myself, what does it matter what I die of? Or when? Isn't disease just a tool in the toolbox? I look at the obituaries and see a notice for someone 90 years old, or 7, or 58, which hits closer to home. I haven't found a pattern in the numbers yet, though I look every day.

We're all living while simultaneously walking towards our death. My journey with Metastatic Cancer has me learning to walk alongside it, we're becoming acquainted. There's comfort to be found in familiarity, more opportunity for fear to fall by the wayside.

Consciously, I try to walk alongside death, making choices of how to spend each day. Some days are for pushing blindly through, like getting Dana off to college. Some days are for resting, the price to pay for pushing through those busy days. Some days are for forgetting, for pretending that every day will be as common as today, when I feel well.

The doctor calls to tell me to stop my pill chemo, my blood work shows my liver is stressed; another bump in the road that I couldn't see. I stumble and cry. Then I remember, again, that every day is new, different, and I catch my breath and find the rhythm of death's gait, or is it life's? Quietly the skin of contentment spreads over the warm surface of my anxiety.

Today I am living and grateful to simply be running errands.

HOW THURSDAY BECAME MY FAVORITE DAY
Or Joining the Oncology Support Program's Memoir Group with Abigail Thomas

It was early September. Dana was off to college in Chicago and I was filling my time in totally new ways. The first memoir group I attended was at Abigail Thomas' house in Woodstock. I joined the others sitting in Abby's eclectic assortment of lawn furniture on the patio outside her kitchen. Her three dogs wove through our legs, sniffing, tail-wagging and barking with great enthusiasm. I saw Barbara who'd invited me to join, and she introduced me to Perri, Craig, Annie, and Phyllis. I recognized Roberta from days when our girls were little. Abby came outside with her bracelets jingling, a heartwarming smile, wearing layers of comfy clothes including a Robin Hood green sweater announcing, "*Pleeease* make yourselves at home." I felt sincerely welcomed into the tribe as she presented a scrumptious homemade apple tart which we ate while Abby read poetry and assigned prompts for next week. The prompts were given to inspire us to write something that we wouldn't have thought of otherwise. We took turns reading the stories we'd brought. I read "Good News Again" and caught heads nodding with understanding. This is a support group and I felt safe to write about cancer here. I added Thursday afternoon to my list of things to do each week that had nothing to do with doctors.

From the first day it was more than just reading, it was listening to the stories of others, riding the waves of their voices and words was addictive. I was moved, over and over and over, and soon my week revolved around Thursday and scheduling doctors and lunches around memoir group. How could something else be more important than to hear the voices of these new friends telling their personal stories? Our Thursday memoir group became a family of support and encouragement; a consistent place to share what's going on with ourselves.

I felt something click with writing now, I just needed to let myself write all the words down, all the stories down, I felt my roots deepening into the creative process. All the years in fashion, when I was limited by my finances and fabrics, I did the best with what I had. It was at the Tonner Doll Company that I got better at doing a project again and again, to make it the best it could be, but there I was working with someone else's idea. Now, with words, I can write as much as I want, using as many drafts as I need to hear my voice telling my story in the clearest possible way.

On Thursday, I've gotten to know my fellow memoirists not through discussions of our daily habits or preferences, no, no first dates here. We listen to our darkest secrets and triumphs, childhood traumas and illness and love. We meet through our stories, the things we choose to share with the group. It is an inside-out learning of each other. One day a week we disclose something that we hadn't shared before and it makes that day special. I wouldn't miss it for the world. No, I could do lunch with you any day but Thursday.

REMIND ME WHY I'M HERE

It is September 21, 2012 and I am pulling years of journals from my nightstand. I begin to read the one leading up to my breast cancer diagnosis: April, May, June, and July 2009. I sit to anthropologically study my mind in the months before I was diagnosed. I am looking for clues, I already had cancer, my nipple showing visible change for a few years, but the yearly mammograms did not show the multitude of tumors in my lovely, dense tissued breasts, or the spot on my spine.

I read through my dreams, stories about my children, and about making love with my lover of eleven years. I read that I knew he wasn't "*the one.*" I talked about how grateful I was for my job, my co-workers and my disappointment for being passed over for the big project at work. The high hopes were placed on the new woman and I had a hard time swallowing it. Over and over, page after page, I began to question "What is my JOY?" I no longer knew. What do I need to accomplish in this life? I wondered. I know I have creativity to be released, projects and ideas unexpressed, unfulfilled, and only talked about. My journal is foreboding.

I read about visiting my friend Therese, an acupuncturist, about my thyroid condition. She recommended that I add kelp to my diet and teaches me to make nettle infusion, which will boost my thyroid function, but intuitively she guides me to these perfect detoxifiers to accompany the upcoming chemotherapy, surgery, toxic tests and radiation.

I read up to my breaking up with my lover, the movie we watched that night and how it screamed to me to stop fucking around, put both feet under me, focus, love myself and remember why I am here and what I need to do. I still have parenting and learning to do with my children.

Then the hammer hit home. I am Stage-Four Metastatic from day one. I realize now, in retrospect, that I had no clue what that meant, even when explained to me. The doctors softened the blow and I remained optimistic. I returned eagerly to work when I was able. I wanted to be normal. I received a clear PET scan in September 2011 followed by a "Mets to the brain" diagnosis in late January 2012 after a week of clear sailing through doctor's appointments and "You're good-to-go" praise. Brain metastasis, which is what Ellen had at the time; Ellen who taught me "everything I never wanted to know about Metastatic Cancer," Ellen with a port in her brain, Ellen who was in hospice and died months later.

I had brain surgery in early February to remove my brain tumor and stereotactic surgery three months later, when it began to grow back. Again, I rushed back to work as I took Tykerb, a 'targeted therapy' that crosses the blood brain barrier; something that couldn't help Ellen. I couldn't see how I could survive financially without my job. The whole company has been a huge support to me and I felt needed there. I rushed back, still recovering from radiation, on strong targeted therapy, anti-seizure medication and an estrogen suppressant. This time though, I knew I wasn't normal; I wasn't up to speed. The side effects added up, I was tired and arthritic. I went on a leave of absence from work and receive a stipend from Social Security Disability. I have time to rest and focus on self care. I procrastinated worrying about money by selling off a portion of my doll collection.

DRIVING TO THE ONCOLOGIST
9/12/2012

I will avoid the longest traffic light in Kingston on Wall and Pearl Street by turning right onto Greene, following the curved road that brings me onto St. James. I pass an old stone house; a squirrel scurries in front of my car and then a cat, but slowly, un-catlike. I slow almost to a stop, to allow this infirmed beast to cross in front of me. I follow it with my eyes and see its owner on the porch of a two family home, bent, practically in tears, calling her pet, cigarette in hand, her toothless mouth forming a thank you for not running over her beloved cat. I drive another two blocks, stopping at each sign. A heavy woman is wheeling a baby carriage, carelessly, in the middle of the road and I drive around her noticing she is wearing full coverage headphones, she's deaf to my approach.

I turn wide onto Broadway, around a shirtless man, looking worn out, older than his years, as he rides his bicycle towards me. I approach the YMCA and get into the right hand lane to turn, then a left past the cemetery, and a right into the parking lot for my oncologist. Today I will get my blood retested to check my liver function. I am busy enjoying this picnic of energy I have after two weeks off my pill chemo. It is surprising how suppressed I have been. I enjoyed it like I was on vacation: painting the back of the house and making love with Robert, dinner in NYC with my Parisian friend Katia, and Leon Russell in concert. I also joined a new writing group, attended our Metastatic Support Group, dinner with Katy in Woodstock, Thirsty Thursday on our neighbor's porch, and tonight back in NYC to visit Danielle and Tommy. We are going to the Susan Tedeschi-Derek Trucks Concert. Then I will attend the retreat at the Omega Institute for Women With Metastatic Breast Cancer, followed by a writing retreat on Martha's Vineyard with girlfriends and a week-long visit with Dad and Mary back at my house. I hope to be back on chemo by then, but right now, I'm tasting life and all it offers, as it comes at me. Winter will have its own contractions, with cancer adding its own measure to the mix.

THE 1ST ANNUAL RETREAT FOR WOMEN WITH METASTATIC BREAST CANCER

September 2012 Sponsored by BREAST CANCER OPTIONS at the OMEGA INSTITUTE

We were all women with metastatic breast cancer brought together by Breast Cancer Options at the Omega Institute in September 2012. We were twenty-eight women, from Long Island to Albany, meeting for the first time, excited about being at such a lovely retreat center, in the fall, but also nervous about meeting so many new people with the same disease.

After checking intow our rooms, we gathered into a circle in a building surrounded by trees and introduced ourselves. We heard 28 variations of diagnoses, progressions, treatment plans, drug reactions, and indefinite futures. There is no one-size-fits-all solution for our dilemma. I looked around the room at many women wearing hats and wigs to cover bald heads, some women dozed from the strong medications they were taking and others needed lots of assistance getting up for dinner or to get back to their rooms. But me? Two weeks before the retreat my oncologist told me I had an elevated liver enzyme in my blood work and I was taken off my targeted therapy drug, Tykerb, for two weeks. I was almost back to my *normal* old energy, feeling enthusiastic about being at the event and walking around the beautiful grounds. I was high *off* drugs.

In our opening circle, our facilitator, Nancy,

dimmed the lights before guiding us in a centered breathing exercise with our eyes closed. We were encouraged to speak into the circle whatever we felt about having metastatic breast cancer. We took turns slowly, with long pauses after each person spoke. I had just written a piece called "Good News Again" which expressed my current philosophy about having cancer and I said into the circle, *"Sometimes having cancer feels like a gift."* I was thinking about all the people I've been meeting that I'd never have met without having cancer. I've also often thought about how I hope that I'm the "one in eight women" with this disease and that can cover a wide range of "Eights" in my life, spanning out from me like spokes on a wheel, so my daughter, sisters, nieces and girlfriends don't have to go through this. I said, *"Sometimes I feel chosen to have cancer."* The last thing I said that evening was, *"I don't fight cancer. I'm learning to walk along side it."* I'm uncomfortable using the status quo cancer quotes with battles and wars.

The next day Nancy broke us up into small groups and I quickly found my teammates: Mandy, Rose, Debbie and Jean. We answered questions that Nancy provided to break the ice. Mandy has been well for six years since being diagnosed metastatic, but was diagnosed with her initial cancer in 1994. Rose has been through layers of diagnoses, one breast, then the other, then metastatic more recently. Debbie was having trouble with side effects right now and Jean had a large moon face and weight gain from steroids. I remembered it well; being on steroids after my brain tumor and watching my face grow daily, even after I went off the medication. I had been rebelliously bald and stated "I'd never have to wear a bra again" after my bilateral, but the full face on steroids was my Achilles' heel. I heard my mother's voice commenting on my chubby cheeks whenever I looked into a mirror. On the last day Jean shared a photo of herself, a second grade teacher, with soft brown hair and a big smile and I could see it was her, but could it be only six months ago?

We had a woman come speak to us about the latest pharmaceutical developments, Cindy from the MBCN website spoke to us about networking and advocacy. We wrote in our journals and ate meals at large community tables in the Omega dining hall. Our acquaintances and friendships grew rapidly within the circle. I loved sitting next to Pat, Penny, Darlene and Gloria.

    A day later, Nancy had us make another circle. She felt that perhaps there were people that had not expressed their feelings in the first circle and would like to have a second chance to express them. She was right, as several women spoke angrily, "Cancer in *not* a *gift!*" "I don't feel chosen by cancer, I feel *cursed!*" and then someone said, "I will *fight* this disease every day of my life! I will *not* accept it." I spoke last. I acknowledged that not only one or two of the things that I'd said in the previous circle, but all three made some people angry and I was sorry for that, but that's how I feel. I realized I needed to be more sensitive to the many stages of grieving taking place at the retreat. We are not all at the same level of acceptance, nor do I remain stagnant emotionally. Rose was a spitfire with both jokes and anger about her fight against cancer, Carla, not forty, with a young son and husband at home, was reeling with her brand new diagnosis of metastases after finishing all her treatments and reconstruction. Linda B. was livid about having cancer and this was a forum for her to vent the unfairness of it all.

    Talking around the circle I heard about Bjorna's problem on the drug Zometa, and Kim joined in. Jude spoke about having a bad reaction to Faslodex, she got a severe case of neuropathy within two weeks of her first injection and needed a walker. Quite a few women spoke of Xeloda, including quiet Mary, wearing white cotton gloves to protect her dry, cracked fingers from infection. Clare, our oldest member, was diagnosed metastatic 17 years ago without recurrence. Jude and Bjorna needed to leave each morning to get their chemotherapy. Lydia was the frailest, but no less determined to kayak out into the lake; it was on her bucket list. Betty and Barbara had multiple tumors on the brain treated with all-over brain radiation and complete hair loss. I'd had one brain tumor surgically removed, followed by specific Gamma Knife radiation. I looked around the room and there was no contest going on, anyone of us could die soonest or live the longest, every one of us shared surgical procedures or chemo drugs or follow-up metastases, but not one of us was exactly like another.

I sat in an Adirondack chair in the partial shade of a tree, overlooking a large lawn at the Omega Institute. The wind blew under the branches lifting them up gently, exposing me to the sun. I was soothed by the soughing of the trees. I'd spoken to my oncology nurse who told me, "Your blood work revealed that your liver function is back to normal, so resume the Tykerb again, only we'll try you on four pills a day instead of five." So there I was, taking a few minutes of solitude, giving a silent toast to welcome back my Tykerb. I sat listening to the trees and a young man to my right playing his guitar. I was happy to be there.

It was both feet into the fall season there at Omega with yellow trees and a cool breeze. The light dappled through drying leaves while the wind gave a crisper sound, so different from the voluptuous sound of the summer wind through the same trees. I was there, enjoying a fall moment. I began my Tykerb again, day 1, month 7. I felt so lucky to have this drug to help me and so grateful for all those women joined together in this life, sharing their voices and knowledge as we hold hands on the edge.

A SPY ON MY OWN CANCER
October 23, 2012

My PET scan was Tuesday morning; it was a follow-up to the one I had eight months ago, to check if the breast cancer had metastasized beyond what had appeared in my brain last winter. I was unpurposely lethargic getting out of bed Wednesday morning, until Robert called with an idea to meet me in Beacon. "We could meet and go to the DIA museum. Are you game?" he asked. It sounded to me like just what the doctor ordered. I got up, called to make my echocardiogram appointment earlier, filled the tank and drove south to Beacon. Robert was late to the train, but I was happy to work on my writing while waiting in the comfort of my car. I heard the train pull in and drove over to pick him up. We go to enter the DIA driveway and see: "CLOSED. Open Thursday through Sunday 10am to 6 pm." "Well, I had the hours right," he said when I laughed. It was a gorgeous sunny fall day and we were both prepared to enjoy it.

We poked around in shops, admiring the art of Hudson Valley artists. We stepped into a restored fire house called The Glass House and looked at the incredible variations of glassware, all colors and weights. We watched two women in a studio, blowing glass. We wandered up the old staircase into a photography exhibit with large photos of nature. The panoramic vistas are rich with acute details of moss, the texture of rocks, and the action of flowing water.

My cell rang and I answered. "Hi Carol? It's Gwen from Dr. Andrade's office. We see that you have an appointment to see the doctor on Monday, but he would like you to come in sooner. I have Friday at 3:30 available." That can really only mean one thing is what I'm thinking. "Sure Gwen, but is there anything you can tell me now?" I ask. "No, I wouldn't know anything about your report; you'll talk to Dr. Andrade when you come in," she replies. I hang up, call River Radiology and leave a message that I need to pick up a copy of my PET scan report and disc tomorrow, Thursday. We exit the empty gallery with a strong suspicion as the logical assumption.

We finished up our visit to Beacon with a late lunch and tea. Sitting at the window counter in a little café, we looked out at the fall colors on the mountain and watched kids returning home from school. We walked back to the car discovering a gourmet oil and vinegar shop and stopped to take pictures of the late afternoon light on the old buildings. I accepted Robert's offer to drive me home, grateful to relax and enjoy the ride. I disliked admitting that I was tired. He drove us west on Route 84, into the sunset. We watched the amazing, bright colors behind an explosion of clouds, that looked like Medusa's hair, colored purple and red. It changed continuously, each detail noted by one or the other of us until it faded from view. It was then that we realized that we had followed the sunset well past our exit. The colorful view was a dramatic closure for the day and one of many times that I have missed that particular exit to the thruway. Nature is such a good way to find perspective and it did help, for a little while. Anxiety crept back in slowly; I did not sleep well.

Like I think this is new; being anxious and venting about the surrealistic nature of discovering my body holds cancer yet again. I am in my third year and entering my third round of cancer re-diagnosis. Tomorrow will be the "official" diagnosis, when I visit the oncologist, but I picked up the results today; I can at least empower myself that much. My body grows cancer behind my back and I feel like a spy trying to get the results. "Oh, I can't give you a copy of the report, but it's on the disc I gave you. It's company policy to not release the hard copy of the report for ten days following your scan," she tells me, smiling apologetically. I take the disc home and print out the report. The company policy has not caught up to the capabilities of the modern consumer.

I read to myself, *"IMPRESSION: EVIDENCE FOR TWO NEW BONY METASTATIC LESIONS IN WHAT APPEARS TO BE THE POSTERIOR ELEMENTS OF T12 OR L1 AND IN THE RIGHT ILIAC BONE JUST ABOVE THE ACETABULUM."* I have experience with cancer metastasizing to my T1 already and my organs appear to be good for now.

I call Diane to ask her, "What is the iliac? And the T12 or L1?," while I simultaneously research these bones on the internet. Now I know my doctor will tell me tomorrow that I have more bone "Mets." My friend Diane asks me, "How do you feel knowing this now?" There is that word again: "feel". How do I feel. How do I FEEL? I usually answer her with a verb, not a feeling. Today I feel impatient, ANGRY, tired of bullshit; I want to write my feelings, but not feel them. I would rather keep busy. After my last diagnosis I was all stressed out worrying about going on the drug Tykerb, but I have adjusted. Will I be put on a new chemo? Or radiation? I have done this before and I guess I will do it again, testing my body for the strength to deal with more side effects. I go to my emails and gratefully find my new metastatic friends from the retreat having a dialogue about bone Mets. Debbie and Denise are answering Jude's questions about their drugs, the effectiveness and the duration of time that they have been on them. Such good questions and responses are reassuring; I could be like them and still living years from now. I am in the chronic disease department that will continue to involve a cocktail of drugs. I might evolve a mouth full of sores that make talking difficult or neuropathy in the extremities that require a walker, but I won't die today. This is just a damn in-fucking-convenience. And you know what hurts? The tendonitis or arthritis in my wrist, exacerbated by one of the drugs

I take! The cancer lies secretively, quietly and only shows up in the scans. Luckily, I have no fractures and there are drugs for me to ingest to try to slow this down.

November 1, 2012

I dreamt of being in college. I was so out of place. Everything was done so differently now; you traveled around campus and the building we were in, on a conveyer belt. The belt was enclosed though and you had to wait for an opening, then jump inside and scramble to find a space. Every portal was different, different sized holes to enter, different seat designs.

I was working with the teacher on a project, kneeling on a table in the center of the room. I had on old lace edged, low crotched bloomers and I pooped out the side of them, onto the floor and continued working, pretending nothing happened. The TA came by and noticed it. The teacher said clean it up. He knew I did it, but did not tell the TA. The room was lit theatrically, under lit, casting shadows above each brick. It felt like an old tavern.

I caught the conveyer belt awkwardly again, scrambling up and over other passengers, mostly children and young adults with a few teachers. I went to the introduction of my next class, a draping class and inspected all the work details. She introduced the class and dismissed us. "No pulling grain lines in muslin?" I asked surprised, expecting homework to be assigned, to push us to achieve. She looked at me with a scowl. I walked out with the rest of the students, but I noticed all the details in the room especially the notions and fabrics, while they rushed off. I wanted to begin and excel; learn something I never knew before.

Jude came over yesterday. We took a long walk up Pearl and around the big loop and returned to the house for tea and cookies. At four-thirty I ran upstairs to put on a costume and makeup. Jude put on her turtle costume and we stood outside and handed out candy. It was so nice to have someone to talk to. She left at 6:45. I closed up at 7 and Bobby came over. I made up his face and threw the Alladin turban on him and we went to the Shiber-Cochran's house for the annual Halloween party.

Faith had most of the band this year, so adult types were confined to the kitchen. Lisa and Mike wore regular clothes saying they were Kingston Republicans, Kate was Frida again, Carole a version of herself, Karen and Mark were dressed in black wearing silly CVS blinking orange mesh wigs. Then Lynn and Doug joined us and we did the annual group "poem" and drawing. It was fun. Happy Halloween.

November 2, 2012

What a heavy day I had yesterday! Bobby picked me up and drove me to my Zometa infusion. It was fine. Then he dropped me off at Diane's for our work. She made notes for me afterwards because my wrist hurts to write. I cried and Diane hugged me, comforted me. She was happy to help me feel, but I am so uncomfortable reaching those feelings, the depths inside me, that I try hard to stay away from them. I am afraid they will drag me to depths that I will not return from. But I sit here today, in the comfort of my bed, typing, with Mila cleaning herself beside me.

I drove myself to memoir group yesterday and read "1973-1983 Ten Years in Three Word Sentences." Sharon wrote a piece pondering how death is so like birth, Annie read a poem about being raped by her husband on a beach and Roberta gave the next chapter about her brother's suicide. All this honesty and grief; it was a deep, deep day.

Bobby took Mom and me to Santa Fe last night and we had a nice dinner. Mom got a margarita and was soft and silly around the edges. We were both conscious that I couldn't hold her up because *I can't lift anything heavy.*

I cleaned out the spiral cupboard and laid matting down to keep it cleaner and got rid of a few items too. Stitched a shopping bag repair and vacuumed the downstairs, inspired by my 'Meta-Sista' Rose, who still makes meatballs and cleans her entire house after chemo. I don't feel fully productive though; like I'm waiting for the worst to happen, waiting for pain or sickness or new turn of tragedy. I need a schedule, but I don't make one. It is 3:30 and I have not showered. I'm feeling depressed, in a version or a shade of my own making.

November 4TH, 2012

I woke dreaming that I was living in a motel room, but keeping everything in my car for safekeeping. Today it seemed like I was sleeping in the lobby: there were two people in my bathroom, a couple unpacking their car thru my room; I was getting fed up with it and yelling for them to all leave my rooms. I needed to get in the bathroom! I needed to get my day going! This was not a subtle dream as I woke up needing to pee and needing to get up. We turned the clocks back last night, so I can afford this indulgence, but not if I intend to accomplish anything today.

"Team fall cleanup" was fabulous yesterday. It was so fun and relaxing and we got the whole yard put to bed for the winter. Susie stopped smoking. She is using something that her doctor referred to as a crutch, but she is happy to be off them. Leslie, Susie and I were talking about retirement and Linda said "AH-hem!!! Some of us still need to work!" Jim cut back all the trees and shrubs s efficiently! We (Mila and I) are ready for winter and the temperature fell to a very unsubtle hint that it was around the corner.

I have been missing contact with my son and finally called Mike Friday morning. "Hi Mom. How are you? I'm at work, could I call you back later?" I said I was calling to let him know I was thinking of him. He called after work on his drive to his Dad's for band rehearsal and told me about his great day.

Yesterday I spoke to Dana who is happily spending time with Shish who's visiting her at college. She sounds so happy and I am grateful. She said she is getting her work done and he took her and her friends out for deep dish pizza the night before. He's thinking that he might stay longer because of the post-Sandy Storm gas crisis, but I think perhaps they are having a very good time too. Matt called about the gas up in this neck of the woods because of the shortage where he is too.

I begin my Tykerb today: month 8.

I had dinner at Charlotte and Tony's. She made a delicious risotto with scallops, Brussels sprouts in caramelized onions and bacon, kale salad with pignoli nuts and parmesan. Dessert was an almond-chocolate 'candy. DELICOUS!!! All of it! And wonderful conversation too. I am so grateful to have such fabulous friends.

November 6, 2012

I dreamt that I was a passenger in a vehicle. It was a white jeep with only two seats with an attached trailer that had two more seats. The driver and another person were in the front seats, and since I was the guest, I jumped in a back seat, in the little trailer. It was white on the inside too, neat as a pin and reminded me of the interior of a small boat with pillows matching the upholstery. We were driving along on a small dusty road when the two people in front had a disagreement. The driver got out, with the car still running, to go to the bathroom. The jeep continued moving at the speed of a child's battery operated car, so theoretically, he would finish his business in time to jump back in as it continued moving along the small dusty road. I was peeved to be put in this danger, and sure enough, we watched in slow motion, what could go wrong. At this point it was with TV show detail: the camera focused on the foot pedal of the car and how the car hit a small slope, the pedal moved just slightly, the slope increased, the pedal fell slack to the side as the car increased speed and the slope led up to the main highway that had three lanes in each direction! The driver was not getting back in time and we couldn't go on the highway driverless! I knew the car had voice control too, so I yelled, "Stop! STOP!" The second yell was strong and efficient enough that it came to a complete halt just before hitting a wooden sign, also painted white. I don't know what the sign said because we were below it, only seeing the posts that held it. The driver jumped back in. We weren't supposed to go on the highway and he veered the jeep back to the slow dusty road. Everything had been white, all the other vehicles and signs, with white sand dunes flanking each side of the highway. The road was black and the sky was clear bright blue. It was a beautiful day.

This is my first dream after my Faslodex shots yesterday and the Dream Circle at the Oncology Support Program that I went to with Jude. I was disciplined enough to get the computer out and type this up!

We had a very good Metastatic Support Group today with a lively conversation: Bob, Tom, Suzanne, Me and Rosie. Rosie played my videos for the group. We talked about depression, getting out of bed, then veered into dangerously divisive political territory, and back out again.

I had dinner with Charlie at Stella's Restaurant tonight. We ordered a Caeser salad with chicken rottini with broccoli rabe and sausage; we split both dishes and a glass of red wine. It was really nice and synchronistic: I called him just as he had dialed my number.

I came home and got ready for bed when Mike Schneller called; Kate and Rennie invited us over to their new home to watch election results! We all went in our pajamas. Mike and Lisa picked me up to drive around the corner where we watched election drama and theatrics for an hour or so. Kate and Rennie unpacked dishes as we watched. Their home is lovely!

November 7th, 2012

I dreamt of an emergency situation; some impending, but unknown doom. I dreamt I was on a floating raft in the shallow water of an enclosed pool, in a small enclosed wildlife preserve. The water was rich with sea creatures moving under the clear water. I was looking at as much as possible because our time was limited. We would be told anytime now that is was time to leave the water. We were waiting for airplanes overhead. We still had time though and moved to a new pooled section by pulling my raft out of the water, walking on a narrow stone paved path that separated the pools, and putting the raft in the new pool, looking at the new wildlife under the water. There were all sorts of amazing fish and amphibians to look at, all colors and shapes, swimming amongst the flora and fauna. Two people said they would be right back, "Go ahead and keep looking," they told me, but I knew they *were too nervous to stay. I was unsure what to do without them, they were my guides, but I was calm and continued to look at the life, so close, just under the surface; such an opportunity that I might never have again. Soon enough, I will search for another guide, I thought, but for now I will enjoy this opportunity and I looked in the water again for new things to see. There were patches of taller grass to navigate with this section of the pool.*

Barbara Sarah suggested that I study <u>Naikan, Gratitude, Grace and the Japanese Art of Self-Reflection</u> I have begun. I am reading it and remember the book of Gratitude that helped me out of my depression and anger when Chas and I were separating and divorcing.

November 10th, 2012

I went to NYC on Friday to visit my new endocrinologist and, after a thyroid sonogram, was prescribed a thyroid medication for my goiter. Cousin David escorted me from the bus to the doctor, then to have lunch with Danielle and all the way downtown to Robert's.

Robert and I went to see <u>This Must Be The Place</u> with Sean Penn over at Sunshine Theatre. We walked behind a young couple and I felt I was walking behind myself; the 'me' of the 1970's, the 'me' with long legs in tight black jeans and long blonde hair. Robert noticed it too and said so this morning, but he said, "She didn't have your gait."

Back at his house we kissed, standing in his dimly lit apartment. We enjoyed our shared kissing; always a gift between us. It led us to the bed were we removed our clothing, sometimes helping each other and sometimes just doing it ourselves. We began slowly, I'm not confident that I can proceed and he is sensitive to my condition, but slowly, gently we engaged, at a new pace. My confidence was there, my comfort, and I reached orgasm; soft around the edges and sweet. We laughed to share it; to share our friendship. "We always could make each other laugh, couldn't we Carol?" We always could talk about it too; another gift of our friendship.

THE YOUNG WOMAN IN THE PHOTO 1977

There is a picture on my wall of a beautiful young woman with long blonde hair and a slender body. The photo was taken by one of her lovers. The two of them had escaped the city for the weekend; they walked, exploring the woods. She sat on a fallen tree and her lover squatted in front of her, looking up from behind his camera. A canopy of trees surrounded them. The tall young woman in the photo wears a thinly strapped red bodysuit that leaves her breasts barely covered. I notice her open smile that exposes her slightly crooked white teeth. She is energized by his adoration. I look at this picture and feel love for her too, her and her cocky confidence.

This lover worked at her shop and when he stayed for the night, he'd slip out the back door only to reenter through the front gate with the other employees. She lived in the back of her store, sleeping on a bright red captain's bed. When alone, she sometimes laid naked on her single bed to bathe in the light of the full moon that reached for her through the narrow alleyway.

She thrived on sexual energy and secrecy. She was a ninja lover that had learned to make a sport of intimacy. That was a time I thought I had few inhibitions, living a Gemini life, concealed openly in the East Village.

November 11, 2012

I am so grateful to wake up in my own bed and that I'm still able to be independent. The sun pours around the edges of my window shade and lets me know, gently, that it is time to get up. I allow it to tell me several times, before I listen and obey because I can; there is no rush.

It is time for breakfast. My solitude is a gift. My heat is busy heating my house, Mila is curled beside me and I have one cool leg sticking out of my covers to relieve my intensified hot flashes.

I was able to feel such comfort today in my warm bed with the sun shining in my windows. I did two sun salutation stretches before feeding my hungry cat and fish. I called to see how Joe was faring during the storm and reached out to Carole, to include her on my walk. I called my mother too, to check in on her and we talked about Thanksgiving.

I sent out a "sorry" to Carla about her new bone Mets. It made me cry to hear about it. I cried for her and sent a note to support her. I reached out to Jude to ask how she is doing; her mom passed last week and her son is visiting. I took myself for a walk up Loundsbury, quietly pondering my life.

November 12, 2012

I dreamt it was Thanksgiving and I had everyone over to my house; everyone I had ever had for a holiday and more! I was only slightly more ready than if they all came today! First to arrive was my nephew Mike, Jamie and the new baby. I was thrilled to see the baby! So new! But she could sit up already, grabbed a pen and drew me a picture. I went to the basement to get her more art supplies. While I was down there I saw that my dining room table was down there with all the leaves in it, fully expanded, but in the basement! Hmm, what was upstairs now? Friends from work followed me down and had wine glasses for water which they left on the table. Bobby came down to see if I should come up to greet the company; I had been downstairs for quite awhile. I carried wineglasses up off the table, trying to remember whose was whose, but no one claimed them. That meant I would have to wash them again. More work. Should we celebrate down here at the dining room table or upstairs on whatever? I began to pick up Christmas decorations left out on the floor and bags of candy that were left over from Halloween. No, it looked to like a basement down here.

I began to go up, but everyone began to come down and picked out a chair. I looked at the full table and the cloth was upside down, first things first, we have to fix that. I picked up two jackets flung over a chair, resting in a bowl of pasta with tomato sauce and hung them up with spaghetti dripping off a fur trimmed collar. I had no drinks. I asked Charlie to run for wine and Bobby to get other drinks. Charlie's whole family was there, alive and dead. His sister-in-law Alice's late mother too, all of his sister's kids, boyfriends and friends included; I ran upstairs and the young people were having a great time hanging out together outside. WE NEEDED TO SET THE TABLE! Had I even cooked? All the Pistone elders were sitting, waiting for the first course and I'm setting the table. It was an honor to serve them, but I was not ready, I had not known they would all honor me with their presence. They chose the big table in the basement and sat patiently. I was wondering what I was thinking being so unprepared. I had to serve a very large meal that would be stretched to the point of needing magic to do so, but somehow I was not fixated in panic. We would eat as best as I could do it. Getting people to help me was like herding cats. I would have to figure it out. I was still putting on a front to mask my anxiety of how I could pull this off. I had no freaking clue they were all coming. Maybe I was dead and this was my service. That would explain all the dead people at the table. I was dead too, still rushing to please everyone and serve an army of unexpected guests.

The Holiday stress is creeping in.

SUPPORT

November 18th, 2012

I now belong to several support groups for people with cancer. This is helping me to live beyond the boundaries of my own suffering. My suffering is put in perspective when visiting Tom in the hospital with severe back pain from metastases in his fractured spine. We have people who join our metastatic support group enthusiastically, but never come back. Perhaps because they are like I'd been before, in denial of the severity of my predicament, unable to handle seeing other people in an advanced state our disease. I feel seasoned by the laughter in our metastatic group while we share the study of life through this particular lens. We listen to each other's current diagnoses and worries, but share the other aspects of full lives too. Nancy is in Hospice and expressed that she is in a different place than the rest of us, but she shared her wisdom about pain control from her wheelchair.

Our Thursday Memoir Group with Abigail Thomas has members that have or had cancer, but there is evidence of other traumas layered into people's lives too. Child abuse and the suicide of a loved one are experiences given a voice in this safe environment. We listen to each other, talk about the writing, but don't sit and discuss the history of what brought us to this group except for what we put to the page and read.

Most recently I joined a Dream Circle and the participants all share the cancer diagnosis. Within two sessions we are sharing dreams that would have been hard to confess to strangers earlier in our lives.

We seek to understand the messages of our subconscious. Cancer is putting the moment front and center. Healing is taking steps bigger than chemotherapy, radiation and surgery. Communication feels urgent.

Yesterday I was part of our new Breast Cancer Option's Women with Metastatic Breast Cancer Support Group which spawned off of our retreat last September. For most of us this was a mini-reunion. We had four new women there that were so grateful to join us. The one thing they all had in common was, "Before today I never knew anyone else with this disease. I thought I was the only one." Two of the women needed to share every detail of their journey. We all listened attentively. I think we have all felt a great relief getting to know each other over the last two months. Another new participant spoke of refusing a new treatment because she would lose her hair for the third time. She was vehement about it and "Tired of all of this." She was drawing the line here. Barbara and Jude showed how their hair was coming back again; Rose spoke of her second round of hair loss being about one week away, "Next time you see me, I'll be wearing hats again!" Mary was sporting a cute wig. The choice was clear and Rose spoke it, "Either you're bald and living or having hair in your coffin." Celia had been quiet, but spoke next. I noticed she was the only woman in the room who still had a large, exposed cleavage. She was grateful to be here, she said, but after she spoke, she went to the waste basket to throw up.

We will meet again in January, but keep our connection on Facebook and through emails to share the constant re-diagnosis of such a large group. It is an amazing experience, really. I have said many times over the last three years that cancer has given me many gifts. I do not choose to be sick, but I am grateful for the life lessons I continue to learn about human existence.

November 25th, 2012

I am sitting home, alone post Thanksgiving weekend. Connie and Richard took off a half hour ago and I finished vacuuming, removing the leaves from the dining room table, and generally pushing things back into place. I feel a righteous energy flow through me; putting things "right."

Kate called to see if I wanted to join her and Rennie for turkey pot pie. I said yes! I will bring the pumpkin pie for dessert. They invited Lisa and Mike Schneller too, for dinner. Lillian made pecan bars to add to dessert. I held Mira while final dinner preparation was completed. It was sweet, but I am tired and anxious about the MRI of my brain tomorrow. I am not paralyzed by it; it is just under the surface. I am living in the present, conscious of the luxury of being well, while knowing that what is seen tomorrow could change everything. It is always this way, but I am conscious of the potential.

THE GIFT OF GRATITUDE

Since I've been undergoing treatments and big diagnostic tests for cancer, I've had a hard time planning very far in advance. Last Monday I had an MRI of my brain and waited most of the week before someone told me the results. Aileen answered the phone and said, "Carol, I was just going to call you. Dr. Bruce took a look at your MRI and said you are all clear. There were no signs of any brain tumors." I yelped and a cheer ran through our memoir group. My heart lightened. Let the Holidays begin! I will decorate for Christmas! I have three months ahead of me before the next scan and I'm going to enjoy them fully. I still have Metastatic Cancer and metastases to the bone, but every positive result overrides the current negative results. I feel like Tarzan about to swing through the jungle, holding the vine and now, with these results, I'll go ahead and jump off the branch, "Aaghaaaa! Aaarrrrooooo!

My Mom knows how to do this Holiday particularly well. She came out of the Depression, the youngest of three children to older parents. "Our parents were worn down by the time your Mother was born and they spoiled her," my Aunt Margaret once told me. Their father was a very resourceful man, a plumber by trade and he grew a big vegetable garden in the back yard. Mom said they didn't lack for much, even in the hardest of times.

For her children, Mom created a fairy tale Christmas. Dad would bring a tree home and it would sit on the porch in a bucket of water until we were ready to set it up. Our living room was prepared, chairs moved, and then the tree was brought inside. Dad placed it in the old metal tree stand and screwed it securely with much debate about it straightness. One year Mom brought Dad's selected tree back to the Little League on Partridge Street because it was so crooked. Another year Dad bought a tree that was so bent that it was almost horizontal. That year our neighbor, Mary Jane came over with a hammer and string to fix it. Mom had ideas of perfection and didn't like any detail to fall short of her expectations.

Then it was time to decorate the tree. Using the wooden ladder, Dad had to wrap the string of lights around the tree having the tallest child or Mom handing them back around to him. Mom took each ornament out of the tissue paper and told us a story about when and where it came from, before she supervised their placement on the branches. Some were recently purchased from the Five & Dime, but in time became part of our childhood memories. Every year someone would make something to add to the decorations. In kindergarten Bobby and I each made a pair of traced mittens out of wallpaper strung with yarn and each year we got to hang our mittens. I turned a ketchup bottle into a red candlestick holder in Girl Scouts and Mom pinned sequins and beads onto Styrofoam balls as per the instructions from The Ladies' Home Journal. In high school Connie made baker's clay angels for everyone. They all became family treasures. The most revered ornament is still an old, dry chenille bell with two-inch long fringe hanging off of its circular edge. On the front of the faded red bell is a soft portrait of St. Nicholas. The other day I asked, "Mom, how old is the bell?"

"Okay," she said calculating the answer. "It was on my Christmas tree forever and I'm almost 85 years old and I think it was on my mother's tree before that and she would've been 125 this year, so it has to be at least one hundred years old. Your Gramma's childhood tree would've been very, very simple by today's standards. They decorated with oranges and nuts. Your

Gramma used to tell the story of a poor family that came in to admire their tree. The children came in and stood looking up at it; the youngest, a little boy, stood pointing at the tree saying, "I want that 'ornnie' up there on that tree!" mom told me the story yesterday, but I heard that very story on my Grandmother's luxurious lap every Christmas, and other times of year too, when any of her grandchildren asked her to tell it.

Mom told me that my Father's family had a tradition of putting up a Christmas tree, but only one child, out of the five children, got a special gift each year. Dad grew up without things. He was a newsboy by the age of three, but we suspect he was used for sympathy by his older brother to sell more newspapers in front of the Queensbury Hotel. Dad never had the happy traditions or memories that our Mother had, but once Mom got the Christmas ball rolling, Dad would jump on board hiding gifts, assembling toys, partially eating the cookies left for Santa; as young children we didn't see or feel his reservations. Our early Christmases were filled with colorful lights, sparkling tinsel, stacked gifts wrapped by aunts, uncles and grandparents, along with gifts left by Santa under the tree, all beautifully displayed. We hung our stockings over the fireplace on Christmas Eve with our photos taken in homemade, matching pajamas.

Mom said her family's stockings were hung Christmas Eve and filled by morning with nuts, an orange and a piece of candy. "We would get up at 4:00 am," she told me, "and go to 5:00 am mass. We weren't allowed to look at the tree before that. It stood behind the closed door to the dining room, displayed in the bay window. We could look in our stocking, hung over the fireplace, but couldn't eat any so we could receive Communion. I'd run out ahead of the family," she added, "and jump up and down trying to peek in the dining room window to see the presents."

One year, when my children were young, I decided to make baker's clay stars as Christmas gifts for our friends attending our Caroling party. I recruited Mike, Dana and my friend Robert, to ambitiously manufacture a ton of them: rolling out the dough, cookie cutting the stars, drying them, painting them, varnishing and stringing them. After Christmas Caroling that year we gave everyone a star and many friends still have them. I still hang ours too and think of the old days when my children were young.

So I will decorate for the Holidays. Dana is coming home from college after her first semester and Mike and his girlfriend Sara will join us for Christmas Eve dinner, our tradition.

My brother Matt carried the decorations down from the attic for me. I'll dust and polish the banister before wrapping the garland around the railing. I'll gently un-wrap the ornaments one by one, remembering each person that gave it to me with a prayer. I have the frail paper cut outs of an elephant and a lion that Richard made for me in 1980 when I had a Christmas party in my newly renovated apartment. Molly had been a student of mine and gave me a pair of traditional Chinese silk ornaments from her first trip overseas. Paula was a big fan of the Tonner Doll Company and each year she sent the employees doll ornaments dressed in fashions from different decades. I collected about eight of them over the years and hang them from a garland over my tree near the window. Paula generously bid and bought a one-of-a-kind doll that Tonner auctioned off for me as a fundraiser when I was first diagnosed in 2009; she died a year later of breast cancer herself. Interspersed between the dolls are glass ornaments that my friend's son made for me before he went to prison and I hook these on the garland with prayers for both of them. There is the Rudolph from Charlie's sister Maria, and Alice gave us the little gold church, Gannon gave us the small drift wood painted as Santa. Sally who babysat my children with all the comforts of Gramma's kitchen when they were so young, gave us the small jointed wood moose that hangs of the tree and the St. Nicolas that she made sits on the piano. I place them with prayers for her growing family now that she really is a grandmother.

My sister Connie gave us many cloth ornaments to place along the bottom of the tree when the kids were toddlers and Chrissy gave us hand-blown glass balls to hang at the top. Bobby brought us back cut out tin decorations from his trip to Mexico and I hang my mittens I made in kindergarten next to the baker's clay "cookies" varnished with pictures of my children: a picture of Dana dressed in her favorite five-year-old princess dress and Michael blowing his trumpet. Each one is placed with a prayer. I hang the ornaments Anne and Ray gave to my children over the years and I am so grateful for their generosity, there is even the hat ornament that Debbie gave me at work and I hope she is happy despite the dissonant ending to our acquaintance. The baker's clay stars and mini disco balls are sprinkled about the house.

So as my neighbor Billy told me last week, "Carol! You have to decorate for the Holidays. It'll make you feel better!" I have to agree; so many prayers of thanks and gratitiude with each ornament that I put on the tree, reminds me that I'm not alone in this life. Please accept my deepest thanks for your being part of it, of this Holiday and the bigger picture too, part of the world that we all share.

December 19th, 2012

It was a very big day: Dana's boyfriend, Shish, picked her up in Chicago and drove her home! I helped unpack the light things out of the car and we shifted things around in the attic. There is a whole lot of shifting going on around here.

I went to Diane's yesterday to video of "The Gift of Gratitude," but I was having difficulty reading it. We took several takes before I was able, with Diane's help, to figure out what was bothering me. I shortened the piece on the fly and read only the beginning, about cancer, and the end, about gratitude and felt pleased enough. I explained first to Diane, and later to the Oncology Support Program Mets Group, about the adrenaline rush I get from a good scan and how I wrote that piece when I was high from the results. Reading it now, however, two weeks post-results, the smoke is already creeping under the door infiltrating my bliss. It was hard to get it up to read the whole piece, it felt too long for YouTube, but shortened was fun when I recaptured my original motivation. Diane asked me the right questions and was patient for the answers.

December 20, 2012

I dreamt an epic dream this morning. I was just sailing along in life. I went to Chicago to see Dad and Mary, but my luggage was stolen. My friend called and told me where to find it. I walked to a location, a small walkway bridge over a ravine in the city, a rather desolate place, and there was my Gucci leather duffle bag. The location was a notorious gang hangout. An open plaza surrounded by tall high rise office buildings on one side and a lower skyline of houses and trees on the other side. The bag was open and most of the things inside were gone, but my keys were strewn about in the dirty water. I recognized the beaded string attached to my keychain, that Dana had made me when she was little. I picked up my keys, leaving the rest behind. I found my rolling luggage in a similar similar location. It was odd that no one was around; not a soul in sight.

I was back at Dad and Mary's explaining about finding my keys, wondering why I didn't bring the rest of the bags with me, why had I abandoned them? A woman runs up to the door and hands me the newspaper. I look at it; it's the Daily Freeman with the headline about my trip to Chicago and about my luggage being stolen. It put me at increased risk that whoever stole my luggage could know my name and address too. It was like I was being handed over to a gang. My friend sent me the paper to warn me, but I'm not sure about what? It's all a mystery and I'm having a hard time wrapping my head around it. My friend seems to have a better understanding and perspective of the situation. I am clueless, but feel the urgency to figure it out; my life is in danger.

Today it hits me: how much I have planned next week, actually this week! Memoir group today, Saturday night is Christmas Caroling, Sunday is Shish and Dana's dinner party to introduce his family to ours, then Christmas Eve dinner at my house, Christmas day with Mom, then go to NY for a few days and come home to Cousin David, Aisling and the girls visiting up here. Wow! Am I ready? Can I make it? Keep up with the plan that does not include cancer as any aspect except for its constant companionship?

December 22nd, 2012

I dreamt about being in a boarding house and it was hard to find my apartment. There were so many personalities in the house, so many tourists. I did find my room, but then it was hard to find again. It was a tacky hotel with white "faux" antique patinas on the doors and furniture. There were so many tourists, or refugees, walking, milling around, and looking for their rooms. Okay, now we weren't one of them because we found our room. I looked out into the hallway, unsure about why we were there. Where was our permanent home? There was a light shining from the bathroom that gave an inner glow to our rooms. They were rooms that would have white tinsel trees to decorate for Christmas. Everything had the false lushness of the 1960's.

I had an apartment and I told the real estate agent that my daughter and I were going upstate for a long weekend. We walked up to the bus station and the women behind the counter said, "No, you can't go there."

"Why? What do you mean we can't go there?" I asked.

"There is weather coming," one of the women replied.

"The weather? We're worried about weather? The buses won't take us?"

"That's right. All the busses are stopping. We have a blizzard coming anytime now and it will be really bad. You need to go home and get ready." They were dressed in summer clothes, as we were, but they were urgent and serious. It seemed impossible to me that this storm was around the corner and we didn't feel it coming. We walked back home to North Main. I opened the French doors to my apartment and was surprised to find them unlocked. Why would I forget? It's good we came home, I thought. Then I saw the realtor, in a mink coat, the sign of success. "I thought you were gone!" she said. I was happy and surprised to see her. I explained why we were unable to get out of town. She seemed more knowledgeable by wearing a fur coat. We still wore our summer clothes.

Yesterday, Dana and I ran off early to her dentist appointment for her long overdue maintenance. I got to see our dentist and he said he saw my YouTube video. It was sweet. Then Dana took me out to breakfast at Duo. So tasty.

PRE-CHRISTMAS RANT

Then I sat in my reclining chair. Dana went to sleep at Shish's. I was alone again in the house. I read and then made popcorn and watched The Hedgehog on my laptop. It was a wonderful movie with beautifully realized characters. I stayed up too late feeling hesitant about sleeping. I can be tired during the day, but delay going to bed. I am not sure why, but it continues to be so. Everything is in a flux that I cannot smooth. Dana's things, in boxes, are everywhere and not much more can squeeze into her little room. I have unearthed things with no place to put them. We are women in flux. Change is everywhere. I am adjusting.

My soul is pouting though I try to control my outer appearance. Dana and I are not going to be able to please each other; someone is going to be pinched. I studied martyrdom, so I assume it should be me. This day is at odds with everyone in my immediate world. Dana is cranky, and I am uneasy. Shish found her a whole kit of Dremmel accessories and that was what Charlie was getting her, now he is stressed that Shish could get her girlfriend stuff that her father cannot and I already find the whole gift giving thing stressful. I have the added stress of possibly, but not definitely, having added guests for Christmas Eve dinner. I am vague and un-showered.

Dana fell asleep for a long nap and did not finish making the cookies she started. Boxes still stagnate in the living room though I have begun to move them towards the studio.

Connie worked on Friday; she and Richard arrived Saturday and joined us for Christmas Caroling at Kate and Rennie's house. She had a "minor" headache, the average person would not know; they were active Carolers. Connie drove Mom home earlier and Richard enjoyed a bit of wine and stayed till the end of the party with me, when I drove him home quite giddy.

Kate and Rennie were so sweet to offer to host my traditional Caroling party at their house this year. It has been my celebration for many years now, but my friends knew it would be enough for me to do Christmas Eve dinner. I felt responsible to help in every way that I could and wanted to get there just before six o'clock. I got dressed for Christmas Caroling in a humorous mismatched red plaid outfit with my green Doc Marten's boots. That began to lighten my mood, but Dana was not ready to leave which left me scrambling to the car carrying cookies, cheesecake, our caroling music books and silverware to drive around the corner to the party. I began swearing and slamming the cabinet doors. I wanted to scream, I wanted help. I was acting mad, but if I really thought about it, I had to acknowledge, that I really felt sad. I am sad to lose my daughter, though I like Shish very much. I picture her saying, "Uppie! Uppie! Uppie!" as a tiny girl wanting me to pick her up and now I hear her telling me, "Mom, I've been on my own at college for three months now. I'm not used to being directed and told what to do!" My children aren't interested in my Christmas Caroling party. I guess this is how it works. Was I different to my mother? I place myself as the main road, but they need to fork off on their own. I am uncomfortable with this precarious balance; I feel like I am standing in a row boat and any sudden move will tip us out. Any exposure of strong feeling will alienate.

When I arrived they were almost ready; Kate was whipping up a kale salad and I watched her assemble it because I was making one for Christmas Eve dinner too. I had just seen the woman at Mother Earth's serving kale salad and took a copy of their recipe for the dressing. Kim,

Jody and Diane all saddled up beside me to ask how Kate was going to dress the kale salad as they were all planning to make one for Christmas dinner too. Adams Market had the kale prominently displayed as we each entered the store for our holiday shopping. "Where's Dana?" was the other popular question.

Dana made it to the party after awhile and mingled, catching up with her many friends and their parents, but she made it clear to me the day before that she did not want to stay and sing. They had stayed up until 5:00 am cleaning Shish's apartment in preparation for the "meeting of their families" and they were tired. Shish would come to pick her up, say hello to people and they would leave. His mother, Anna, would be at his apartment and there was much to do before Charlie, Mike, Sara and I joined them for dinner the following evening. Dana would be helping Anna cook the Armenian meal. Dana had already been scorched by her grandmother's fear driven fury about "The 29-year-old-Armenian-tattoo-artist-boyfriend," but Shish was looking forward to meeting *her*. He entered the party in full swing, after a busy day at the "office" and headed right to her with his long arms open, embracing her with his full charm. He shocked her with his forthrightness and left Gramma like Maggie Smith in a Downton Abbey episode with jaw agape. He told me the night before, "Carol, I get it! I am a grandmother's total nightmare! To hear your wonderful granddaughter is dating an older, fat, Armenian tattoo artist? I'd freak out too!"

I find myself repeatedly saying, "I can't make this shit up!"

So Sunday morning rolls around and I pop over to Mom's for coffee talk, but Connie is full-out sick with a migraine. Luckily she brought her lasagna already prepared. I walked in the door as she called for a bucket. I ran to the basement to grab it and Richard ran it upstairs to her. Mom, Richard and I sat and chatted for a bit, but all my prep was going to be solo and I headed home to set the table for Christmas Eve. I spent the afternoon doing that, and then dressed festively for dinner in Newburgh. Charlie picked me up at four with some wine and I carried my homemade cheesecake and cookies. The drive to Newburgh was pleasant and Shish's neighborhood was borderline sketchy. We walked around back, up the back deck staircase to the second floor and knocked. We could see them all in the kitchen, Dana being very pleasing and focused on her task. They could not hear us though and we resorted to calling on our cell phones. They got the calls as they turned and saw us, which confused them, "Why didn't you just knock, Mom?"

We had a lovely dinner festively arranged on a long folding table in the living room. The dining room is where Shish and his roommate have their art studio. Taxidermy animals hung off the walls and two extra large cats, Rico and Kitty, roamed the apartment. Dana looked stressed being perfect for Anna, helping cook dinner. Charlie and I joined Mike and Sara in the living room in front of the huge flat screen television with the Food Network on. Anna's hummus was the best I have ever tasted. We made small talk until dinner was served and then feasted on the abundance of Armenian delicacies Anna and Dana had made for our pleasure.

I sit in my bed next to Mila and pray for my kids. Pray that Mom, Dad and Mary, my siblings, Chas, Robert and all my cousins and friends are happy and well this Christmas. Life is amazing.

HAPPY FUCKING HOLIDAYS

Delirious dreaming: the spiraling open of a Christmas tree skirt, continuously spiraling open; ivory ribbed cotton with large cloth covered buttons, reminiscent of Victorian bloomers. I pick up one corner and it spirals open taller than the tree itself. Continued delirium where I fold everything smaller. I am in a small car and when I get out of it to park in a small lot I remove the driver's seat, fold the car in half and ride the seat only inside a small chapel that looks perfect for a small performance, but there is no backstage, only a spiral staircase going up. At the end of the pew section is a garage that has a small trailer deli in it. Cars drive inside to place an order. Two small cars park inside and then a large van pulls in too, packed with large people, and they can't exit their vehicle. I exit the building, step outside and can't find my car. They look so different when folded and which one is my seat? I have to use my key fob to open the trunk and then I am sure it is my car. My seat had folded so neatly into the size of a sandwich box and looks like a Victorian button or the Christmas tree skirt folded up.

I made it through the Christmas season before coming down with the flu on New Year's Eve. Luckily I wasn't planning to join any festivities that night. My body aches to sit or lie; to move brings doubt of my strength, but I move nonetheless. The coughing gods have temporarily relieved my violent retching. I sit here breathing in and out unobstructed. My body rests in the ache. I look around at the Christmas ornaments like they are delirium, put up in a frenzy of holiday optimism that lays flaccid inside me. It is easier to close my eyes than to look at it all around me. I do not have the strength to take them down; I am not supposed to carry anything heavy so I can't get the storage containers from the attic. The decorations will mock me until I put them away. I am satisfied to be on this side of the holidays. They can stay up those decorations, go ahead and mock; you can't hurt more than the day did. You can put the same cast of characters in a room, but you can't predict what they'll do.

I am recovering slowly from Christmas Eve. I did not rip down the decorations in a tantrum of self-hatred and loathing. That was very restrained on my part. I knew I would regret the drama of ruining heirlooms, though the kids would not care as much as I would. I sat in my chair with my pity party. I did not say what I felt. How could I? Who would I tell?

On Christmas Eve day I was up early beginning dinner preparations. Dana and Shish stayed overnight with me so they could sleep in. They began their appetizers and other contributions for dinner when they got up. I tried not to be stressed out about timing, and lightened up by playfully taking photos of Shish's solid tattooed calves standing barefoot in my freezing kitchen. Dana saw me and hissed, "What the hell are you doing MOM?" I was a tourist in my kitchen taking pictures of her boyfriend's calves. I was trying to feel confident about my thrift store gifts that were purchased under my mother's mandate, "WE ARE EXCHANGING GIFTS THIS YEAR!" I was struggling with the pressure, expectations and potential disappointments.

Dana and Shish finished their cooking and showers as the guests arrived. Dana said she had to run out for a last minute gift at Bed, Bath & Beyond; Shish, Mike and Sara joined her. "We'll be back by six, I swear Mom." Meanwhile Connie forgot the extra sauce at Mom's house and ran back to get it, sneaking relief of her migraine for another hour. Charlie looked around and said, "Where the hell did everybody go? It's time for dinner, for God's sake!! It's just plain rude!," as he stormed out the door.

The kids were re-entering the house as Charlie turned on his car. He was sitting outside as I told Dana and Mike, "Call your father. He left upset and hungry because you had all disappeared." "No way! He just saw us come in. Mom, I told you we'd be back by six and we are." How can no one be wrong and everyone is right? We all know Charlie gets low blood sugar. Dana told me she had not gotten the other part of her father's gift and I knew she could not be empty handed for him, of all people. She proceeded to wrap gifts as we got dinner on the table.

I sat on the inside of the table, farthest from the kitchen, symbolizing how out of control the whole event was for me. I did not take the seat at the head of the table, the seat I held for all these years of holding our feasts. My nephew Mike and his wife Jamie brought their adorable baby daughter, Giulietta. Mom and Connie had each made a lasagna, Dana and Shish made the creamy, cheesy, green bean casserole. I made the massaged kale salad, pies and cheesecake. Mike and Sara brought beverages and the happy news of their engagement. We had half of Sara's homemade apple pie leftover from the Armenian feast at Shish's apartment the night before. My gifts were disappointing, especially to Dana, and I'd had it for the holidays.

I forget that I too am susceptible to the Holiday blues. I generally think of myself as optimistic and cheerful. I dressed festively and wrote a piece about being grateful around Christmas, reminded by all the ornaments that I hung with prayers of thanks to all the people in my life who have helped me. I took my time decorating after my clear MRI of the brain and looked forward to my daughter coming home from college. The reality was harsh; the holiday expectations continue to pressure for unachievable perfection. Christmas Caroling is the highlight of my Holiday festivities, sharing food and song with family and friends that want to partake in the real spirit of the season. The rest is just too much.

January 4, 2013

Work with Diane: I am recovering from my cold/flu; she touched points that I could have screamed from the condensation and compression of the illness and also the sadness of falling off the pace of my life and all that was keeping me well. I miss my support groups and writing, my dinner with Mike and Lisa on Tuesdays; the list goes on and on and I am sad. Diane reminded me not to turn it in on myself, but it is too late for that, that is how I got sick in the first place, but maybe I have only had a cold and not added to the cancer. We did guided imagery. I have the feeling of spinning in the torrent of water going down the drain. Head over heels, out of control, spiraling out of control. "Just go with it," she recommended. "What do you see?" The swirling of the water, the suction.... "Go with it, let yourself go and tell me what you see." Its black, darkness as I slide along with the current; up and down small curves in the pipes. At the end I am stopped by the filter. I am still a body and so I am trapped between the current of the flow and the filter. I see light above the water level outside of the filter, but behind me is darkness. I wait till the flow of water subsides and I clamor on my hands and knees to climb back up the pipe through the sludge. I grab the long strands of Dana's hair stuck in the drain to climb up and out the last long stretch. "What do you see now," Diane asks. Light. I am small enough to sit in the sink in my white bathroom. It is white, light, quiet; peace. I hold my knees to my chest and rest after my journey through the pipes and the adventure of my return. I am not ready to leave and pass bodiless through the filter. I still live and as I breathe, my body regains its natural size; each breath restores proportion. My guide, Metatron, reminds me to keep an open heart, like the space around my small self in the white bathroom; I visualize a space of white light, peace around my heart to protect it from closing against love. The pain of loving my children lures my heart to close against it; to close them out. It hurts to be susceptible to this pain, but a border of peace could protect it, strengthen it to remain open. I need to speak my truth. I need to remind my children about my illness and what I need from them to help me around the house. If it is no longer of interest to them to help me, then I will consider letting it go, selling home.

MY WHISPERING HIP

My right hip has begun to communicate with me. It's become a regular occurrence. It is not saying much, just whispering. I cross my legs and I hear my hip; I uncross them. I find myself standing, thrusting my right hip forward, leaning weight on my right leg when my hip reminds me to balance on both feet. In the shower, balancing on my right leg, to wash my left foot, I become conscious of the tenuous position and I contemplate buying a stool to sit on for feet washing in the near future.

Tonight I sat at the kitchen table talking to Dana, who is nineteen now. We have been proud of our affectionate relationship and that she has been able to plop down on my lap and hug me anytime. I had to speak up though, about my hip, and I preferred to do it before she plopped again. "I don't want you to feel rejected Dana," I said, "but I don't think you can sit on my lap anymore. My right hip is irritating me and I am afraid to aggravate it. I'm sorry Girlie." "Don't worry about it Mom. It'll get better and then I'll sit on your lap again!" was her response.

Stage-Four Metastatic Breast Cancer lives in my right hip and spine. I am on shots of Faslodex in my ass to subdue my estrogen and the infusion of Zometa to fill in my bones. The pill chemo, Tykerb, crosses my blood-brain barrier to quiet the Her2Neu positive proteins that encourage cancer growth everywhere, including my brain. I am in a good place, a quiet place of subdued cancer. I am fortunate that there are targeted drugs to throw at my variation of this disease so that I can continue my life. I try to be conscious every day that this time is extra. This new day is a gift for me to share and learn. I have time to work on sharing a little more time or wisdom with my children, though they don't need it right now. I am in the sidebar of their lives, but if I write, then maybe one day, they will pick this up and know that I love them and that I was thinking of them as I passed through the last sixth of my life.

  Earlier in the day, Bobby drove Mom and me down to Matt and Atiya's newly rented house in North Salem. My brothers assisted our 85-year-old Mom up the outside stairs and I paid attention to each step myself. I toured the old farmhouse, admiring the wide plank floor boards and wrinkly glass windows. Then Matt and I stepped outside. We walked far out by the horse pasture. We walked past the large dressage barn and over towards the fenced in area, where Whiskey stood waiting for Matt and the carrots that he held in his hand. Matt told me that usually they had to walk down to the bridge to cross the stream. Now, though, the stream was frozen so he stepped down on to it and slipped slightly on the thin layer of new snow. It was gorgeous outside, a perfect day for a visit and walk. I drank in the refreshing cold air, the blue sky and the long winding stone walls that lead up the hill through woods. A thin layer of white lay on the fence rails and tree branches. I looked all around soaking up the beauty; hesitating about taking that step onto the ice, but Matt's hand reached for mine. I accepted his strong grip, but laughed nervously at the weight of us together on the frozen stream where twenty feet away, the water flowed, gurgling over rocks. We glanced, smiling at each other and quickly separated. It was nice to see my brother happy and proud, showing me his new residence. "Look at how this horse has trained me to bring him carrots," he said. "He bit Mira today, but here's a carrot to feed him." "No thanks, Bro," I replied. I thought about how I like my fingers. I know my reticence is the opposite of my youngest brother's daring, adventurous ways, but he has developed patience for me and the cancer in my bones.

MOM'S WORRY

We sat and talked some more, enjoying each other's company. We had eaten dinner and watched a movie on her TV, but now the evening was ending and my Mother began to complain, beginning with all her worries about Dana. She disapproves of Dana's boyfriend. I sit up out of my relaxed position and explain all that Dana is managing to do for herself, all that she is successfully working on and towards, but Mom worries that Dana isn't helping me enough; she should be home and doing more things for me. She wants me to reel my daughter in and demand her to stay by my side. Mom worries about my health and I know that she worries that I will die before her.

Dana was home during the hard and thick of it. During most of her high school years, Dana was the one that held my head if I needed to cry and told me it was all going to be okay. I have Stage-Four Metastatic Cancer, but Dana said it was all going to be okay. We had a role reversal and I never saw her cry. She wanted to be strong for me. Dana needs to establish a life for herself now, a life that she wants and is drawn to. There will be time enough for my children to rally around me again and help me, as I need it.

It seems to get heavy as I leave. The conversation leaves the moment and goes into the spare room of my Mother's worry. I used to argue with her, not realizing that it was just a room cluttered with her thoughts, all the thoughts that have no place else to be. As I prepare to leave, she flings open that door, releasing the pent up thoughts to fly about like litter on a breeze. Her thoughts swirl around me and this time I do not swat them, but see them for what they are; the clutter and dust of my Mother's worry. Dana has been the closest grandchild of the last ten years; all the others are grown and unappreciative of the olden times when their Grandmother took care of them. My Mother tries to hide her grief over losing her closest granddaughter to adulthood; she wants to refuse, yet again, the inevitability of growing older.

 I stand by my Mother's side door, ready to leave, as the dust of her disappointments spiral around my head. My Mother cannot control the room of her worry, its opening or closing. I open the door and walk into the fresh air of a brisk, late winter night and I compliment my Mother's decision to fix her little side porch. She stands in the cold air accepting the compliments that she deserves. That is the note that we can end on. She has more love than she has places for and it makes her pout, pushing out the very people that she wants near.

SURVIVNG TOM
Part One
February 2013

There have been many visits to the hospital to see my friend, Tom, over the short time that I have known him. The first was when he returned from vacation and they found metastases in his spine. More recently, his chemotherapy made him violently ill. This time, after weaving my way through the labyrinth of hallways, I found that Tom did not have one of his usual rooms with a view of the Catskill Mountains; he was in the first room of the Oncology & Hospice Care ward. I found Tom sleeping vulnerably with his mouth open, reminding me of a bird fallen from a nest, his top sheet twisted in his lap. I placed the small container of homemade cookies on the table across his bed and sat in the chair beside him.

I looked around the room and saw signs of other visitors; a back pack and pocketbook in the chair near the doorway. I reached over and touched his hand. He stirred, groggy on pain medication, but opened his bright blue eyes that looked happy to see me. He held my hand in both of his as he flashed his infectious smile.

"How are you feeling today, Tom? Are you in pain?"

"Yes, Carol, about a ten, about a ten," he repeats, short of breath. Tom is talking through the pain in total stillness; the tumors in his spine have broken vertebrae. His chemo has been discontinued and he accidentally took his pain medication too close together. He holds my hand while asking, "How will I know if it's time to let go, Carol?"

I am a novice at this conversation about death, but it is time to learn. I have been asking myself these questions and I am also seeking answers. "Do you believe in God?" I asked, knowing that he does. "YES," he states quickly. "I think we ask for God's guidance, Tom. God can help us to know when it's time to make that decision." I want to help him and make it easier somehow. I hope that I am accessing my sage spirit, and not my ego that would pose as wisdom. He pats the edge of his bed, asking me to sit nearer.

"I wish that we had met twenty years ago, Carol," he said while holding my hands. Then he surprises me by pulling my head to his chest, holding it there while I chuckle, and respond into his hospital gown, "Tom, we would have fought all the time! We are on opposite sides of the fence!" He is from Cincinnati, Ohio and likes sports and racecars; I have lived an artist's lifestyle in New York.

"No, it would have kept things lively Carol; it would have kept things alive." He held my head tighter to his chest and added sadly, "I miss this so much, Carol. I miss this so much." I know that it is closeness and physical intimacy that he speaks of.

I sat up and stroked his arm, looking at this friend, this man I have only known since last August. I joined the Metastatic Cancer Support Group in July while Tom was away; the addition of his positive energy helped me to commit to staying in the group. The core of our group has formed fast bonds; we find comfort in our shared wisdom, humor and fears. There is no time to waste.

He looked at me as we sat holding hands and I said, "Tom, we *met because* we have Metastatic Cancer. It's amazing that we get this life changing disease and it brings us together with people we would never have known otherwise. I believe we are meeting at the *right* time, Tom. We have been helping each other to live and maybe we are also here to support each other as we approach death; intimacy has taken on a new form. It's time to open up to the love of the universe. We are *surrounded* by love if we open to it," I conclude, realizing I am trying to jam as many of my pearls as I can in this small window of time. I looked up from his hand to his face, to make sure he was still awake. He was; he sat with tears in his eyes as I continued to stroke his arm.

His grandsons were giggling as they ran into the room and I stood up to meet them and Tom's daughter, Amanda. The two and four-year-old boys jumped up onto "Paw Paw's" lap and saw "Cookies!" They gobbled them down leaving Tom in a bed of crumbs and love. It was nice to meet the part of his family that he's talked about so much in our support group. I took their pictures and admired the older boy's toy truck that 'Paw Paw' gave him. He turned to his grandfather, who reminded him of the name of the truck. I was a witness to Tom's legacy and suddenly very conscious of death's approach. I could see Amanda loves her Dad and so do the boys sitting in his arms watching the cartoons on the TV. They've been a big part of what he's been living for.

Part Two

It was the next morning that I was told that Tom had signed DNR and DNI paperwork with his daughters present. That was a huge step towards his youngest daughter's acceptance of his approaching death. We missed Tom at our metastatic support group's post-Valentine's day party; he had really been looking forward to it. I remember when Nancy offered to throw the party, and the date was set, that I wished we could do it sooner, so everyone in the room *that* day would be able to be there, but life is planned for the living and the optimistic, who plan ahead.

We all drew Valentines for Tom, and a bunch of us went over to visit en masse and shared a lively conversation with our friend. He was having a better day; his pain was well managed. I was part of the last group to leave. I was catching a bus to New York City for some fun; conscious to do it while I can. My furlough was ending; my three month scans were the following week.

I returned to the hospital on Thursday. The light was dim in his room. His youngest daughter, Jennifer, caught me going in and said, "Oh, he's sleeping!" I said I would come back, but she flipped on the overhead light and invited me in. His eyes opened, startled; I leaned over him and we kissed. He was sitting upright on the bed with wet hair, a fresh hospital gown and his urine bag on his lap. He introduced me to his 'baby girl' and pointed out the gray hairs she had given him over the years.

"Tom! You're looking fresh and coiffed too!" I said gaily to my friend, who sat sleepily smiling. "Yes, Roger, my big son-in-law, picked me up like a sack of potatoes and put me in the shower today. I said, 'WHOA! Easy Roger,' but it felt so good to get cleaned up. I made Roger promise not to 'man-shave' me, but he did my face just right." His eye lids were heavy behind his glasses.

"How's your pain tonight Tom?" I asked. "None," he said, "but I, thisss…..?" and he dozed off. It felt like he was going to say he did not like being so sedated. I was glad Tom was not suffering, but he could not stay awake to visit either. It is such a fine line to walk; being present in our last days, but not suffer more than we have to. He was more cognitive last week when we spoke on Saturday, but he was in pain of a level ten. Tuesday his pain was well managed when our support group visited, but today they were trying to find the balance again. I know that I don't have a clue about what is best, but I do know that being on this side of the hospital bed is way different than being in it; making choices of this magnitude could not be easy to do. I am contemplating the above as I sit holding Tom's hand, massaging his fingers.

It was another Saturday, and after I shared the entertaining ritual of wedding dress shopping with my future daughter-in-law, her bridesmaids, Mother and Aunts, I drove myself towards home. It was foggy and raining when I decided to stop and visit Tom as I passed near the hospital.

Otherwise I wouldn't see him until Monday and that is a long time; there had been talk of moving him to a nursing home.

I got off the elevator and they saw me first; they were behind me as I turned towards his room. Tom was being pushed in a wheelchair by Amanda and her friend, Keri. We took another spin around the ward, chatting. Back in his room, Keri confidently picked Tom up out of the chair and listened to Tom's direction as she gently lowered him to sit in the chair for a change. Amanda finished arranging blankets and tidying up; she had arranged all our Valentines on the windowsill along with family photos. Amanda explained to me, with Tom listening, that he is on pain medication, but only gets boosts of morphine if necessary, so he can remain more cognitive. Keri said good bye and left. Amanda was preparing to leave too, but had hesitated. Tom dozed in his chair.

"Is he in hospice care now, Amanda?" I asked softly as we stood at the end of his empty bed. I was trying to clarify his situation and understand the nuances of expectation. "Yes, Carol, he is. His oncologist has used his diagnosis of pneumonia and his need for antibiotics as a reason to keep him right where he is, so they don't have to move him. There are no empty beds in any facilities nearby."

I was relieved to hear that he didn't have to be moved. Amanda's eyes were moist as she explained that she needs to go home for few hours. One of her boys actually told his teacher in school on Friday, that "My Mommy doesn't live at my house anymore." I could tell she was stretched thin as she looked at her Dad dozing in his chair. "Go home. I'll stay with him awhile, Amanda," I said. She left to prepare for the arrival of the rest of Tom's family from Cincinnati.

I sat on the hospital bed, near Tom's reclining chair in the corner. The TV was on mute. I contemplated what to do, watching my friend sleep. I pulled up a chair by the foot of his recliner and began to massage his feet. He smiled a sleepy smile and without words I knew he was enjoying being touched, but I asked to make sure. He nodded slightly. The nurse came in with his medications in little paper cups and lined them up on his tray. "Are you a massage therapist?" she asks. "No, just a friend," I replied. Tom woke up and he swallowed each pill as the nurse told him what they were for. He had asked not to be given drugs when he isn't clear about their purpose; part of remaining conscious of his choices.

I noticed that his eyes were drawn to the TV and I followed them to the movie: <u>A Few Good Men</u>. I suggested that he turn up the volume and we began to watch it together, but he quickly dozed off again. I leaned back on his bed watching the movie, my head next to Tom's loud, but rhythmic IV pump, and just feet away from his struggling breath. He held the remote in his hand upside down, muffling the voices of Tom Cruise and Demi Moore, but I watched it anyway.

His sleep apnea, combined with morphine, had me sit up more than once to see if he was taking his last breath, stuck on the intake for what felt like an eternity, but he woke again and we talked. There was a puddle of urine in his lap from a leak in his colostomy bag. I hadn't noticed until suddenly there was an aide there to change his robe and clean up; he had buzzed her. I said it was a good time for me to leave, but he asked the aide to give him ten minutes. He took my hand and said, "I am so sorry Carol, I didn't mean to offend you. I shouldn't have taken it for granted that you'd be comfortable. I lost my modesty several years ago from all the invasive things I've had done. I didn't mean to offend you, I'm sorry."

I assured him that I was not offended or overly modest, but that it was simply time for me to go take care of myself, get dinner and rest. I had a long day. I kissed him goodbye and went to tell the aide that she could help him now.

Driving home I realized that it had touched the buried nerve of an experience I had when I was a young teen. I was a candy striper volunteering at a nursing home. I walked through the hallways delivering flowers and helping where I could. I became very friendly with an elderly woman that was always alone and she found comfort in my attention.

One day, the large nurse that came in to give her a sponge bath told me to leave, but the woman asked me to stay while she was bathed, and held fast to my hand. I told the nurse I was fine with staying, but the nurse berated me, embarrassed me like I was a pervert for being interested in helping the woman while she was naked. I left and never went back because of the guilt and confusion I felt. I was innocent of her charges, but here it was popping up after leaving Tom. I was nervous about my humiliation, not his.

Part Three

The rest of his family arrived from Cincinnati later that Saturday night and visited Tom before settling in at Amanda and Roger's. Tom's sister spent the night with him in the hospital and he asked her to call me at 8:30 Sunday morning. It was early for me, but I am so glad that I answered. I was confused at first as to who it was. Tom lost his voice months ago, but a recent injection in his vocal chords had restored some of his volume, only higher pitched. When I realized it was Tom, we had a sweet chat, with his sister in the background correcting his facts. I told him I would visit tomorrow and looked forward to meeting her. "You'll love my sister, Carol, she's great." It was our last chat.

On Monday afternoon his family filled the room and we introduced ourselves. Jennifer got up and offered me a seat near her Dad. His sister told me that Tom had asked for me again at 2:00 am, but they didn't call me and he fell back asleep. He was mostly quiet now.

Tom is propped up in bed to help with his breathing; there are no more liftings, showers or outings in wheelchairs. He has traveled far this past week. Amanda sits on the other side of the bed and wipes her father's forehead. She touches his bag to check for fullness. She's not afraid to care for him and seems open to the honesty of the time he has come to. He twitches strongly and furrows his brow. I reach to touch that furrow, and selfishly hope my touch can help to ease his strain, to help him, to make a difference somehow. He is still fighting, struggling, though he woke during the night and yelled; angry to find out he was still here.

I held his hand and watched him struggle with each breath. It looked hard for him to be dying by the way his shoulders pumped up and tensed with every breath. Birth came to mind; the pushing, the strain, and I saw Tom's dying as his struggle to birth his own soul. For some it might be easy and open, if they're ready. For others death is a struggle, I can see Tom trying to fit through to the unknown; to release from the fears and responsibilities that hold us to this life.

I went back over in the evening, to sit with him again. At home all I could do was pace with expectation, like the expectation of birth. It was more peaceful to be there with him in the hospital, listening to the long, struggling draws of air into his lungs, seeing his glasses, unneeded now, folded on the bedside table. I witnessed his full face slowly transform into his death mask; skin loosely covering bone, his mouth contorted by sagging open for so long.

The nurse touched his leg and told him the medication she was giving him with such respect that he woke and lifted his head to acknowledge her presence. Then he suddenly yelled, "See how they hold me hostage!" His sister spoke calmly to him and then his daughter; they asked if they could kiss him. "Yes," he whispered. They took turns and then I asked too. "Yes," he said. "Good night Tom. I love you." I kissed his cheek and then his third eye. "Sleep well." I said good bye to his family and wondered if it would be easier for Tom tomorrow when his family went home; maybe he needed quiet to die. Amanda escorted me out to the hall where we hugged. She walked me to the elevator and I hugged his sister too. I could see his reflection through the love in their eyes. I was grateful, yet again, that he was surrounded by love. I got on the elevator and exited the building through the maze of hallways. I am still reading the signs to find my way out. There is no clear exit.

Epilogue

Tom's family went back to Cincinnati on Tuesday as planned. I thought I had said good bye to Tom on Monday night, but I was drawn back to his bedside for several more visits. I talked with his daughters and their friends who kept a vigil by his bed side, and I learned a little more about my friend from the stories they told. It struck me how Tom and I had bonded without the formality of detailed histories. The girls told me he was a good father and worked construction. He had no health insurance when he was first diagnosed and relied on clinics for treatments. Before he left Cincinnati, the doctor told him he had three months to live. His son-in-law, Roger, invited him to come and stay with him and Amanda in Saugerties. He was in his third year of living with them when he entered the hospital this time. He said in group one day, "I am a fighter," and he was. He held on for two long weeks.

Amanda was there on Saturday night, alone, and told her father that she loved him and that she was going to go home, shower and spend time with her family. She was going to leave him alone for the night; she thought that might be what he needed. The nurses called her in the morning to tell her he was very close to the end and she returned to the hospital to be with him. She lay next to him in the bed and told him she loved him and that she would be okay, that Roger would take good care of her so she could take good care of everyone else. Tom died within minutes of her reassurances on Sunday morning, March 3rd, 2013. She made some calls, including me. I said I was not going to come, but I got up and ran over. They had just taken his body to the morgue. Amanda walked me into the empty room, but I was going to cry and I was glad his body was gone. He wasn't there any more either. I kissed his daughters good bye.

On Tuesday Amanda and Roger came for our Metastatic Support Group memorial for Tom and lit the candle. Amanda sat in Tom's chair for our sharing of stories. Such sweetness people can bring into our lives, giving us gifts of all kinds. The quantity of time that we spend together does not always measure equally to its value.

My friend Tom let me look over his shoulder as he reluctantly approached death's door. I am grateful that he let me share his transformation; I had never been strong enough to share this experience before.

I remember the one visit that I made to my friend John Berger, while he was dying of AIDS in 1984. He was emaciated, lying in pain on the couch, sun shining over his shoulder from the window behind him. I chatted all sorts of nervous gibberish and present-day trivia, unable to acknowledge his approaching death. He looked at me with kindness and compassion. He knew he was dying and seemed to forgive my ignorance. Having Stage-Four Metastatic Cancer is teaching me to face this study of life and to train for death's inevitability.

HOLDING ON, LETTING GO—THE BEGINNING

It was during Tom's last days, and we were going around the room at our memoir group, reading when Abby blurted out, "*God, you're good!* We should put together an anthology!" The buzz ran around the circle; everyone seemed energized by it. There was something that we could do to mark this extraordinary time of writing together. We were surrounded by so much fragility, that I for one jumped on the opportunity. I began to collect our suggested writings for the collection. Craig promised to proofread it. Annie and Sharon talked about marketing ideas and book readings. Ruth sent out emails for our first separate meeting. We worked hard and had our first public reading at the Benedictine Auditorium to raise money for our printing. We packed the house.

MY PEACE ON CANCER

I was too young to note the publication of Rachel Carson's Silent Spring, but I did celebrate the first Earthday picking up litter as I walked to high school. In 1971, Nixon declared a "War On Cancer," but I didn't notice; I was sixteen then and I was sure I was going to be sixteen forever. Cancer was on the fringe of my life. Our culture was becoming more ecologically conscious, but the emphasis of The War On Cancer dug deeply into the trenches of the cure, which is more profitable than the cause.

This War On Cancer reached my own family when Aunt Betty, Uncle Al and then Aunt Janis *lost* their *battles*. There was an unspoken feeling that they did something *wrong*. There was a *reason* that they got it, a *mistake* that they made. Uncle Al worked as a plumber in vats of dye at a paper plant, and it poisoned his liver. Aunt Janis sat quietly smoking cigarettes while she knitted, ignoring the changes in her breast until it was too late.

Flash forward to 2009 and my own diagnosis of Stage-Four Metastatic Breast Cancer. In the language of war, I was handed a live *grenade*. "What did *I* do *wrong?*" I asked my doctors and people asked me, "Did they *say* why *you* got cancer?" I don't have a history of breast cancer in my blood relatives, or the BRCA gene. It could have been swimming in the Hudson River as a child when PCB's were high, or sewing a ton of cotton kimonos and breathing in the dust of the fabric's chemical finish. I also loved corn as a child, was it sprayed with DDT? *Or* is it my "long-held anger and resentment" as Louise Hay states in her book on healing, but wouldn't there be even *more* cancer in the WORLD if *that* was the case? There's a long list of possibilities, but my doctors assured me that it was not my fault. I wish that the biopsies of my cancer had tags to tell me which toxins warped my cells.

When cancer became personal I called Diane and she helped me face one of life's *many* worst case scenarios by teaching me how to breathe and to allow the news to enter slowly. I learned techniques to relax and I learned to *choose* what I needed to do to live. I chose to welcome my chemotherapy and surgery. I learned to imagine healing and protection, to open to the help and support of everyone involved in my cancer journey.

My body needed to rest and it took time to learn to accept that there would be couch days. I had to accept that I needed a new measure of my value. I attended an "Unconditional Healing" retreat with Jeff Rubin who *taught* me that healing is more than getting cured; healing is about living emotionally and spiritually undiminished by disease. I learned to be grateful for my rest. I was grateful for the mindfulness of meditation and the distraction of movies; the generosity of friends that cooked dinners for my daughter and me. I was grateful for my daughter's maturity to accept our temporary role reversal. Life did not turn out as we expected.

Living with disease is a now another aspect of my life. My doctors make recommendations for treatment through cyclical scans that measure and map where the cancer is in my body. I gratefully accept the longevity of the treatments they offer. I see the drugs and surgeries *not* as toxic weapons of war, but *tools* for my survival. Then it is up to me to learn alternative ways to deal with the side effects of treatments that extend my life. This does not feel like a war to me, but like a Master's Degree in Being Human, with a minor in a Personal Study of Illness.

"Carol, be BRAVE," family and friends encouraged me. It struck me early on that I would do what I needed to do for my children, but I wondered, "Is that *BRAVE?*"

"Keep FIGHTING Carol, you'll win this BATTLE." These comments made me squirm, but everyone meant well, so I accepted their encouragement.

"FIGHT THE FIGHT, Carol, You'll be a WINNER!" Eventually I was struck by the LANGUAGE of this WAR I was DRAFTED into. It doesn't express **my** feelings. I didn't *VOLUNTEER* and I don't want to FIGHT. I want to live in PEACE. I reject this expectation that I'll automatically speak the language of WAR because I have cancer. I understand the barrage of test results can feel ASSAULTING, making the language of WAR tempting.

I'll never forget talking about this with my metastatic friend, Tom, when he told me, "I'm a FIGHTER Carol. I've always been a fighter." He needed the language of WAR to express his feelings of frustration. When he imagined FIGHTING, he felt power over his body. But in his last days when Tom asked me, "How will I know when it's time to let go?" we were able to talk about death. I sat quietly, holding his hand when he pulled up out of a deep sleep to apologize, "I'm SORRY, Carol, I'm so sorry; I almost QUIT." These are disturbing words from the lips of a dying friend. He was so used to FIGHTING that he equated dying with QUITTING.

So *please*, try not to think of me as a LOSER when I die and don't call me a chicken for not FIGHTING. Cancer is NOT the local bully that is picking a FIGHT with me. Cancer is not something that I can petition against and WIN a court case over. The image of fighting a BATTLE to defeat cancer or death is exhausting and only defeats my tranquility. I choose to LEARN and write about my life right up to the end. No one will DEFEAT death; not with WAR, or PEACE for that matter.

TODAY IS APRIL 3rd

I dreamt I owned a house. From the outside it looked like a rough summer cottage with a tacked on screen porch, but the inside was bigger. The colors were gray and white, washed out or unpainted; not like my real house that has warm yellows and creamy whites. I had a servant at this house; a thin woman with straight, shiny, black hair who came running in with a wet sheet that had been hung outside, before the rain. I said to go ahead and hang it inside the kitchen, off that clothesline near the ceiling.

Then I looked down at my tiny baby that lay in the palm of my hand; she was too small to carry in the crook of my arm. She had no clothes; there were no clothes small enough, so she was naked and adorable and I kept her in a small, empty brown paper bag that had handles that I swung like a cradle. I took her out frequently to admire her; she was precious to me. I held her in my hand while talking on the phone to my Dad and Mary. I looked out the kitchen window and I saw the religious order of Brothers and Sisters that shared my property. They wore brown robes tied with rope and sat with their backs to me, on folding chairs, saying prayers towards the shrubs. They simultaneously moved the beads of their rosaries in one hand and then moved around to different locations during the day. I got the feeling from the dream that I did not step outside very often, but relied on the people who came to visit and call me.

I stayed up reading John Steinbeck's <u>East of Eden</u>, until close to 1:00 am and I lay in bed this morning until 9:30. I lay here thinking, and I witness how far away my lightheartedness jumps when I approach radiation for the third and fourth body parts. It is fraught with ominous possibilities, but I have done well with radiation before, so why not this time? I went to bed with an itchy red patch of skin surrounded by a large welt on my buttocks from my Faslodex shots on Monday and that was worrisome too. But why worry? I have had such "a good attitude" towards all of this before.

It was supposed to stop, though. There was to be an end to all these treatments so I would move on past this study of cancer, and blossom into a new phase of my life. I did not plan on studying this topic for the duration, not really, though I talk that way. I plunge deep down and find another layer where I am exposed in my disbelief, which has made it all easier to bear, easier to take one step at a time. But I begin again, today; take one step at a time and one day at a time. First, I have today and tomorrow which do not include radiation.

Friday I will head back into the city and the sub-basement of the Columbia-Presbyterian Hospital to have my "simulation" during which they plan the angles of the radiation beams and I receive my tattoos for this round. I will also find out new, small indignities, like if I have to go panty-less lying on the radiation table and whether I lie face up or face down, but that is not until Friday, and Charlie said he will drive me down and back. Then I have the weekend and a few more days after that. I will then experience five treatments, but only one at a time. I have remedies for diarrhea; I'll rest, eat good food and bathe in the love around me.

This too shall pass; I can only control how I choose to approach all of this. I've come too far to drop the spirit of adventure now. There's still more for me to learn. Please God, give me more endurance to live a rich and healthy life. Please hold me above the grayness of despair, the empty hallways of gloom; let me look upon this chilly spring day with the optimism of a daffodil and experience the simple joy of being in my own home at this very moment. There are so many things to turn towards with gratitude. So what if my ass sticks out on the radiation table? They have seen so many before mine showed up.

THE LAUNDRY LIST

Diane called to ask how I was feeling. "Is this a trick?" I asked her. I always have a hard time speaking my feelings about cancer and she is well versed at prodding me. "Let's see," I say, "I am doing laundry, washing dishes and going in for radiation to my spine and hip beginning Thursday. It's just on my list of things to do." I know it is an inadequate answer, but she is reminding me to unbury them. Keeping busy is not a feeling.

I've come a long way in four weeks, since my doctor suggested my fourth round of radiation. First I postponed the appointment with the radiation oncologist for two more weeks. Then I discussed my flailing thoughts with friends, "Don't all the radioactive tests I get, added to the previous radiation of my T-1, chest wall, and brain just increase my cancer eventually? How do I know when I've had too much? Maybe I'd be better off just stopping now and ride it out." My thoughts spiraled in a web. What I meant was, "Maybe this could all go away now? Maybe I could stop and I'd just be fine?"

Barbara returned from Nepal and came by to deliver a gift. I caught her up on my news. "The doctors want me to do radiation for the bone metastases on my hip and lumbar."

"Radiation?" she asked. "Good; that's good. It will buy you time and postpone pain." I love Barb's matter-of-fact statement. It *is* about buying time; for me, it is about buying time.

Charlie drove me into the city for my consultation and then again for my simulation. It helped to see familiar faces from my previous treatments and to see that my ass wasn't going to be sticking up in the air. So, for me now, coping is putting it on my laundry list and arranging lunch dates in the city.

I went to therapy today and Michael also asked me, "How are you feeling?" When I responded neutrally, he said, "I don't know, but if it were me, being closer to death, I might feel angry about having to leave before the party's over."

"Well, the party will never really be over, but what I worry is that I won't finish growing up first. I worry that I haven't accomplished what I am supposed to accomplish in this life; *that* upsets me. What am I supposed to accomplish? How can I go if I'm still not sure what my gift is?"

I told him about my dream on April 3rd; the little baby that I held in the palm of my hand. It was a precious little naked baby that I carried in a small brown paper gift bag with handles. I swung the bag by the handles to comfort her. The answer burbled up from the depths; I still hold the seed of my potential in the palm of my hands and that is precious to me, but kept simply, and unspoiled. She is content to be with me and ride out the time I have left.

RADIATION: Round Four

"**H**i! I still have the card you gave me when you graduated," Errol said as he came over to hug me. "My wife loves the picture; said it's the first picture she saw of me working. Glad I had on matching scrubs that day! You're next," he added. I changed in the dressing room, removing everything below the waist, as per my instructions. I double tied my hospital gown over my sleeveless tee shirt and walked to the nurse's station feeling vulnerable.

"Ms. Dwyer, it's so nice to see you again; well, not really *here*, but you know what I mean," Brenda said as she prepared to take my vital statistics. She and I had spent many afternoons chatting before chest wall radiation three years ago. There are things we know about each other that aren't discussed today in this brief catching up.

Errol escorted me to the simulation room and I bumped into Marguerite; we embraced. She was my favorite person in the whole place; she gave me comfort on my darkest day of radiation in the spring of 2010.

Today, I lay down on the radiation table as Errol placed stiff wedged forms under my legs and torso. I asked him to prop up the torso form a little more and he asked me to place my arms crossed on my chest. My back from the waist down is unprotected on the hard table. The air is being sucked out of the new poly-pellet canvas wedge under my torso; he quickly pushed against it, sculpting it to my body. "I remember that you like pictures, Ms. Dwyer. Would you like me to take a few now, on the machine?" "Yes," I said, happy to be remembered for my compulsive photography.

"Now could you put your arms over your head, Ms. Dwyer?" My shoulders tensed and were exhausted quickly. My back and shoulders were uncomfortable, but I assumed that my shoulders were not used to being held up or stretched, for so long. It is Round Four for me; I became casual about my comfort in the familiarity of experience.

"Okay, now for some new tattoos, Ms. Dwyer."

"Thanks, Errol. Could they be more interesting this time?" I joked.

"They were *all* tiny butterflies. Here are six more for your collection."

That brings it up to about eighteen or twenty small black dots on my torso and neck; another simulation is complete.

★★★★★★

I arrive by bus the following Thursday for my first treatment. I feel anxious about the discomfort that I felt last week on the table. The Radiation Oncology Department looks fresher from the new renovations, but this part is not new. I lay down on the table as Miguel and Ramir read Errol's notes about my precise placement; my body in the molds that are secured with braces to the table.

"Lay perfectly still, Ms. Dwyer. We'll need to take a few x-rays first. Lay perfectly still and let us line up your body to the machine." The technicians pull the sheet under my body to move my dead weight, lining up my tattoos to the infrared beams. I remember trying to help them when I was new here, but I am dead weight now; *that* is being helpful. The technician to my right gently strokes my skin upwards to line up the tattoo by my pubic hair. My arms are crossed over my head. "Something is sticking into my shoulder blade," I stated uncomfortably.

"Don't worry. This won't take long, Ms. Dwyer. Stay perfectly still." I lay still as they abandon the room, my eyes closed, breathing consciously, calmly; I hear the machine as it passes over me. Something is pressing into my shoulder blade and just below; numbness spreads up my arm followed by its sister, anxiety. I'm not praying for the healing of my cancer, but distractedly waiting to bounce off this fucking table. The technicians are in and out. I turn my arm to see if it still works. "Just a few more minutes, Ms. Dwyer. Please lay perfectly still. I'll look at the form when we finish. Lay perfectly still now."

My arm is dead. The bones of my spine are flattened against the hard table, reminding me of being yelled at in gym class for lousy sit ups, my boney spine crunching on the hard gym floor. I wish the pounds I've gained in my waist were turned around to cushion my spine.

"We're almost done, Ms. Dwyer. We're almost done."

The treatment ended and I complained about my shoulder as my two technicians helped my stiff body sit up on the table. We stared at the 10" long ridge that stood up into my shoulder blade for the past forty-five minutes. "That's the problem, Ms. Dwyer, she said as she pressed the ridge down into the form. Tomorrow, I'll lay a cloth over that too."

This form, taking only one man's labor, was quicker than using a suction sculpting method; not like the original form they made for my chest wall radiation. That form took two guys holding it to my body while the material set, drying to my precise shape.

They helped me put my hospital gown back on. I exited the radiation room and went to get dressed. I remember my mother telling me as a child, to "Keep your underpants on, *except* in the bathroom," and as I walk without underwear down the hallway, I feel quite vulnerable, like a panty-less child.

✶✶✶✶✶✶

Tommy and Danielle were there to pick me up and take me back to their apartment. I laid down on the couch, exhausted, my hips cramping, contracting; a frustrating ache like having the flu, but only in my lower body. I rested quietly on the couch, slightly nauseous. I heard Tommy 'shhhhh-ing' Pucci, their dog. I listened to the street traffic, the bird on the tree outside their third floor apartment. A beautiful day except in me, something is missing from me; my energy's extracted. I rejoined them for dinner and buoyed with the distraction of company and conversation. I managed to sleep with Pucci, doing his healing canine work by my side.

During my consultation with Dr. Chao on the previous Tuesday, I was reassured by the familiar faces of people who work here: Raoul, Errol, Margarite, Janet, Brenda, Miguel. When the memories of my optimism were reflected today, Friday, approaching my second treatment, it is being infused with deep sadness; yes, everyone was familiar, but I had not planned on coming back. The surprised greetings and hugs were winding down and I was filing in line for the 'treatment,' just like everyone else. The Radiation Oncology Department had been receiving a face lift in my absence, the reconstruction is almost complete and it looks less like the sub-sub-basement that it really is. The Feng-Shui of the nurse's station has changed, but I have changed too; I am no longer the dewy eyed novice at the cancer game. I know what "Stage-Four Metastatic Cancer" means now. I have invested almost four years and I have many metastatic acquaintances and friends that have died.

I watched my YouTube video that I made last week, before radiation. I listened for my wisdom to wash over me now, now that I don't feel such patience or confidence. Now that nausea shakes my roots; the spasms inside my bones rattle loudly, echoing their reverberations in my mind. My final spiral is just one accident away, one slip downward. Is this the beginning of my spiral, I wonder; or will I have another reprieve?

I had slept on Thursday night, but that was the last of it until I found pain medication left over from my bilateral and brain surgeries and took one at 6am on Sunday morning. I do not like to resort to prescriptions, but I guess this is what they are for. My anxiety has grown about going back to the radiation table. I heard that another metastatic friend has died. Penny died Friday. Her daughter wrote that, "Mom got to see the daffodils bloom again this spring, before letting go of this life." I too have enjoyed the daffodils and wonder if I will see them next year. It feels best to be conscious of such things, just in case, just in case the world ends; even if it is only *my* world.

THE HAMMOCK

Awake on Sunday morning, ready to enjoy another piece of this long Memorial Day weekend with no place to rush to; basking lazily in bed in what I call my "hammock," the period of time *hung* between scans. They changed one of my drugs two scans ago after tumors showed in my hip and spine. My last scan showed more bone metastases; doctors prescribed five intense radiation treatments to prevent spinal pain and to stop, or slow down the cancer there. Now I rest in the 'hammock.' This is the time that I live for, swaying in the breeze, innocent of disease.

I'm not looking at the calendar, but the anxiety of the approaching scan licks the edge of my mind like the tide coming in. Go away! I want to enjoy the innocence of this time in between, but alone, undistracted, the darker thoughts slip under the door. The next scan will measure if, or where, the cancer sits in my body; whether it's being held in check or spreading; whether the drugs need to change or treatments increased.

I couldn't feel the cancer in my bones; it was the PET scan that revealed my raffle prize. Bone metastases are upsetting, but I'm relieved that the brain Mets haven't reoccurred. I'm careful not to aggravate my bones with aggressive activities and look forward to swimming this summer, to continue yoga and walking. I can write about being young, energetic, adventurous, and sexual. The drugs to eradicate or slow down this disease do the same thing to many aspects of life that I used to hold dear. Feeling comfortable is important now; I relate to the appetites of the elderly.

I feel well, but that is not a measure of health anymore. *Feeling well* is handling the side effects of the drugs I take with the help of vitamins, supplements, rest, the support of family and friends. I never forget my health is compromised, but the first few weeks spent in my hammock, feel euphoric and optimistic; I am grateful for the reprieve. As the next scan approaches, the ropes of my 'hammock' begin to fray. Friends see me as strong and brave. They ask, "How are you?" I reply with, "I feel fine," because I do, but add, "I have a scan coming up." That statement is a small window into the erosion of my confidence.

SCAN DAY
June 13, 2013

Here I am, right now, sitting in my recliner, my bored cat trying to lie across my arms as I type. I just had an MRI of my brain and a PET scan of my torso. On my way home, I stopped at the supermarket to pick up a few things. The magazine racks reminded me that the world is still turning with new super models, Hollywood and sports stars sharing their tips about weight loss, abs and white teeth. I don't need their advice; I have everything I need, both good and bad. I am not worried about "healthy eating to prevent cancer," or how I'll look in my swimsuit this summer; I'll be happy to swim.

This was my fourth cat nap, on a rainy day full of napping, but the only one with my cat sitting across my lap. I didn't sleep well last night, anticipating the early morning scans. I dreamt, woke, dreamt, and woke before finally rolling out of bed for my appointment. I napped in the MRI machine with hammers around my head. I rested in the Quiet Room, preparing for the PET scan, while the radioactive isotope spread throughout my body. An hour later was my nap in the PET scan.

"Does it say in my records how many of these scans I have had here?" I asked my technician. "Yes, Carolyn, you've had eight of them," he answered while the nurse checked my IV.

Eight radioactive PET scans in less than four years; part of my cancer statistics. I used to be "normal" and would have thought that this was nuts. Now, I go in and just do it, nap and relax. Today is another day; whatever the test results are, they are already; the only difference will be that next week I will know the results. That will end this reprieve and hopefully begin another.

A MOMENT WITH MIKE

My grown son, Mike, stopped by to visit me this week and after catching up on current news, we talked about that painful time when he went to live with Charlie across town. His perspective is so blunt that he reminds me of analyzing my own mother at that period in my own life. We see the things our parents do wrong so clearly and how they hurt us and try to control us. He told me a few incidents that I have blocked from my memory, my yelling and screaming with frustration. The one punch sentences he delivers cut through my gray memories leaving streaks of clarity between. We have a strong relationship and we share love, "But Mom, I had to leave you in order to grow up. I had to push off; you had to annoy me for that to happen and I think I am healthier for it."

I feel lucky to have lived long enough to hear it from him.

NEW BONE METS; NEW CHEMO
June 20, 2013

I showered and dressed for my birthday and was finally headed out the door for my acupressure appointment with Diane, when the phone rang. "Hello Gwen," I said. "Yes, I can come in today; all you have is 1:30? Okay, that's just before my Metastatic support group across the street." My visiting friend looked quizzically and I explained, "My scan results are in and I assume, since I am being asked to come in to talk to the doctor, that the results are not that good, hence the appointment. Good results are reported over the phone." I ran out the door, drove to Diane's office and shared the news about the doctor's appointment with her. She asked if I wanted her to go with me. "I'll be fine," I told her. "I've done this so many times now that it's not a big deal. I'll just go find out about the changes."

I entered the doctor's building as the rain began to fall, hoping that it would stop before I had to go back out without an umbrella. There was a man walking up the staircase. "You can pass me if you like. I'm moving slowly today," he said. "So am I," I replied as I sped like a serious turtle past him, explaining I was late for my appointment. I got out at the next floor and he continued upstairs. I went into the doctor's and told Gwen I had arrived. I chose my chair, sat back; a few minutes later the man from the stairwell walked in the door, out of breath. I'm guessing he has "chemo brain" as he sits down slowly; we are in an oncology office.

The huge flat screen television was on in the waiting room; there is nowhere to go to get away from it. There was a tragic story about an 18 month old child's abduction being sensationalized on the big screen with suppositions that the mother had something to do with it. The child's photo was shown over and over, the same accusations made over and over too, but hinting at new revelations if we sat through the next barrage of commercials. I looked up at the clock over the man's head. I don't want to be late for my metastatic support group. I look forward to the group every other week and today we are celebrating my birthday. The time is getting close.

The man from the stairwell caught my eye and he shook his head at the television report. I wrongly made the assumption that we shook our heads about the same thing, about the redundant tragedy playing out for our entertainment. I was wrong; the man began broadly proclaiming that the perpetrator should be shot, "Just taken out and shot! Whoever took that baby? Jail is too good for them! We pay $50,000 a year to feed them and they don't deserve it! They should just be shot. The same with those lazy welfare recipients! They should go to work for that money!" I looked away, breaking eye contact, but he rambled on.

"Please call me for my appointment!" I was begging in my brain. "I want to go to my support group, I want to find out the results of my scans and I want to get the fuck away from this fucking moron."

"Carol you can come in now."

"Thank you for calling me in, Jody, or I was going to kick that asshole in the shins. I don't care if he does have cancer." She acknowledged that the man I spoke of *is* intense sometimes.

Jody led me into a small room to wait for the doctor. I could hear Jody tell the doctor that I was ready. My doctor's voice traveled the short distance down the hallway as he reviewed the report out loud, "Well, it looks like the right hip has cleared up some, but now her left hip has a new tumor. So it looks like she has three *new* areas; a couple of the radiated tumors have shrunk, but one is bigger...." I listened of course and felt like leaving, now that I already have the news, but I wait to see if there's more; also to hear his suggested treatment. I'm pissed. I've been so calm that my anger surprises me. I'm disappointed to hear my news traveling through the hallway; the fucking cancer is still there, spreading. I had placed my hope on a clear spell; I wanted the summer off, but I wasn't going to get it.

The doctor speaks to Jody some more before he shuffles down the hall and picks up my file from the wall bin outside the door, just to the side of being visible, peruses it and comes in saying, "Hello, Carol. How are you? Blah blah blah, more cancer in you sacrum, blah blah blah, your right hip looks like it responded well to radiation, but you now have metastases in your LEFT hip, blah blah, and the tumor on your right sacrum cleared but spread to the left side, blah blah blah. Do you have any pain? Blah blah, Zeloda, I've had a lot of good results with patients on this treatment. Blah blah it's a good chemotherapy, blah blah... I had one woman with a VERY large tumor blah blah...who responded so well on this treatment."

I hate hearing about other patients' tumor size and how they have responded to treatments. I'd rather speak to my metastatic friends who actually take the drug, though we all respond differently, I want their support right now, right across the street, they are waiting for me with a birthday cake. That's what I want. I am fucking disappointed and that is a good place to be with those feelings. Everyone in the group will know how I feel. They don't know people who feel this way. They have personal experience and real support and this guy in the white coat, who means well, is making me late.

THE BIG KETTLE
May 29, 2013

An acquaintance offered to help me recently, by sharing her healing techniques that cured her illness. Another friend has stated that it was her *positive* approach that made all the difference in her health, especially her bout with breast cancer that she *won*. Survivors sometimes seem to have all the answers for those of us that are failing the War on Cancer. I've felt that some think that those of us that are metastatic only need some guidance to be cured like they were. But I have a positive attitude and Metastatic Cancer. My positive outlook might not extend my life, but will definitely help me enjoy what remains.

Over the years, I've also generously distributed unsolicited advice and judgments about eating well, yoga, exercising, and how you caught that cold, but my worst offenses, or biggest contributions, revolved around my "successful" pregnancies, *natural vaginal* childbirths and *breast feeding*. I'm sorry if you were a victim of my expertise while I added to this stew of good intentions, boiling together with misinterpretations, in this big kettle of life.

People mean well trying to show me how they succeeded, but it still riles me and I am stirred into the kettle, alongside the zealots and righteous ministers of all the "right ways" of the world. We spin together in the pot, dizzy, trying to get out and away from each other.

NEW COURSES
July 3rd, 2013

I had dreams of being guided to take new courses, to learn a new way to be. I was told to study the sunrise, the sunset. Another class taught me how to disassemble a car and to reassemble the rusty parts across the expanse of my healthy, shaded, green lawn. I dreamt about having cancer, waiting for the other shoe to drop; any day life could change from the complacency of this phase to a new phase, that will make this period seem glorious. I need to see the tranquility I already have, not wait for some new disaster to point it out to me. I woke up having bitten my lip.

Cancer is the course I've been studying. I wanted to graduate by now with a degree; it's been four years this month. I've learned so much, but I have far to go. I knew I'd be fine after chemo and breast surgery, but brain tumors shook my confidence. I didn't doubt that I would survive the experience; it was just that this cancer didn't seem to be going away. I wanted to be different from the other cases. The metastases are spreading in my bones now; I began a new, chemo to detain it. I recline in my chair greeting the side effects stopping by to say "hello," brief glimpses of red, sensitive finger tips, diarrhea, and a flatness of mood; nothing that will kill me. It is not time to let go of life, but prepare? Is there any way to prepare? It will be shocking no matter what, but I talk about it with my family, friends and support groups.

My cousin Fred died yesterday. I didn't know about his poor health, so it seemed sudden. It is odd to see how the world goes on without him today, a blip on the screen, like I will be one day.

Leaving my job at Tonner Doll Company was a mini death, an experience of letting go. I left the high speed pace of work that I could no longer keep up with. I miss the adrenaline of deadlines, but I need to live out my time in a slower lane. The price, besides having cancer, was to see them carry on without me. They could not have been sweeter about it. They welcomed me back several times, held a spot for me for as long as they could, but I had to let go. I go back to visit my co-workers, feeling ghostly sometimes, walking through, watching them work. I know the detail of what they do, I appreciate the quality of their work, their focus, but I'm no longer part of it and it continues without me.

There was a time that I was very possessive of my particular jobs there; I loved to make the doll hats and was able to feel creative and accomplished owning that task. When I visit now I particularly notice Melanie, Suzanne and Maria's hats and how well they construct them. I see that I held that job securely through of the grace of my co-workers. They were always capable, but allowed my ego to hold that specialty. I am grateful for that. Now I have let it go. There is much to let go of in this life; I have the privilege, or the torture, of taking baby steps.

GRIPES
July 18th, 2013

I had dreams, but let them slip away. I crept out of bed, or creaked I should say; my bones and joints speaking in foreign languages of aches and pains. My feet feel round and sensitive as they touch the floor. Whose body is this anyway? I don't know her.

I am feeling lost in my world, my body. Where did my life go?

The house is stagnant around me. Nothing has moved for months. My bedspread flung off my bed in this heat lies over the railing. I have no clue where to put it. So it stays on the railing. Where is my concern for order? For responsibilities?

"I am depressed," I admitted to my nurse, Jody, after my Zometa infusion. She sat down in the chair across from me and said, "It's to be expected, Carol. You're on a cocktail of drugs, strong drugs, and you need time to adjust. Do you think you need an antidepressant? Do you want to talk about that?"

"No, I don't, but thank you." It seems absurd to pile one more drug into the mix, to add a drug to help me avoid the confusion caused by the mix of other drugs. I should be grateful to know why I'm depressed, but I'm not. I have this image of turning towards dying instead of facing life, but really it's all in the same direction. My life is in front of me, and so is my death.

What's bothering me is that I am only half here. I am half not here. I wake up at night, like a vampire. The morning is aching bones, lethargy, depression. I am sad to be so cautious; I don't dance anymore or ride my bike. I can extend my existence without pain by practicing caution, watching my step, not taking risks.

I need to know what I am living for. I forgot. Why am I living now? I have been a clothing designer and fine seamstress. I have enjoyed color and texture and shape of clothing; it's been a large part of my life. It's like I've decided to use duct tape instead of needle and thread. My life is duct taped together now. Drugs are seeping into my bones, but that's the point, right? I have cancer in my bones so they are helping me. Hold that thought. Stop here.

TIME

August 5th, 2013

Time is flying! I've thought that for years, as I began my work week every Monday. The weekend was never long enough. Then, suddenly it'd be "Hump Day" and then the weekend again. I'd get used to Michael's naptime and it would change. In kindergarten he asked to be called 'Mike,' and now? My son has five tattoos and is getting married next month.

I see babies in the grocery store and can't keep myself from telling their parent, "*My baby*, Dana, is in college now. They smile politely, looking for the cereal and I know that someday, when they walk in the grocery store and see a baby in a stroller, they will realize that their precious time passed too.

Life is still measured from season to season, birthday to birthday, or New Years, but "Back-to-School" as a measure for me has faded fast, replaced by the appointment for my next PET scan. The new weekly measure is not paycheck to paycheck, or weekend to weekend, but the refilling of my pill cases with my medicine and supplements. I find myself cocky, rich when the supplements come in and I fill the first week's supply. The second week is fine, but by the third week I am surprised by how fast the pill bottles have emptied. It's already time to reorder the Xeloda, Tykerb, Levethyroxine and my anti-seizure pills. I'm almost out of vitamin D3, calcium, milk thistle and curcumin. How long will this protein powder last? Full of hope, I add some to the list.

I know that the chemo is staving off the growth of cancer and the supplements are supplying my body with the nutrition that it doesn't get from the food I eat, but where does the time go? All this time digested by millions of people and then excreted, producing adults who make books, buildings and dinner, but is that the real byproduct of time? Is the final measure of time the things that we produce? I sit in silence, in a kayak on the lake, watching the loons. It doesn't create a byproduct, yet that time also passes. In another year, if I am lucky, I'll be back to the lake again.

The mystery of time is a lifelong wonder for me. I look on pictures that show the physical beauty that I once lived in, but time didn't stop, and I continue to age and disintegrate; I pause at the universality of it. We can lift, tuck, reconstruct, but no one really escapes the aging of our bodies… until death. All that chaos, jealousy, passion and anxiety, beauty, pleasure and peace crashes past, to expose that our lives are just tiny waves of time.

Thursday, September 12th, 2013

I dream that my friend wants surgery, but no one will perform it on her, so I offer to do it WITH her and her husband. We meet on a busy northbound avenue in NYC. It's dusk; the street lights are turning on. I set up a large, but portable, cutting table, a block below a very busy corner. She's eager and grateful as she mounts the table with her husband's assistance, but I want to place a piece of gray plaid flannel underneath her and align the large black perpendicular lines to the edges. This plaid's pattern is so large it doesn't repeat on this surface and darkness obscures the subtle accent colors. I want her lined up with the lines, even and blocked, so we begin again. She is ready now, but, "There are a few issues," I point out. "We're in a very busy street, it's not sterile and it's very poorly lit," I say as I look around, and smell, the filth in the unwashed street and the overflowing garbage can. A bicycle messenger whizzes south, jumping on the sidewalk almost knocking down her husband. I am unsure of how to proceed and I want to do more research with them. "Let's go up to the main library," I suggest. "Let's learn some more about what we're planning to do." I turn to her partner and say, *"I'm nervous about how much I'll hurt her when I put her stitches in, she'll scream, and we're in a public place. I don't want to be arrested!"* I'm not backing out, just clarifying these real concerns, and reminding us that we're in this together; we're all responsible. Deep down I am hoping that a real doctor will step forward to try and help her. I know I'm unqualified, except for postponing the inevitable sorrow of having no more tools at hand to survive.

I slept long and well today. I feel satiated and ready, less depressed. I had a rambling session with my therapist yesterday, talking about all the losses around me. He said, "I saw you; you almost cried. Why did you hold back?" I told him, "Because I am afraid I won't stop." There is *too much* to care about. I want to be stoic or numb. My 85 year old Mom has the flu; three inspiring friends that I met because we all have Metastatic Cancer, are dying, illustrating three possible ways I myself might die. Two other very close friends are moving to Philadelphia in three weeks. My brother Matt has a new job and is suddenly moving to California, after recently moving closer to me, with plans of being more available to visit and help Mom. There is no blueprint for what will work out and what won't. I float on my raft in the ocean like the Life of Pi, experiencing the spectacles, storms and then the calm. I eat and sleep and interact with friends. I float.

Here I am, waking up again to a new day; my second day off chemo. It's pill chemo, which demystifies it somehow. I take it like the other drugs in my regimen and I adjust to the side effects or not, depending on the week; one week on and one week off. Each of the weeks on has been different, so every day is still new, but sometimes it takes me days to realize I'm okay, that the shoe is not dropping now, that I can walk farther than I thought, or enjoy another swim, perhaps the last of the season. Time stretches out before me like the wet, frothy residue of the ocean receding from the shore. I sit and write, trying to sculpt the words to my liking, my meaning; trying to expose my truth. Every day is new, but it takes till afternoon to see its potential before me. I let others rush around outside, driving past, checking in, but my world is slowed down. I am cautious of biting off more than I can do, committing to more than I have energy for, but suddenly I become impassioned about a topic and raise my voice or move to the music, or feel life as it used to be. Today I am grateful that the drama of cancer is not raising another tentacled arm into my life. My boat feels safe for another today.

2nd ANNUAL BCO OMEGA RETREAT for WOMEN WITH METASTATIC BC

September 23, 2013

I felt a great/deep relaxation in this room and in my body. When we were leaving this meditation I saw in front of me light rain falling in a puddle; evening light, the soothing sound of rain; a cleansing rain. Perhaps it was the accumulation of our sorrow, some so deep, but spread over all of us to share, and when combined it is a gentle soft rain. No storms today because we have others to share our sorrows and fears.

What does living with uncertainty mean to me? Look like in my life?

Living with Mets has brought uncertainty front and center. I know uncertainty exists for everyone----no one knows what life holds for them, but mostly we think we have control. Mets has opened a window to uncertainty. I see the broad view and sometimes I can hold it before my hand tries too hard to hold it and it flies away. Then I need to begin again. Begin again to face all the uncertainty in my life; for however long I can live.

Small group discussion of Living with Uncertainty: Charlotte, Maureen, Denise, Mandy, Joanne and me: "Unwavering Faith," was Denise's quote for our small group discussion. That was my favorite phrase. Denise, so succinctly states, in two words, how it's done. I am not religious, but unwavering faith hits home. I trust I will live as long as I am supposed to learn in this life, to prepare me for the next one.

September 24, 2013

I dreamt of soaking my feet in pickle juice. I had two plastic bags filled with pickle juice as I reclined, but I held the bags just so, so the bags wouldn't spill. I wore my slip. Charlie and I were married, but sexual restraint had already crept between us. I was a frustrated wife grooming myself for no one. I visited work in a long hallway room filled with bolts of fabric on both sides. I loved looking at the colors as I reclined awkwardly on a cutting table, holding the bags of pickle juice on my feet. Was this a new pedicure treatment?

After the meditation I was aware of the walls that still pop up to separate me from others. I build them up and I can take them down. Maureen led a breakfast discussion about miracles, angels and unexplainable connections to spirit. I wanted to be separate, not join, but resistance was futile. I know better than to listen to the walls my mind builds. I sat between Louise and Joanne. I listened and shared, connected. I spoke about the Archangel, Metatron's support, along with my late in-laws, Anne and Frank, Aunt Marg and Uncle George, my late grandniece Chloe and how they held me into life. I witnessed my prejudice of organized religions and let the wall I tried to create, collapse and connected to these beautiful souls who are participating together for a spiritual experience.

Walking back from lunch I thought about how we gather at this retreat, like merging paths on the same pilgrimage of this life, sharing the burdens, keeping each other warm. We walk slowly together before dispersing again to mingle with others who think they are well.

We just relaxed on the floor. I had traveled far away and yet so close to me.

I was a child, precocious. A teen, defensive, bold and insecure. Older and adventurous; to me now, bold and quiet, trying to hold on while letting go. I am being. Nancy's soothing voice

brought a relaxed me back into myself. I am up now. Can I stay as the imperfect me? Not rush off to fix someone else?

Carla and I spoke to Beverly and Ann Hutton about dreams at lunch.

After our relaxation on the floor, while the rest of our group was at the main hall receiving healing body work, we sat and each pulled an angel card, but first I asked, "How do I keep my heart open to my children…to not be numb to the sorrow of leaving?"

I pulled the angel card: DREAMS.

I said how I often begin my pieces of writing with my dreams. Carla spoke of long range plans, dreams, but I said when I think of dreams, I think of night dreams. I forget that I can day dream! It's free and natural. There are no consequences for un-met dreams, no crimes or waste. I can dream of my hopes for my children and invest in their futures by praying for their higher good. Whether I am here or not is of little consequence. Dreams do not have a shelf life or expiration date.

Then I walked into the main hall and walked to Corrine for energy work. She does cranial sacrum work, reflexology and more. I told her about my bone Mets, brain scar and more mundanely, my sinus condition. She propped my head up and everything that she did was wonderful and cleared my breathing, but it crept back in, like a cloud. The image that came to mind was "Ghostly," the ghost of my nasal passages. I was breathing through my mouth, but when I left the building, I became clear again. What do you want, Oh Ghost of my nasal passages? What do I need to learn from you? You creep in like the mist, or come upon me like a bag over my head. I have gotten beyond my fear of drowning; suffocating that way, but breathing, remembering to breathe, appreciating breath, allowing the unstoppable flow of breath? I remember a lover telling me to breathe as I held it; expecting to orgasm without breathing.

I was holding in fear, the fear of letting go, of loss of control, fear of failure and pressure to succeed. But back to now? What am I afraid of?

I was stressed approaching this retreat and all that I didn't know about it. I was afraid of meeting old friends near the edge, new friends near the edge. Eight of us from last year's metastatic retreat have died and Jude, Rose and Pat are strained. Carla and Mandy have returned from last year, so have Denise, Louise, Linda Roy, Linda and Darlene and me. We came back, reconnecting and newly connected to new friends. It is a new dynamic present. One that is more hopeful.

What am I afraid of? What takes my breath away? Love? Lack of love? Sometimes I'm scared anyway, despite all I know.

September 26, 2013

Thursday, I walked to the lake with Karen and Mandy to see the morning mist rise.

We are not old and new groups now, but a combined sisterhood. This is one group, a group open to other women. I am moved by our ceremony for our sisters who have died this year and by our new sisters that gathered to share the ceremony with us. The tree is planted. We sent love and light and shared the same. The sun shone on our tree and someday my picture, my name on a rock, will be placed in my memory. I am grateful to share my live presence around this sugar maple and to be able to lift the shovel of dirt, ashes to ashes, dust to dust. I am at peace to know there is a physical place I will share with my sisters when my time comes to pass through. It's a place for our spirits to mingle. I feel it will be a powerful energy circle for other women walking this pilgrimage to visit and be healed in their hearts.

One year ago today, we had our closing ceremony for the first annual BCO Retreat for Women with Metastatic Breast Cancer. There's no description wordy enough to cover it, but it has been a spiritual high, huge laughs, meditation, writing and crafts, sharing, mingling, kayaking (the 1st annual Lidia Memorial event), gratitude, dancing, an artful group shot, and closing with another fabulous meal.

Isis came to visit before lunch and took the group shot arranged by Louise, with my assistance. Then I led the way outside for a spontaneous topless small group shot, all of us leaning over the porch railing. It was a spectacular event no matter what it looks like! I asked who was with me and Ruth said, "I'll do it, but I didn't have a mastectomy." Several others too, but I said it didn't matter! Join in! Eileen, Ruth and I got in place, Beverly joined in by Ruth, Carla between us, I saw Estella and Josette. Then Mandy surprised me, as I removed my shirt as the symbolic CHARGE! when she slipped in to my left for the photo. I know she was out of her comfort zone! I don't even know how many women joined the picture, and we were cheered by our friends on the ground, along with the golf cart drivers!

Tonight at our SHARE event, Denise read her card to herself from last year, Mandy read a story she wrote about her father's death, Ruth read "Scan Anxiety," Kathy about her eyebrow, and at Ruth's suggestion, I read "Exposure 1973" (1st section). Louise showed us how to make origami frogs, Charlotte read scripture and wrote it out on a large sheet of paper in big letters. Darlene thanked everyone and said she was so happy to have more energy this year, and have less weight, than last year. Robin read a piece called "Kiss My Booby Goodbye," Karen Longhair read a poem that helped her through the rough of it. Then Josette got up and told us the whole sad story of her life. We fidgeted, but she needed to speak out loud how her 18 year old brother died in the back of her car after partying with her and her friends. It was uncomfortable, but she needed to speak the whole rest of her life too. Natalie showed us her magazine called The Pink Paper. Maureen got up and told the story of "helping" Robin with her breakfast and accidently pouring cayenne pepper on their oatmeal and eggs.

A lot of people cleared out, but a bunch stayed and danced including me, Beverly, Louise, Nancy, Kathy, Natalie, Josette, Maureen, Estela, Karen, Karen and Karen. We had a great time and laughed, being completely silly. It was funny watching Nancy trying to reel us in with more spiritual music which made us even sillier. But she succeeded, and we all laid down on the floor listening to "Calling All Angels." There was lots of love.

What hits me today is how happy our group has been on this retreat.

How we have shed our discomforts like the miracles of Jesus, in our joy of being together. Last night many of us danced, not everyone could, but we had fun, while no actual physical miracles took place. Our spirits were lifted and connected. I saw Mandy sitting with Charlotte at dinner. I saw Robin giving two classes on EFT and after Maureen's story shared at our SHARE about the cayenne on oatmeal, Robin said, "You never know what'll happen when you're offered help."

Mandy didn't stay to dance; taking her shirt off in public had already taken her way out of her comfort zone.

I am home now, walking around in circles, unpacking a little, making my nettle infusion for tomorrow and looking at the project of organizing the huge chest of drawers that Matt dropped off the night before I left for the retreat. It all feels like ages ago. Even leaving Omega and hugging everyone goodbye, feels like ages ago. I am back in my chair, but differently; I'll never quite be the same.

I called Abby to let her know I was back. She said she printed out my pages earlier in the day and sat and read them immediately. She loved them and said they were flawless. I went to visit with Mom and catch up. We made a date for tomorrow, brunch at Sissy's on Wall Street and then the Farmer's Market. I sat in my chair and caught up on emails, Facebook, messaged with Karen Miller, who is going to join our metastatic group at the oncology support center.

September 28th, 2013

I dreamt of being with girlfriends and we were having fun. I was able to shed my worries and live in the moment. We played all over the house, the attic, the basement, the living room. We were cooking and there was a mink slithering around the house. It ran down into the basement and I blocked the passageway that it had been getting through to be upstairs. I went into the dining room and there was a young bear. It was large for a youngster, like it had an adult frame without its full adult strength, or adult weight. I could see from its frame that it would be a powerful bear and it would not be safe to live with it in my house. I did not have much time to get the bear out of my house. I was wearing a little black dress and the bear was wearing the black fur that would only become fuller as it aged. I had a doctor's appointment and I sat on the examination table in my little black dress. The doctor entered the room very seriously. I swung my crossed ankles. He told me this was serious and I smiled. He was frustrated that I wasn't taking it seriously enough; he wanted me to prepare for the worst. My old girlfriends came in the office with the food we were preparing before, at the house. The party moved to the hospital. I didn't get serious, or invest in the worry and the doctor realized that he made a mistake this time. I was okay for now. It was someone else's scan. I was in a reprieve and we celebrated gratefully. I had been prepared more by happiness than by worry. I still had a vicious mink in my house and a growing bear to deal with. Life was not easy, but fun was to be shared when the opportunity arose. My little black dress was getting a lot of use; my classic style was in full force.

INCH BY INCH
October 3, 2013

In the beginning I was stunned. I had no fucking clue how to absorb the words. They had no meaning to me. I heard it like my mother's disappointment or a teacher's bad grade, "Carol, I'm sorry to tell you, but you do have cancer, Stage-Four Metastatic Breast Cancer."

"*Stage four metastatic breast cancer*" rolls out of my pen now and off my tongue and off my chest, except when it knocks me upside the head, slams me in the chair and holds me down, bound with the assistance of drugs. How does the weight lift again? Inch by inch, immeasurable; sometimes by noticing the sun in my bedroom or sharing meaningful words with friends, but now, after layers of dramatic treatments, I spend a lot of time numb, armored against feelings of being on the fringe of life, not fully involved, but not dead. If I catch a look at those feelings, I realize I'm detaching prematurely, trying to protect my loved ones from grief.

WEDDING PREPARATION

"You must be so excited about your son's marriage next month!" Yes, of course I am. How could I not be? But why does this feel fake to me? How could this measure of time, of life, and of my son's rite of passage leave me numb? *That* is my mystery, NOT "How do you live with Stage-Four Metastatic Cancer?" That's not a question that I ask, I just DO. What do I need to do to prepare for the wedding? That's what I try to resolve. Dress? Check. Rehearsal dinner? Check. Which members of my family have RSVP'd? Check, uncheck, check, uncheck. Feelings? Skip that one; what's next to do? I am numb.

I'm feeling the restraint of time, energy and the lack of confidence that I have years to get to know my beautiful daughter-in-law, Sara. Will I have enough time to evolve a relationship into my Mike and Sara's busy lives? I turn instead, to work with my cancer support friends. I turn to writing about my life, to understand it, to explain it, to love it, and to examine the feelings I already had. I let my children live their lives that feign innocence of my mortality, and theirs.

HOLDING ON, LETTING GO

Marjorie, Abby and I worked on the lineup of stories for the book and handed them over to our book designer, Austin Metze, after Craig had proofread it enough times to recite the book by heart. Austin suggested the name and cover artwork and we were on our way. It was printed by October. We had our second public reading at the ASK Gallery, and used Bob's camera to shoot a video. It was so exciting and energizing that I did more than I should, but loved feeling like my old self, lifting chairs and designing the space with Charlie, who made a recording while listening to us for the first time. He told our kids, "You should've seen your Mom; she was like her old self!" We planned more readings and sold books and paid our bills. We'll be able to fund our second book next year.

CARLA
November 12th, 2013

I ran to the oncologist for my pre-chemo blood work then across the street to the Support House to talk with Doris about book business. I took myself out to lunch to read over the Advanced Directives for the workshop tonight, stopped at the post office to ship books and went home.

    I was tired and sat in my chair making phone calls, slept. I am finishing up another round of the chemo cocktail I'm on for Metastatic Cancer and I'm looking forward to the week off to recoup some white blood cells and energy. I want to visit Nancy tomorrow, who is in hospice at St. Peter's in Albany. I called Nancy to talk. It was brief. She's on morphine. I feel the strong current building around her and if she's lucky, perhaps the current will take her gently from this suffering. I want to hug her first, kiss her head and thank her, she's been my guide, teaching me since the day I met her a year ago in our metastatic support group.

    Then I got up and walked to my desk, sat to look over my bills and straighten out the reimbursement confusion, all the stuff I wish someone would do for me, but not really. I actually appreciate that I can still do it myself. I had the email open, communicating with new memoir participants and book orders. A new batch of emails finally came through the sludge of cyberspace. They rolled down my screen while I hit delete, delete, delete for anything political or spammish, only reading the ones from friends. Then I saw one from Todd, Carla's husband.

I yelled, "N-O-Ooooooo! NO! Not Carla, NO! Not Carla!" I have been coping with dying friends calmly, expectantly, but not Carla. This winded me. We met last year and reunited this year at both of the Breast Cancer Options and Omega Retreats for Women with Metastatic Breast Cancer. We were "sistas." We posed topless in the raucous group photo on the front steps of the 'Cabin in the Woods.' That was only in September. She posted last week on Facebook, asking Paula for the number to call so she could counsel new-comers to this sisterhood. She is our tenth sister to die this year.

I knew she was just dismissed from a clinical trial she'd been hoping would work for her. I knew that her liver was not holding up well, but Carla looked so voluptuous and strong that I believed she *wasn't* going to die. I was as blind as if it was my own death that sprung up on me. Not young Carla with a seven year old son that she loved so much and a sweet partner of a husband and so much to live for. She was still so present in September that she complained about not being able to go back to work *yet*. Last year I had annoyed her with my acceptance and gratitude, but she was newly diagnosed metastatic. We all came away understanding how unique each of our situations are. There is no "ONE WAY" to do this metastatic thing.

This year at retreat Karen stated on the first day that she needed to cry and I said, "We have that in common too." She was my roommate for the week. We'd stayed up late talking, but didn't cry. I sometimes worry that I'm numb. I was prepared for Jude's death; we'd shared conversations about it since we met, including one long walk in Montrepose Cemetery. We had closure. She seemed at peace when we last spoke, but Carla?

Carla, you made me cry and scream and wail. I stomped my fucking feet and wailed. The cats ran upstairs in fear. It made me *angry*, Carla. I wailed, but wailing is dry sorrow and now I am congested with tears. What are these tears waiting for?

FOR PEARLS PASSING

Strung like pearls on a necklace

We walk out of this world

Strung together here

The clasp opens

We leave alone

Joining again on the other side

A brief separation

Always softly linked

Like pearls on a necklace

Or beads prayed on a string.

NANCY'S GIFT
November 22, 2013

Tuesday afternoon was a special support group. Our friend, Nancy Henry, had died the day before, Monday, November 18th, 2013. She was not only a wonderful soul, but the longest standing member of our Metastatic Cancer Support Group. She held the lantern of living for us to follow, and now, Dean told Rosie, that she died "a beautiful death." Rosie said, "We'll spend most of our time together today as a memorial for Nancy." I boldly sat in her chair, realizing only later that night, that it had been Tom's chair before that. Tom died in March. I won't sit in that chair every week; we'll have to share it.

Rosie lit a candle and read one of Nancy's poems from an older issue of *Celebrate Life* and spoke of the many things Nancy and Dean, did for this Cancer Support Community. Rosie also told us that Nancy wasn't always as patient as we knew her in recent years. She told us Nancy was quite needy when she first arrived. None of us were here then. I read a poem that I wrote in honor of Nancy, Jude and Carla called "For Pearls Passing". I had been so saddened last fall when Nancy went into hospice and thought we might lose her then, when I hadn't even gotten know her, but she lived and we learned by her forthright explanations of living compromised by illness. Kathy read Nancy's poem, "The Way I Live Now". Ruth, Jerome, Suzanne, and Bob were all present too, waiting for a turn to speak. Lisa was there to observe us because Rosie is leaving the helm of our group after our next session. So many changes to absorb all at once it seems, though we've been expecting both.

We heard the knob of the French doors jiggle and it opened slowly. We watched a woman appear, crooked, with long, thin, gray hair, dressed in baggy black clothing. She stood for a minute looking at us before she stated, "I need to talk to someone about my symptoms. I have bone pain and I need to talk to other people about these awful side effects I'm having." We stared at her in the doorway of our cocoon, our laughter interrupted. Rosie spoke of the memorial that we were having for our friend that we lost this week and asked if she would like to join us, we could talk about her issues at the end, but the woman persisted. "I've been in pain for weeks and I need to know if anyone else has these side effects. I'm sure it's the side effects of the drugs I'm on. The pains are all over my body and come and go as they please." Rosie asked, "What's your name?" "Jane," she replied. "Alright, Jane, we'll get back to you after our memorial, if you'd like to stay." She entered the room and sat to my right, bent in her chair, miserable. Someone mentioned how special Nancy's partner Dean is, how special their relationship was and how long he has cared for Nancy. Jane complained, "Well some people have supportive partners and help, but…" Rosie patiently asked, "Jane, would you like to stay and wait till the end or you can leave and come back for the next session, if that's better for you. This memorial is important for the group." I encouraged her to join us. "You're here now. Wait with us and we'll introduce ourselves. You'll find lots of us living with bone metastases, on the same drugs and discomforts." Kathy continued her memories about Nancy. It was a lovely group, an honor to Nancy and somehow fitting to get a new member this day, not only a new member, but such a raw one; we could witness the solidarity of our contentment and happiness in being present and alive. Jane was illustrating the misery and suffering that we have to choose everyday not to be. Maybe the energy of our group can help her, but I'm not willing to let go of the joy I find here, for anyone.

At the end of our memorial, we introduced ourselves to Jane with our brief diagnoses and history. We spoke of the laughter and joy we experience in our group, shared recommendations on how we deal with our own powerful worries and fears. Kathy recommended finding a hobby. Jerome suggested helping others as a way to rise above our discomforts. It went around the circle. She has plenty of people in the same boat, bone metastases, Zometa infusions, but no one willing to commiserate about *"how awful it is to be me."*

We all have rocky roads and insisted on enjoying the company we share. When we were all leaving I thought I saw her standing a little taller, Suzanne noticed that Jane smiled. There is always hope and we shared it. The full power of our group surrounded her without losing our joy. What a circle we share. Nancy's energy was very present sharing a glow of compassion that made Jane feel like a parting gift, someone to replace her, not with the attained wisdom Nancy shared, but with the need of our earthly support, to distract us from Nancy's departure.

WHAT THE LIVING DO

(Title borrowed from Marie Howe)

I meet friends to go to the wake of our dead friend and hug all of her family members. I kneel in front of her in the casket. I look at her sleeping in her purple dress and touch her cold arm, packed with the final chemo, formaldehyde. I look at her full, bright red lips and thank her for having lived. I walk out and mingle before driving back home. In my pajamas, I fix dinner. I think about all of my dead friends and stand at the stove realizing that I am still living because that's what the living do.

There is this proof that I still live. I wake up in the morning and wiggle my toes, brush my feet together like a cricket and open my eyes to the sun curling around the shade. I know I am alive, not to *any* day, but *today*, a new day. I feel the cool air on my body leaving the warmth of my bed. I feel the urge to pee and relieve myself, with my cat purring by my feet. I can still touch her soft fur, because I'm alive, and when I shower, I enjoy the warm water on my body, this body that still lives. How can I grieve when I am alive today? How can I be sad when I know that Jude, Carla and Nancy are somewhere safe? They don't suffer now. I know that in my bones. The birds chirp outside my window and the sun shines. Their peace is my peace. My illness was their illness. We remain part of the same universe. They have transformed from physical beings, leaving energy behind to comfort me. Please know I love you sisters and I will join you one day, but not today. Today I will be busy living.

I notice the bright color of the stockings I pull up my legs and brush my teeth to care for this body that still lives here, in this world. I smear makeup under my eyes to mask dark circles, because here in the living world, I care about my dark circles. I eat something basic to sustain me, knowing that I must to live, and then, another time it is with relish that I enjoy rich flavors that seduce my tongue to live and enjoy this life more fully. It is so much more than paying bills and going to work; life is enjoying work and loving children and friends, sunrise, and conversation. Life is about letting go of friends that need to die now. Life is breathing in a deep breath and remembering that this is a temporary gift, this breath, this life, the color of my stockings, the caring to put on makeup, the caring for others. Hold hands if you can, or stand shoulder to shoulder and support a head there when you can, and hug in grief and share tissues. These are all things that the living do.

THIS PORTAL
December 8th, 2013

I picture the dying being swept up through a large portal in the universe. This portal mirrors the same three months of time between my scans. During my recent span of renewed freedom, I've been glad to be announced well again, but I've also lost many friends.

I flew through these days of freedom, conscious always that my friends Jude, Carla, and Nancy have died. My friend Lisa's father left, too, and the last time I saw him, I felt he had something that he wanted to say. It's not the first time that I felt a conscious proximity to the portal. He died one morning with hot coffee waiting for him on the counter. He died sitting on the couch, and I could visualize him slipping out of his body and out of this world. Then I saw in the paper that my son's grade school coach left suddenly at 53, and my surgeon's father, 94, died after a steady decline. Let's cap off this portal with the great Nelson Mandela's death and call it a day until after the holidays, when I get my next set of scans. I have no such power of negotiations and see more obituaries appear in the newspaper every day.

And what if my scans don't give me *more* of what I want? How earthly my human desire is for more of this health that I have been enjoying these last three months. Acquaintances have been surprised by my energy, the energy balanced by resting and doing less as I adjust to the new chemo cocktail that inhibits cancer. I know that people are dying from my circle and I hold my arms open to let them go. They are free now and I think I'm not afraid. Jude told me, "Carol, I can see it. I've been so sick that I see how easy it will be to let go." I can see it too.

I see me teetering though, because I feel well and don't want that to change. I still want to surf as the exception, my ego high on a wave of life. I also know the feel of the hospital bed and the whirring, clicking hushed sounds there. I remember the comforting care of the nurses and friends. Nancy showed me most recently, that peace can enter in the final days of suffering, when life is too hard to hold on and your fingers, my fingers, will have to ease their grip. But today I am alive and well and taking chemo to help and I will get up and live each day that puts itself in front of me. I don't feel guilty for my life when others have died. I'll die too, but not today.

I'll be scanned in less than a month. Ruth is waiting for her scan results. Josh has already begun radiation for his new brain tumors. Karen is facing the difficulties of employment, housing and liver insecurity. Roberta is in hospice and has told us, "I don't' believe I'm dying!" and she was helped out of bed to another reading.

So out of respect for all my friends still living and the other loved ones who died before me, I will enjoy my life today. My day to die is not here yet, but will surprise me in the future. There must always be that surprising corner. I want mine to be past many portals from now. This scan is too close.

ENOUGH
January 9th, 2014

So what's good enough? What's long enough? I've had an interesting life span of 58 years. Is that long enough? Six members of our Memoir Group read to an audience of senior citizens yesterday, a group for which I nearly qualify, but not quite. These elders ranged in age from mid-seventies to mid- nineties. I stood at the microphone, reading my work, looking at the faces to see if they heard me. I saw understanding in the audience, nodding of heads; I made eye contact. I know we have a lot in common, I practice daily with my Mother, working to understand her aches and pains and limitations. We are more similar than not, my mother being eighty-five and me completing my fourth year of treatments for Metastatic Breast Cancer, currently on chemo.

When we were through reading, the eldest man stood and said to the wizened woman next to him, "What a shame these people have known such suffering." He shook his head in pity. The woman looked at him questioningly, she was hard of hearing, and he added, "They're so much younger than we are; to have to face such hardship so young." He walked off to get in line for lunch, using his cane for support. I looked at them and thought, "They suffer just walking and trying to hear. It seems there's so much suffering to grow old, maybe it's not such a blessing?"

I know fourteen people that died last year, but because of my age, I have many more friends still living.

The elders I talked to yesterday have family perhaps, but a dwindling stock of equally aged friends. My mother speaks of this loss often; she only has a few old friends that still live. She is the sole elder in our clan, the only one who knows most of the people in the old photographs, the only one who remembers the older family history. I feel this as I write my memoir, as I tell stories that no one else would know about me or remember otherwise.

I wonder how long I will live this life that is without pain right now. I lay awake in bed last night with a busy mind worrying about my eighty-seven year-old father in the hospital and concerns about my children. Suddenly, my jaw was in pain. Pain or discomfort, I asked myself. No, it was decidedly pain. Where did this come from? Was it phantom? An illusion? A metaphor? I worried about the drug Zometa that I take for bone strength and its possible side effect of jaw necrosis; that's where my mind jumped. I was quickly reminded about how easy it is to be happy, relatively energetic or content, without pain. Pain is a game changer. Suffering is unmeasurable. It can't be compared. The eldest in the audience walked himself over to the buffet, satisfied with his lot, and I followed, satisfied with mine.

I distracted the pain in my jaw by remembering the deep breathing techniques Diane taught me for pain and discomfort early on in this cancer journey. I brought them back to me and gently listened for a message it could give me. I was reminded of my human frailty. I breathed myself to sleep and woke with no pain, luckily, I only had the residue of its lesson.

PRE-RESULTS
January 12th, 2014

I am home eating my sandwich and my houseguest calls from the other room, "How were your results?" Mom had asked the same on the phone a few minutes earlier and I don't know why I bother letting anyone know beforehand, because they don't remember. I've told them both that I wouldn't know until Friday after 3:30 pm. She added, "Don't you have your memoir group today? Because I was thinking that you might have a hard time running your group if you had just gotten bad news." I took a deep breath and know I can be realistic, but no one else needs to be in advance of any news that I may or may not get in the next few hours.

I'm sitting in my own kitchen with a few minutes until I leave for my appointment. The sun is struggling to show itself, but the clouds keep covering it over. I sit in the gray light relishing this 'pre-results' moment. It has a peculiar privacy to it, knowing I will text, email, phone and place the news on Facebook when the results are decreed. Right now I sit alone with my thoughts, clear of anxiety and worry, full of optimism, and confidence in my New Year's commitment to visualizing two years into my future.

This moment is a pure measure of me right now. I don't know what the science of my body is saying yet, but I sense I'll be okay no matter what the doctor reports. What a pleasurable moment this is, this lucid moment flying free of reports and diagnoses. It opens a window wide onto how life used to be.

RESULTS

I sat in the waiting room distracted by the big flat screen news interview, until Jody calls me into an office where she takes my temperature, pulse, approximate weight and draws blood. I wait a little longer for my doctor to come in. He always enters looking down, reading papers while shutting the door behind him.

"Well Carol, the good news is that cancer is not in your vital organs or soft tissue. Your lungs and liver are still clear. The bone metastases on the right are still quiet; we can presume that the radiation you received there was sufficient. But your metastases on the left have grown. Two spots are not significantly changed, but the left sacrum has tripled. That means the chemo isn't working." We went on to talk at length about the selection of treatments. More radiation to the area is dangerous to the production of white blood cells. He was recommending two targeted therapies in pursuit of inhibiting the hormones feeding my cancer. I've tried Tamoxifen, Femera, Faslodex and then, for the last six months was on a pill chemo called Xeloda, in conjunction with Tykerb, which I've been on since 2012.

"But what about the her2neu+ aspect? What about continuing the Tykerb, that breaks the blood brain barrier and perhaps keeps the Mets from continuing to spread in my brain?" I asked. He explained that the radiation might have been enough there too. Maybe the drug wasn't the main inhibition and besides, he couldn't prescribe Tykerb with the new drugs because there are no studies of their combination; the possible side effects are unknown. He spoke of two new chemotherapies that would be left for my future use, if the cancer spread to my liver or lungs. "I don't want to use them now. I'd hold them for later. They would be too toxic for the stage you're at now, but I'm faced with the possibility of under-medicating you or over-medicating you. How would you feel about seeing an oncologist in New York, someone who is more exposed to trials and studies? You have the oncologist that you saw in NYC or I have someone I would recommend."

Our discussion was satisfying even with not-so-good-news. I felt respected and included with his suggestion of a second opinion. I went out into my car and made the phone call to the New York doctor's office, the same doctor that reported my first round of bad news in 2009. I've talked to so many people with Metastatic Cancer, that I am not shocked by this news. My doctor was happy that my liver, lungs and other vital organs did not show any activity, "It is only in the bone," he said.

THE TALLEST COUPLE IN ALBANY

Part 1

June 2009

Watching my daughter *be* a teenager made me revisit my own experiences of youth and I began to think a lot about my high school boyfriend, Randy, or "Randu," as I called him.

I wondered if I hurt him when I left for college. I'd loved him and wished to clear the air between us. Where was he now? His parents would be older, like my parents; would they still be living? Mrs. Mason had always been kind to me and I had grown very appreciative of her. One day I called their number. Mrs. Mason answered the phone. She said, "Carol, of course, I remember you!" I told her I'd be up in Albany visiting my old girlfriends on June 6th. She said she'd be pleased to have me stop by.

I arrived at their house, recognizing it 36-years later without looking at the number. Mr. Mason was sitting in his recliner with an afghan over his legs; it took him a few minutes to make it to the front door. He smiled a greeting, a weak hello, and invited me in to sit down; his wife would return in a few minutes. I told him that I would always remember his fabulous record collection. In fact, I learned about American music in his basement listening to his jazz and blues albums. Did he still enjoy them? He didn't have them anymore; he'd given them away years ago. He didn't look well and it made me sad.

Mrs. Mason came through the door and gave

me a vibrant "Welcome!" We smiled and embraced, then settled into the living room talking about life and our children. We began with mine and moved on to hers, including Randy. She lifted a picture of him, with his son, off the dark wood mantle to show me and then brought out his wedding album. His wife had three grown children from a previous marriage. She was also blonde, an attractive full-bodied woman who'd found a good man. Randy must have been around forty when they had their own son and got married. He was a year older than Dana.

I last spoke to Randy back in 1976. He was bartending in one of the major film studios, and playing cards with a cast of Hollywood characters. But his mother told me he'd changed careers decades ago and was now working at Sear's, specializing in refrigeration repair. He and his family lived in Arizona. "They don't visit very often because his wife doesn't like the cold," she explained.

I shared my gratitude with Esther for her kindness to me as a young woman. I thanked her for speaking gently, but firmly, to me after catching Randy and me upstairs in his bedroom one afternoon when she came home early from work. I was seventeen and her son had just turned twenty. Randy had quickly gone downstairs and she wisely asked, "Randy, are you two using birth control?" I came downstairs a few minutes later in my Catholic school uniform, and she asked me, "Carol, does your mother know you're here? What would she think of you being upstairs in Randy's room?" She knew my mother did *not* know where I was. She knew that Randy was banned from our house because he was African American. I thanked her now, and assured her that my mother was embarrassed for how she'd reacted back then. My youngest brother, Matt, and my Syrian-Ghanaian sister-in-law have three beautiful children together.

We sat and looked through a large box of blue ribbons she'd won for her miniature African violets and she took me to the basement to see her greenhouse. I was nervous about seeing the couch there, the couch that Randy and I wrestled passionately on all those weekend nights while listening to Howlin' Wolf, Muddy Waters and Aretha Franklin. Esther had her African-violet collection on shelves under grow lights, where the couch used to be. I inquired about her career, to understand it better than I did as a teenager. She told me about her career in nursing and family planning.

A month-and-a-half later I was diagnosed with cancer.

Part 2
October 3rd, 2013

My friend Susie's father had died, and I was in Albany to attend his funeral. There had been a great turnout of my old girlfriends and we reminisced over lunch. Afterwards, on my way to the thruway, I detoured past the Mason's house. It had been four years since I'd seen them and decided on the spur of the moment to call, and find out if they still lived in their home. Esther answered, "Hello?"

"Hi! It's Carol – Dwyer. Remember me? I wanted to say hello and drop something off for you. Is now okay?"

"Yes, Carol. How nice to hear from you. I've often wondered how you're doing. Yes, yes we're home."

I made a u-turn and went back to their block. I looked out the right-hand window until I saw their house, number 79. I buzzed. I could see Ralph shifting in his chair under the afghan; just where I last saw him four years ago. Esther answered the door.

"Oh my goodness! You haven't changed!" she exclaimed, though I knew I had in so many ways. I was happy to see Ralph stand to greet me and I hugged them both. I handed Esther the book I brought for them, the anthology from my memoir group, holding on, letting go. I told them I'd written four of the pieces in the book.

I explained briefly, "I was diagnosed with Metastatic Breast Cancer just a month after I visited you back in 2009. I didn't want to call while I was in the thick of it, but I'm in a good spell right now and grabbed the chance to visit and give you a copy of our book. How are your kids? Randy?"

"Oh Randy came for a visit around the holidays last year, but he was on his own. His wife doesn't like the cold, so why would she visit in the winter?" Esther explained. She welcomed me to call anytime, even just to talk, and then I was on my way home.

Part 3

Friday, January 23rd, 2014

"Hello, Carol?"

"Yes?"

"Hi, it's Randy Mason."

"Haaaa! Oh my God! That's wonderful, how are you?!!"

"I'm okay. You sound the same Carol. I can hear you still have the same smile too. I just read your stories in the book you gave my Mother and I wanted to call and say hello and thank you for visiting her. Thank you for the book, I always knew you would do something wonderful. I really enjoyed reading your stories."

"Thanks Randy. Where are you?" I asked looking about my kitchen table, at the remnants of routine, the newspaper, cup of tea and dirty plate.

"I've been in Albany all week. My Dad is in hospice care at St. Peter's and I've been helping Mom and spending time with Dad. She gave me the book to read and your phone number to call you, and here I am, at the last minute. I'm embarrassed to say, I leave tomorrow morning, first thing."

Sitting in my kitchen sunbeam, I could picture the hospice ward. "I'm sorry to hear about your Dad, Randy. How's your Mom holding up? And you?"

"We're doing okay, Carol. He'd been fine right up to the end."

"I have two things to do today, but then I could come up to Albany to see you. If that's okay?"

"It would be nice to see you and I know my Mom would like that too."

"Great, I'll see you at 5:00. Should I come directly to the hospital?"

He called me close to 5:00 and suggested meeting me at the valet entrance of the hospital so I wouldn't get lost. I stood in the lobby waiting, looking in every direction until I saw him coming towards me from the elevator. I recognized his walk and his smile. I touched his shortly cropped salt and pepper curls and said, "Look at you! You look the same too!"

"A little thicker in the middle, but…."

"Well, we all have that Randy." I was deeply enjoying the richness of this experience, seeing the sifted qualities that remain in a person after almost forty years.

We talked as we walked to the hospice ward; sharing brief synopses of our life stories. He warned me of what to expect his father to look like, but I assured him that I'd seen my share of death in the last few years. A friend of mine died here a just a month ago. I wasn't shocked when I walked into his father's room. Mr. Mason was actively dying.

We sat with his Mother at the foot of the bed and talked while Ralph shook and struggled for breath. Out of the corner of my eye, I saw Randy move his leg the way he always did and said, "Just seeing you move your leg like that reminded me of when I made us matching linen dress pants, remember? Yours were light blue and mine were yellow. We wore them with our tall platform shoes and Hawaiian shirts. We were the tallest couple in Albany, majestic on our platforms, with my long hair and your tall Afro!" We all got a chuckle out of the image, even Mrs. Mason and Randy's sister, Audrey, who just joined us after work. "We'd go out to dinner for Surf and Turf with a nice bottle of red wine – a real class act!"

The nurse came in to relieve Mr. Mason's congestion. Randy and I stepped out and walked slowly to the cafeteria. We were dipping gently into memories when Audrey joined us, chatting away about which car she drove and about a young friend that was doing so well in college. She felt like Randy's little sister again, nervously distracting us in this tiny window of opportunity to talk about our old days.

Back in the room we laughed about how I hung out with Randy and the "guys on the Avenue". I never knew their real names; I knew them by Motor Mouth, Big Head, Ma, Peppi, Turkey, etc. I called Randy, "Randu." He remembered everyone's real name, but had rarely seen any of them since moving to the west coast.

I needed to head home, and let his family decide who would stay, and who would go home for the night. Ralph was having a rough time, I touched his head and said good bye. Randy mentioned driving his mother home. I turned quickly and said, "You learned to drive?"

"Well, I had to out in Los Angeles!" he smiled, knowing all the times I drove us on our dates. I was dying to know how many crazy things he remembered. He walked me down to the car and I got to tell him I was sorry for hurting him, if I did, with my cold departure to college. He stopped and turned towards me. "Well, you did break my heart, but I got over it. Actually, I should thank you for rescuing me." I looked at him quizzically and he said, "I wasn't known for being a nice guy, you know."

"You always were to me," I said.

"Thank you for bringing the best out in me, then. I was headed in the wrong direction. You know, my Mom was always partial to you."

"I didn't know, but it's sweet to know now."

We stepped out in the cold air and walked arm in arm to my car while I said, "We had some great sex, Randy, didn't we? We knew how to enjoy ourselves."

He laughed and said, "Yes we did, Carol. Yes, we sure did."

"What were we thinking the time we fucked right off New Scotland Avenue behind the tree? I think that was our first time, when I told you I got my birth control pills and our passion couldn't wait another block!"

"Yeah, you kept me waiting for a few weeks if I recall, but what were we thinking? That no one would see us? I remember complaining about mosquito bites to my friend, Clem, and he said, "Well maybe if you left your pants on…."

My mind flooded with images of our beautiful young bodies interlocking by that tree, or in back seats of cars, or at Saratoga Lake, or on the modern 60's couch in their basement playroom. I heard the rhythmic beat of blues records running down before we were finished. So we fucked to the scratching needle, until Randy jumped up still erect, like a Grecian urn silhouette painting, and put on another album – and then, after sex, moving quickly to avoid staining the couch. God, we had fun, but I didn't mention these reveries and wondered again how many times he remembered them. We left it at just that one on Scotland Avenue. Then we arrived at my car in the freezing October evening. His father was inside dying and I was outside living on the edge.

I said, "You'll be back soon, for the funeral with your family, I suppose?"

"Yes, I assume so." We shared one more strong hug and waved good bye. This was our once-in-a-lifetime rendezvous. I drove away humming "Sweet Melissa" by the Allman Brothers, from a favorite album of ours back-in-the-day.

Part 4
January 23rd, 2014

He called me a week later, on Thursday morning, catching me in the same seat at the kitchen table, only it was cloudy outside. I recognized his voice, but it was still surprising to hear from him. I knew why he'd called me. Ralph died on Monday and Randy had just arrived from Arizona to attend his father's services the next day. He called me *first* this time. I smiled. He told me the obituary was in the Times Union today, I could look it up online.

"I'm sorry Randy, but I'm glad he didn't have to suffer long. Is your

Mom okay? And you? Did your family come with you?" I asked.

"Mom's still busy with arrangements, but she seems okay and I'm fine. I came on my own. I'll be more help this way."

"I'm sorry I can't make the funeral tomorrow, but I'd love to pay my respects and talk to you again. Will you still be there on Saturday? I could drive up then."

"Yes, I'll be here until early Sunday morning, Carol. That sounds great."

Part 5

January 25th, 2013

I spoke to Randy in the morning and said I'd be driving slowly in the snow storm and to expect me around 1:00 pm.

Then, I spoke to Abby and she said, "Oh, you're going to have so much fun! Maybe you'll get snowed in!"

"No, that's not where this is going, Abby. It's our stories we're looking to share; they're valuable enough, if not more so."

When I arrived, Randy was standing outside, bundled up, shoveling. We greeted each other with big smiles and bear hugs on the snowy lawn before entering his Mother's house. We removed our slushy boots and I went in the kitchen to hug Esther. She was keeping busy portioning food to store in the freezer. Randy asked me if I was hungry, "If you are, we have tons of food right here, there's no need to go out for it."

I was hungry so he selected his and Audrey's favorites from the stuffed fridge, and I fixed my plate with the green balsamic salad, a piece of chicken and some fettuccini alfredo. I followed him into the dining room carrying my lunch and said, "I saw in the online funeral registry that your name was spelled R-a-n-d-y-E and I was surprised. I didn't' remember the E at the end of your name!"

"Yes, Carol, there was always and E at the end of Randye, ha ha."

"Maybe I forgot because I always called you Randu, but I had definitely forgotten the E. I was going to write condolences, but I worried that it was a typo and then I'd be an idiot for spelling your name wrong because the paper spelled it wrong. He laughed remembering me calling him "Randu," like a pseudo-African tribesman of New Scotland Avenue.

"First you need to see the pictures boards of Dad that Audrey made for the funeral. Our brother Gary and I helped look through pictures, but it was mainly her project."

"And was I stressed about it too!" Audrey added passing through to the living room to sit with Esther and Gary who were watching a movie. "I had the wrong tacks and I ran out of time; they had to be done!"

I looked at every one of the pictures on the three boards. There were pictures of the young couple, Ralph and Esther Mason, with 1940's-style hair, wearing trench coats on their honeymoon at Niagara Falls. A picture of Ralph in his army uniform with the hat tilted "just so." His certificates of service at Iwo Jima and a small black and white snapshot simply labeled "dead Japs." Then an island photo of the whole platoon of African-American soldiers. Ralph was another man of that by-gone era, a part of WWII and the American segregation history.

Randye pulled a photo album with stenciled letters off a shelf. Esther had made it as a gift to Ralph years ago. Inside were all the old newspaper clippings of the high school sports he was in, clippings with all his scored points. There were group pictures of his high school basketball and baseball teams, with Ralph in the center of them, the first African-American captain of each team and the only black man. I felt Randye's pride in sharing this and I was amazed to learn this only now. I looked at Randye and said, "I didn't remember that your Dad worked at the post office, either, but do you remember what my Dad did for a living?"

"No," he said.

"You only met him once, so why should you. How ignorant we were as kids! We ignored our parents, but look at this history!"

I sat at the far end of the dining room table behind a large bouquet from Ralph's funeral service. I began to eat. Randye was unsure what to do, not wanting to make me uncomfortable as I ate, but I said, "Come! Come and talk to me while I eat, tell me stories of your adventures." He sat to my side and thought for a moment. "Thanks to you I got into skiing," he said. "You took me skiing once and I got a bug for it, and went to quite a few slopes out west with other friends who loved skiing. We were quite the trio." He began telling stories of his skiing and hiking adventures. We sat talking, his voice bringing up memories with just the sound of it.

Then he told me more stories of his prowess in the early days of living in California. He threw in memories of *our* adventures here and there. "Remember the time we had the house to ourselves and we had a party. I drank too much and fell asleep on top of you? You complained about it to a girlfriend, and word got back to me. I was so embarrassed and asked you to tell me next time! But it only happened once. Another time you told me I was getting a little bit chubby and I lost those pounds fast!" These were things I had forgotten.

"Remember going camping, Randye?"

"How could I forget! Just you and me, alone…." he leaned towards me conspiratorially, hidden by the large bouquet, our voices lowered so our chuckling wouldn't be disrespectful.

"I'd told my parents I was going camping with Nancy and she was going to lend us her car, but at the last minute she couldn't lend us her car. I told mom that Nancy's car broke down, and begged to borrow hers and she did."

"I loved fishing, too. Do you remember I caught that fish? It was tiny, about this big," he held his fingers to measure a tiny fish and chuckled; a chuckle that I heard live, right now, right here in the air around me, and it was the same laugh I heard when I was seventeen. Our heads dipped a little closer now, "I remember you sat near me and drew while I fished."

Laughing, I quickly finished swallowing a bite of salad and said, "Yes, I sat next to you on a rock with little gnats swarming around me, but I worked hard not to be annoyed, to be calm and draw. Then, I woke up in the middle of the night as my face got grotesquely swollen and by morning my eyes were slits, but I had to drive home because you didn't know how to drive yet. I had to keep stopping to rest my eyes."

"I really enjoyed that weekend camping. I was in my glory, fishing and being with you by the Ausable River."

"Oh, that's where we were. Do you remember going to Tupper Lake, to someone's grandparent's cottage? We were all in sleeping bags on the floor, a whole lot of us and his grandparents showed up and made the guy's parents come to chaperone us in the middle of the night."

"Yes, and we were in the same bag, trying to be very quiet, but...."

"And his parents came up and made us pancakes in the morning and we took a boat out on the lake and went swimming. Do you remember how we met? You mentioned that before."

"Yes, distinctly, you were walking down the street with your friend."

"That would have been Annie, she lived on your street and we'd taken the bus."

"And I saw you and said to myself, wow! She's tall like me and pretty, like a model, and I walked you girls to Annie's house. Then you called me the next day, interested in buying some weed."

"I *did?* From you?"

"Yes and you split the ounce with Clem, who was going out with Mary Jo, and he always accused me of giving you the bigger half, but I was fair! You got first pick and I had nothing to do with that!"

"And you called me that week and asked me to go to the big New Scotland Ave Gang's picnic at Thatcher State Park. You came to the house and my mother was shocked because I hadn't told her you were black. It didn't matter to me and I didn't want her to forbid me from going." I can still see Mom's panicked face and Randye standing calmly on the sunny porch with a car full of friends watching.

"That was a great first date, with all those friends around, no pressure, no awkwardness."

"Yeah, but do you remember that I'd dropped acid? I heard from Annie that she'd never dropped acid, so I brought some. I was never the idiot that dropped a whole hit or two, I was content to drop a half a tab, or quarter barrel. Annie and I spent a large part of the day climbing a stream, on big rocks. We watched the softball game on the large field below from a *higher viewpoint*, entertained by the trailing arms, bats and balls, while laughing and splashing in the water."

"No I didn't remember that."

"Later, I remember you and I walked away from the group, up to a steep ledge and made out. I remember it was a high ledge."

"We were safe, not on the edge…"

"And we kissed for the first time."

My thoughts went back to that grassy ledge, our first kisses. I was still tripping, but mildly, noticing the details of his broad nose and full lips up close, the touch of his thick fro, his firm thigh, his smile, and his facial muscles pulling his lips up from both sides to show me his large white teeth. I remember thinking of a stallion, the elegance and physique of a thoroughbred. I was tripping and loving this unique man, this man that was my size, and I remember being so happy, laughing and kissing on the ledge at Thatcher State Park.

Randye spoke, "I thought to myself, she's a bad-assed girl going out with me. Here I am, black, dealing pot, and I wasn't the nicest guy you could meet."

"I didn't know that. You seemed friendly to me, and handsome. Your smile won me; your eyes were kind and honest. I never thought otherwise."

"Do you remember the stupidest mistake I ever made?" he said.

"Hmmm, was I with you when you made it?"

"Yes. It was breaking up with you."

"Ohhhh! Yes, I remember. I think it had something to do with you going out with the guys on a night that we normally went out together, so I was upset. The girls decided that we should go out, maybe one of them knew where you'd be, and there you were, looking good. I saw another blonde, an old girlfriend, jump into your arms; I was jealous, but you were free and out with the guys. There were girlfriend whispers in my ear and I left. The next day we stood on the corner, you were leaning on the mailbox and told me it wasn't working out. You broke up with me and I rode my bike home devastated. I walked into my bedroom, turned on the radio and B.B. King sang "The Thrill Is Gone". I broke down and cried and cried. How long did we last that way?" I asked.

"Was it a couple of days? Maybe only one, but it wasn't long, that's for sure. Haha. I knew it was a mistake very soon after."

"Oooooo! We must've had great makeup sex." We laughed together, quietly.

His faced changed as he looked at me. He was serious now and leaned closer on his elbow, turning his shoulder towards me and said, "But I haven't asked you about what you're going through and how can I help you. Where are you with the cancer now?"

I briefly explained the journey of the last four years: chemo, surgery, my decision not to reconstruct, radiations one, two, three and four, and, now, facing an uncertain diagnosis of over treating or under treating my bone metastases. It's all been an adventure.

"This was perfect timing Randye, getting to talk to you now. I've been off chemo for three weeks and before that I wouldn't have been so able to drive up to meet you; being off chemo is like drinking espresso for me! And next week – who knows about next week and what treatments will be recommended!" I let him know I have wonderful support and that Charlie would be driving me down to the City for my appointment on Tuesday, my second opinion, hoping for some new options. His eyes were on me, deep, sad. We knew there was nothing he could do for me right now.

It was getting dark outside and I told him I was supposed to meet my daughter and her boyfriend later, to see the new tattoo parlor he's opening.

"Are you getting a tattoo?" he teased.

"No, these are the only tattoos I'll ever get." I pointed to my neck. "These are radiation tattoos. I have quite a few of them on this body now." He was looking at my most obvious one and his eyes moved down, catching a sparkle; he touched the pedant hanging there.

"I recognize that," he said.

"It's the only diamond I ever got, Randye. I remember wearing it to my Grandmother's house the Christmas you gave it to me in 1972. It showed that you meant it, that we loved each other and that you were a young man of value, despite their prejudice. My Grandmother admired it and I was proud."

"You were shocked when I gave it to you, I remember your face. You seemed to never have suspected it, or expected it. I paid it off on installments and the salesman asked when I'd be back for the engagement ring. I told him I wasn't sure. I looked between that one and a bigger one, which of course was more expensive, but chose this one. It had more sparkle."

"One night we were on a double date with "Motor Mouth" and his fiancée, Alice, when he flung his arm over the front seat of his old Cadillac to face us in the back seat and asked, "When are you two getting married?" I was so sure of myself and said, "Never. I'm going to college in NYC.""

"Yeah, and I was talking about going to California, too, and I did, a year or so later. Over the years, though, I always pictured you happily married, that you'd found someone and had a family. I hoped that someday I would make a lot of money, come see you, and send you and your family on vacation."

"Oh Randye, thank you. I did do a bit of traveling, hitchhiking in '78 with a boyfriend through England, Ireland and Scotland."

"Of course you were hitchhiking! You were so bold that way."

"In 1983 I went to visit a friend in Paris – the year before marrying Charlie."

"Oh! I always wanted to go to Paris!"

"After that my vacations were mostly connected to traveling with shows he was in as an actor. I didn't want to stop, but I had to leave soon…." I needed to get going for the long slippery, ride home. I went in to sit by Esther and gave her a hug on the couch in the living room. She was watching a movie with Gary and Audrey and I hugged them too. Randye put his boots on to escort me to my car and I suggested a walk before I drove home. The snow was still falling lightly.

We walked down his block, bundled up against the cold, holding arms and chuckling about our history. He reminded me of taking him to sleep over at my friend's house, but I couldn't remember who. We laughed again recollecting, that we'd been the tallest couple in Albany, he was 6'3" and I was 6'. We didn't need platforms. We towered over other couples we hung out with. We remembered driving in a car with about six other guys for an excursion to buy platform shoes in Manhattan. I squeezed his arm and we laughed in the cold, warmed by the comfort of being together.

"I always felt I could be myself with you, Carol. I never felt I had to change or be someone else." I looked at him and we kissed on the lips, giggling, my hood sliding down over my eyes, surprised to feel those lips after forty years. I looked at his short, salt and pepper hair, but the man on my arm will always be that young buck that walked me down this street when we were young. "What a sweet story we share, Randye."

This was on my "bucket list," this reunion – to walk down the street remembering how we use to ravage each other with youthful passion and abandon. We hugged outside my car.

"I love you Carol."

"I love you, too, Randye."

I got inside my car as he leaned over to kiss me once more; I restrained myself from slipping my tongue between those soft lips.

I knew better than to start something I couldn't finish.

March 16th, 2014

I dreamt I had the hairiest legs, blonde like my own, but with hairs two-inches long. I thought maybe it was time to shave.

UNBIDDEN PERIMETERS

I am a person living with Metastatic Breast Cancer. This is an unbidden perimeter of my life. I am not a cancer patient, or a cancer victim, but a person living with cancer. I am a mother, a daughter, sister, girlfriend and ex-wife. Cancer is looming in my bones, reappearing in my brain, determining the treatment of my bad tooth. Everything is colored by cancer, and while it doesn't label me, it does give me boundaries. I'm working with them, making choices with no guarantees. I am pondering the inevitable, The End, but holding the remainder of my life in the quality zone for as long as I can. I am following in the footsteps of many friends who have gone before me.

I woke yesterday morning, remembering my tall, handsome Dad who died last week. Appointments for cancer treatments will keep me from attending his memorial in Florida. I did, however, attend local memorials for my memoirist friend, Roberta Jehu, and my nutritionist-healer, Carol Hornig, on Friday: two consecutive memorial services for two powerful women who escorted my father out of this world. I cried for all my losses and wallowed in bed Saturday morning. I was afraid to leave it. I planned to go to NYC and visit friends who had gifted me a ticket to the Allman Brothers in concert. Should I go to NYC? Should I risk having diarrhea in public? What if my hip hurts? What if the tumor in my brain is irritated by the loud music. What if I have a seizure alone on the subway?

My mother said, "Carol, go ahead, get out of the house. You always feel better once you get going." Abby said, "The Allman Brothers?! GO!" I realized I was shutting down again, depressed; leaving my life that is not over. I pushed through the slog of fear and anxiety and got on the bus. I read and dozed; the bus was packed with college students. Two girls speaking Spanglish sat behind me laughing loudly. Behind them were two guys goofing around in their seats. "Fucking dude, I told you it was a fucking joke, okay? Hahahaha!" I closed my eyes again and took a deep breath, and then another. Behind my closed eyes I saw a bright circle, like a flashlight in the fog, and then it opened. The clouds cleared exposing a bright blue sky and light poured through. It was a vision of a powerful portal that welcomed the energy of these three treasured souls. I watched the circle close gently, the fuzzy focus returned as the voices of the young people surrounding me broke through again.

I walked down the sloped underground tunnel to the 1 Train, inundated by the energy of fast-paced people headed in the other direction. Each person was a walking story, each face scrubbed, pimpled, carved, black, coco, creamy, thick with history, pain, passion, amazing hair, and energy. New York City is a special place to feel the force of condensed life compressed into one place. I caught the train, arrived at Danielle and Tommy's, went out to dinner, and then went to one of the last Allman Brothers Concerts at the Beacon Theatre. The whole day was packed with human experience, energy and love. The music was uplifting and my brain didn't hurt. We sat on the aisle and I jumped up for the bathroom successfully every time. Tommy said it was the best show so far. The walk back to their home did me good. I enjoyed visiting my great friends and slept well.

I woke up slowly in the morning on their guest bed, and contemplated just going home, abandoning my other plan to meet my old friend Katia visiting from Paris, but Katia called and encouraged me to meet for tea across the street from Port Authority. I got to meet her twenty five-year-old daughter for the first time and they escorted me to my bus with many hugs and hand waving. It all worked out once I circumvented my anxiety, my tiredness; once I accepted the ring that pulled me alongside the flow of my life. How lucky I am to have this life so full of opportunity and encouragement. It is all around me; I just need to get onboard with a pocketbook of acceptance and a suitcase full of love. That is baggage I can carry, even with metastases in my bones.

March 17th, 2014

Today I am my tooth – my left, bottom molar which is getting a root canal. The tooth can't be extracted because of possible side effects to my jaw, the big, bad possibility of jaw necrosis from the drug I've been taking for bone metastases. I sat in the endodontist's chair, numb, listening to his deep sighs, knowing that I am, yet again, a special case. The cavity went right through the tooth and surprised him. I'll be going back for a follow up appointment on Friday to finish the job. I sat practicing deep, concentrated breathing, thinking that this root canal is not as bad as the Gamma Knife helmet they screwed into my skull, thinking that I am faced with the possibility of having another Gamma Knife treatment, and hoping that it will at least be an option for dealing with the small tumor on my left brain. Discomfort is all relative.

HOPE

When I feel good
I see hope.
But anxiety, fear, grief
turns it into naiveté.
Judged stupid, useless,
Lost.
But a laugh,
someone else's story shared
whether joy or despair;
their truth perks up my heart,
strips the judge of her gavel.
Sends her packing.
The light is re-lit,
a beacon
of remembered hope,
of today
of tonight
of love
of life to live

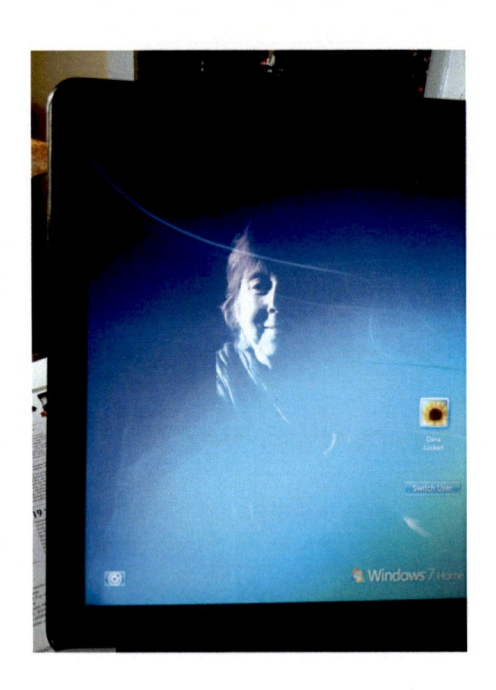

SOMEONE ELSE WILL WRITE THE LAST WORD

I glanced over at my bookshelf and caught sight of a health-care directives folder. I avoid them, don't find the time to finish them, and I realized the whole folder reminds me of a grade-school examination. I look out the window distracted by spring, just like taking a semester's final exam, signaling the end of the school year, the end of childhood. Maybe I just need to write this information out on my own paper, ignore filling out forms, and skip coloring in the lines. I don't want to be kept alive if I'm not living. I have accepted all of the treatments so far as good investments for the extension of my life, a life with quality; slower, but with enough rest it's remained independent and active.

Now my road is narrowing, jostling me to a smaller lane full of parked obstacles, as well as moving ones. Recently I bought time with a root canal. Will I outlive its decay? Before and after it I spent two months on antibiotics with side effects of diarrhea making it difficult to leave the house. I had a weekend of violent vomiting and another with increased diarrhea, which could have been a basic stomach virus, but it felt like an ominous foreshadowing of my future life wearing disposable underwear.

The chemo drug, Tykerb breaks my blood brain barrier. Two years ago, I began with five pills a day, but my liver enzymes went up. So we reduced it to four pills and it held the brain tumors at bay for two years. A new, pea-sized tumor appeared on my recent brain MRI, in the same area I'd had them before. I was able

CAROL DWYER **328**

to have another Gamma Knife radiation procedure. Once again, this will buy me more time; once again I impatiently wait for the veil of radiation exhaustion to lift.

I began my dose of Xeloda the day before I went in for my Herceptin infusion, but my oncologist said to stop the Xeloda when he looked at my cracked fingers and hands peeling like paper. I also complained of my hip discomfort and he ordered an MRI.

I made an appointment to view "green" burial plots in a beautiful local cemetery. Bobby and Charlie joined me for the tour. We walked all over the old grounds and selected several possible sites. I laughed when Charlie always liked another spot, across from the one I selected. It reminded me of when we were married.

I told the manager that I only needed one plot. It will be my place of rest. Mom didn't want to talk about it. I asked my children to come soon and help choose the best site, a place they, too, might find peace and spend a moment in meditation with me. Someday in the future, they could reflect on being there with me alive.

Today I found out the cancer is spreading. My right hip which was quiet since radiation last year, has flared up; I ache in both hip joints and in my back. I turned a corner. Just last week, in support group, my metastatic friends spoke about pain meds to help me sleep with bone metastasis. I was not aware that I was at that door. I needed the information just four days later.

I don't want to leave the party, but I am slowly withdrawing from the busy and loud aspects of life. I ask myself how much is enough? How much life will satisfy me? Will I panic and turn greedy? Will I leave gracefully, gratefully, with peace in my heart? Someone else will have to write the last word.

Death w/ Dignity
Deborah

CAROL DWYER **330**